COVID CURVEBALL

An Inside View of the 2020
LOS ANGELES DODGERS
World Championship Season

TIM NEVERETT

PERMUTED
PRESS

A PERMUTED PRESS BOOK
ISBN: 978-1-63758-143-8
ISBN (eBook): 978-1-63758-144-5

COVID Curveball:
An Inside View of the 2020 Los Angeles Dodgers World
Championship Season
© 2021 by Tim Neverett
All Rights Reserved

Cover art by Tiffani Shea
Cover and Insert Photography taken by Jon SooHoo/Dodgers

This book contains research and commentary about COVID-19, which is classified as an infectious disease by the World Health Organization. Although every effort has been made to ensure that any medical or scientific information present within this book is accurate, the research about COVID-19 is still ongoing. For the most current information about the coronavirus, please visit cdc.gov or who.int.

PERMUTED
PRESS
Permuted Press, LLC
New York • Nashville
permutedpress.com

Published in the United States of America
1 2 3 4 5 6 7 8 9 10

This book is dedicated to my family.
My wife, Jess, who is definitely my better half,
and my kids, Matt, Kyle, and Drew, who all
inherited my love of the game of baseball.

Table of Contents

Foreword

by Orel Hershiser, 1988 World Series MVP

"…three and two to Tony Phillips. Lansford down the line at third with two out. Steinbach on deck. Five–two Dodgers in the ninth," was how the great Vin Scully set up the last pitch of the fifth and deciding game of the 1988 World Series on the national TV broadcast on the night of October 20. As the Hall of Fame announcer was setting this up to the millions watching, I, the person who the nation's collective eyes were on, felt strongly that things were in hand. I had stepped off the mound at the Oakland Coliseum, realizing the gravity of the moment, and told myself that I should take all of this experience in. The vacuum of sound seemed to fill the air, if only for a few seconds. It was just white noise; almost like the intense hum of the ballpark I had experienced a number of times before in my career. This time, though, was different. I remember the emotions were welling up so much that I almost started to cry. I said to myself, "I can't do this," and focused on locking everything back in. I shook it off and went back to the things that stimulated me most on a baseball field—the dirt, the rubber, the grass, the catcher's fingers, and delivering a pitch. This time it was a fastball directed up and in that tailed over the plate, inducing a series-ending swing from the left-handed-hitting Phillips.

"Got 'em. They've done it!" said Scully. *"Like the 1969 Mets, it's the Impossible Dream revisited!"*

After we won, I had a very weird reaction as I just got picked up by catcher Rick Dempsey and gave an awkward fist bump. Then I was mauled by my teammates, and the lady that was in charge of the Disney commercial, which you don't know you are going to get until the very end of the game, was right there. Disney had negotiated before the game for three players from Oakland, and with Tommy LaSorda, Kirk Gibson, and me from the Dodgers. She tapped me on the shoulder, pointed, and said, "That camera...say it!"

It's absolute chaos on the field, but I looked at the camera and shouted, "I'm going to Disneyland!"

Then, fifteen or twenty seconds later, in the midst of the pandemonium, she tapped me on the shoulder again, pointed in a different direction, and yelled, "That camera...say it!"

I looked and shouted, "I'm going to Disney World!" After a bit more celebration, I was seen with both my hands over my head with my glove as I worked my way over toward the dugout to look up at my family in the stands. That is when I finally relaxed and celebrated. Before that moment, it was still odd to celebrate with my game face firmly in place. There was excitement, but it was still kind of semi-work because we had to shoot the commercial and get the line out correctly into the camera while not losing the moment. When that was done, when we began to walk off the field and I saw my family, that is when it really hit me. I had just gone nine innings in the deciding game of the World Series, allowed only four hits while striking out nine great Oakland Athletics hitters, and completing an amazing run through the postseason.

It is easier now, thirty-two years later, to revisit the emotions I experienced during our World Series Championship season of 1988 as I watched the last pitch of the 2020 World Series thrown by Julio Urías.

The number one person on the 2020 Dodgers that I can relate to is Julio, because of his last pitch that resulted in a strikeout and a World Series Championship. Heading into Game Six, nobody on that team knew who would throw the last pitch of that game. Could it have been Kenley Jansen if the matchup was right? Could it have been Blake Treinen? Could it be Julio? Could it have been Victor González? Nobody knew who was going to have that honor and the opportunity to come through with their amazing ability and make history. Not only to be part of a World Series winner but to get that last out as a pitcher is what you never forget. It's what people around the game and the great Dodger fans never forget.

When the Series ended, a lot of folks around the team turned their attention to Clayton Kershaw and expressed their happiness for him. Kershaw has a Hall of Fame resume but had been saddled with unfavorable results in postseasons past. He got that piano off of his back and then some in 2020. He went into the postseason with better "stuff" than in the few past years. I think he went into this postseason with a lot more wisdom on what postseason baseball is about, as far as how hitters attack him. He used both sides of the plate. He understood that even if he wasn't landing his curveball for a strike that he could still use it. There was more variety to his pitch selection, which really helped him. His postseason failures were becoming a large part of his career, and now you can take that context and put "World Champion" on it. Now you can put that title all the way at the top of his plaque in Cooperstown so that no one will ever be able to walk by it and think "*He had a great career but never won a World Series.*" Now no one can say that, and with the way this team is built, maybe he even gets to add more championships before he is all done.

The Dodgers came up short in the 2017 World Series to the cheating Astros, and again in 2018 to Boston. They were well short of the mark in 2019 when they were stunned by the eventual champion Washington Nationals in the Division Series. Those Dodger teams were all really good, but they didn't have Mookie Betts. There were a lot of differences between the 2020 Dodgers and those other teams, but the addition of Betts was big. He came in and emphasized all the details about every aspect of playing the game at the highest level. I think the coaching staff, Dave Roberts, and the front office always emphasized that. Justin Turner is a great baserunner but isn't a fast guy. Mookie has the speed to go along with great decision-making and great knowledge of the game, so you see his impact more than you will with other players. It's one thing for the coaches to tell you how to do something. To have a teammate actually doing it on a daily basis, that is when you truly believe the depth of the knowledge and the depth of the concentration it takes to pull off that level of execution every day. Mookie became that living, breathing example that everybody talks about when they talk about a great player. When Kirk Gibson joined the Dodgers for spring training in Vero Beach in 1988, he had the same effect on our team. There are some important similarities there.

Tim saw Mookie first among our crew when he was broadcasting with the Red Sox before joining us in the Dodgers TV and Radio booths two years ago. I get to watch him now, and he is so good that I almost take him for granted. As a broadcaster, when we look for storylines or for ideas of what we will do in the "open" of a telecast, or thinking about who we should highlight for the game, you almost overlook some of the things that Betts does, because there are so many things he does you want to move onto other players and not just headline Mookie every night. You want to cover Corey Seager, Turner, Kershaw, Max Muncy, and Walker Buehler, and make sure last year's MVP, Cody Bellinger, doesn't get lost in the shadows. Ultimately, and on a daily basis, you actually could headline a broadcast with Mookie, and that'd be absolutely amazing.

In 1988 I was fortunate enough to the named MVP of the World Series. It changed my life, and it will change the life of whoever wins it. Corey Seager was amazing throughout the 2020 postseason and earned the awards he got for being the best player in the NLCS and the World Series. Corey has never been the most outgoing guy, or the most comfortable doing interviews, but he is going to have to get that way because he is going to hear about it over and over for the rest of his career. I don't see him being as shy as Mike Trout, but I see him with that kind of ability to excel under the big lights. I see him maturing before our very eyes because of all the acclaim he has earned. He learned a lot about himself this year. At one point in his career, it was like, the swing is good, but it could be better. The defense is solid, but it could be better. The arm is strong, but he could find other ways to use it. It all came together for him this year due to good health and, I think, by removing some things from his game. He had always been one of the biggest video watchers during games and grinding in the cage, taking so many swings. He found that backing off, not relying so heavily on video, not obsessing on the swings or what happened in the last at-bat, actually helped him because he just went out there, had fun, and played baseball. He became an even more natural baseball player than he already was. I saw more natural movement and more natural rhythm in his offense and defense, and it was impressive to watch him play at the high level we witnessed this season.

As excited as I am about what Corey did and the future he has, I was very happy for Dave Roberts. Dave has earned all the accolades he has received in Los Angeles. In the background, he has built a new way to play "Dodger Baseball" with the roster as maneuverable as it is. He has been able to keep players happy, even though they're changing places in the batting order on a near-daily basis and playing different positions. During the game, when a reliever comes in, someone might have played five innings at one position, but now another is going to play the next four. You might go contribute somewhere else. He has been fantastic as far as this transition into the way modern baseball is played, the way rosters are configured, and the communication in the locker room that keeps the team together. Despite falling short in previous seasons, I still thought he was doing a magnificent job. Now that he has attained the crown, it just upgrades everything he has ushered through with Dodger Baseball.

2020 was a different season entirely due to the Coronavirus. There were so many different elements that were added to this season and so many that were removed. Everybody will always point to the number of games played (60), the two spring trainings, and the delay. I don't think there should be an asterisk on this season, because it was an accomplishment against the best in the world. They all played by the same rules, followed the same daunting schedule, and had to run through the same gauntlet of playoffs. The Dodgers ended up on top. Major League Baseball got it right, and so did the Dodgers. We ended up with the teams with the two best records. Cinderella did not show up, and I think that actually makes it more valuable. They earned it. Weighing it against a 162-game season, weighing it against one spring training and what is considered a "normal season," is unfair.

Broadcasting this season certainly presented challenges. For the road games, working in a place that is built for sixty or seventy thousand people, including the people working, that is empty, and there's no traffic when we left after games because we only had about twenty people in the stadium, was different. I had the feeling that there were ghosts some nights. I think it was harder for the play-by-play guys like Joe (Davis) and Tim (Neverett) because the flight of the ball is so important in regard to the volume and enthusiasm and what's about to happen. It was a little easier for me, the analyst, because I get to react to what I've seen and don't have to call it as it is happening. And I get a replay. Overall, it felt a little bit the same to me, but I didn't get to look "off-ball" like I would normally. I look "off-ball" after the pitch and away from the monitor as soon as the ball is put into play, watching cut-offs, relays, and breaks on balls defensively, along with routes to the ball in the outfield and jumps on the base paths. It was odd, very odd, but for me it wasn't as odd doing the game as it was odd dealing with everything around the game. Eating from the concession machines instead of having a meal in press dining was one thing. You could do your own Zoom call in the hallways of the stadium because you were all by yourself, which was definitely not normal.

During the course of the season, the Dodgers players and staff did a great job following all of the required COVID-19 protocols and were one of the few teams that had no one test positive. The players, led by Justin Turner, established precautions over and above what Major League Baseball put out there due to the fact they felt they needed to be safer than every other team in order to win the World Series. After the final out of Game 6, while the Dodgers were celebrating on the field in Arlington, we learned that Justin had tested positive and that was why he'd been pulled from the game. He had been setting an example and acting in a more responsible manner than anyone, so for him to test positive was unbelievable. I was sad. I was able to process it more once I had more information, but I don't think the introduction of this book is the place for me to discuss that information. I was sad for Justin, and I was sad for the team. In some ways, I was glad that he came out for the team picture. I know that it turned into a controversy, but in the context of everything, he grew up a Dodger fan and had just won the World Series. There is a lot of work that goes into it, and it was a shame that he might be deprived of reaping the full reward. I had the honor of officiating the wedding of Justin and his wife, Kourtney, and am close to them. It was a situation that I met with very mixed emotions. It was the COVID protocols and what was being broken and the positive test that wouldn't allow him to be on the field for the final out. He was the team leader, the emotional leader, and my friend. He should be celebrating one of the happiest days of his life.

The 2020 Dodgers season will be ingrained in people's memories for many different reasons. The good, the bad, and the unpredictable. The comeback series against the Braves, Bellinger's Game 7 home run, Mookie's defense, Kershaw's domination on the mound, all of it.

Anyone can make a list of their favorite moments of the 2020 Dodger season. It would be a long one!

I am sure I speak for most when I say I look forward to returning to a normal season soon and creating more great Dodger memories. This championship season was radically different, and Tim captured the day-to-day of it to provide an inside look at what it was like to be a part of it. I am proud of this 2020 Dodger team and everyone associated with it, as they had to jump through an untold number of hoops just to play the games and go to work. Through all the road-blocks and speed bumps, the Dodgers pulled it off. All the extra work and precautions paid off in the end. If we ever have a parade, I look forward to seeing you there. Enjoy the book.

—Orel Hershiser, a.k.a. "The Bulldog"

Introduction

Who Am I and Why Am I Writing This Thing?

I realize that many Dodger fans don't know me. I am still relatively new and just starting my third season with the club. I am not new to Major League Baseball, however, as I have been calling games elsewhere for quite a while. It is my sincere hope that as time goes on, we get to know each other better and spend some time together around Dodger Baseball.

Broadcasting baseball has been a passion of mine since I was very young. The first game I ever did was a AA game in my hometown of Nashua, New Hampshire, between the Nashua Pirates and the Waterbury Reds of the Eastern League. I was nineteen and still playing college baseball at Emerson College in Boston. It was 1985. After that, I worked in Las Vegas calling AAA baseball for the Padres and Dodgers affiliates for parts of ten seasons before moving to Denver. Before the move, I thought my "career" had plateaued in Las Vegas, that I needed another challenge, and put baseball on the back burner. In the meantime, I was lucky enough to broadcast multiple events at four different Olympic Games. The two Summer Games I was involved in were in Athens, Greece, in 2004 and Beijing, China, in

2008. I was assigned men's and women's basketball, along with baseball and softball. I started to get the itch to get back to baseball again.

One of the many assignments I had while in Denver was broadcasting arena football: the Colorado Crush, then owned by Broncos legend John Elway. That assignment took me to San Jose one weekend, and I noticed the Red Sox were in Oakland to play the Athletics the night before our game. A friend from Las Vegas, Ken Korach, calls the A's games on radio and he left me his tickets along with a media pass so I could come up and see him in the booth. My partner that year was Joel Klatt, a Red Sox fan and former University of Colorado quarterback, and now a star national college football analyst on Fox Sports. While Joel and I were at the game, I went up to visit Ken. As I stood behind him in the smallish radio booth, listening to him narrate the play-by-play while watching it in real-time from his point of view, I knew I wanted back in. That moment was my inspiration. If any of you want to blame anyone for my time in baseball you can point the finger at Korach. Just kidding. Maybe.

The first Big League game I did wasn't even aired. I was called by FSN Rocky Mountain to do a demo game at Coors Field between the Rockies and White Sox that Fox was using to experiment with a different kind of commercial format. I was excited for it because it gave me valuable video that I could send to other teams. The next year, I got a call from FSN RM asking me to go to Arizona and fill in on TV for the Rockies' weekend series with the Diamondbacks. I had been doing some pre-game/post-game work in studio for the Rockies anyway, so I was pretty familiar.

The demo reel I made from the Colorado/Arizona series went to the Milwaukee Brewers, where I became one of three finalists for their TV job in 2007. When I went in for my interview, the first thing I was told was that they had just eliminated one of the other finalists and I was in the final two. Brian Anderson interviewed the next day and got the job, and his career on the national sports landscape with MLB, the NBA, NCAA Basketball, and the PGA has exploded. It couldn't have happened to a better guy, and his success is well deserved. In late 2008, the demo was sent to the Pittsburgh Pirates. I was fortunate enough to be a finalist, and even more fortunate to be selected. I loved that job and that city and planned on spending the rest of my career there. But…life happens.

After seven great seasons in Pittsburgh, I had a chance to continue to work in Major League Baseball and be near my parents, who were both in ill health. WEEI radio in Boston hired me, with the approval of the Red Sox, to work the Old Town team's games on radio. The opportunity to go home and help my parents was the right thing to do, in my opinion. My sister, Nancy, was unbelievable in the dedicated and steadfast ways she took care of my parents and I credit her 100 percent for keeping them both alive far longer than they should have lived. I couldn't help her and my older brother, B.J., all the time due to the demanding baseball schedule, but I tried to as much as I could, and any extra moments I got to spend with my parents were worth it all. My dad passed in July of 2018 and my mom in May of 2019.

I will always appreciate Red Sox chairman, Tom Werner, coming to Dodger Stadium in April of 2019 to personally deliver my World Series ring. He told me that he really missed me on their broadcasts. That meant a lot and shows the class of that organization. Team president and CEO, Sam Kennedy, called me in February of 2019, just before my first spring training with the Dodgers, to wish me luck and tell me, "You will always be a part of the greatest team in Red Sox history." Sam and I remain in touch.

Now, I am in Los Angeles with one of the best groups of broadcasters I have worked with. It is such a refreshing change to be around and work for people that understand baseball broadcasts and broadcasters. They are also a great employer. I feel like I am part of the company in a way that I never did in Boston. It is much more like Pittsburgh in that regard. I am honored and privileged to be able to occasionally sit in the same chair that Vin Scully so eloquently occupied for so many years, and the talented Joe Davis gets to on most nights, to do what I love, which is to go back and forth and broadcast Major League Baseball on radio and TV.

I have been proud to be a Dodger since I was seven years old and put on a Dodger uniform as a bat boy for the Nashua North Little League Dodgers. Two years later, I was eligible to play for the Dodgers, and two years after that, when I was eleven, I caught a fly ball in left field to end a game that resulted in my teammates and I getting to celebrate a city championship. After playing in high school and into college, I briefly played for a semi-pro team called…the Nashua Dodgers, named for Brooklyn's minor league team that played in the same stadium in the 1940s. Dodger greats Don Newcombe and Roy Campanella had played on that team, which was managed by Walter Alston. I have been crossing paths with the Dodgers one way or another throughout my life and career. Another path was crossed while broadcasting AAA baseball in Las Vegas in the '90s and early 2000s for the Dodgers affiliate. Now, I am happy and proud to work for one of the best organizations in all of sports.

Now that you have some clarity on my background in baseball, I hope it will give you an idea of the perspective I bring regarding the game and the ancillary things that accompany it. My idea is to help you get a better understanding of just how different this season was than what my colleagues and I have experienced for so many years, and what we hope we can return to soon—the countless charter flights, late night buses, numerous hotels, and long hours of work on game days have all been replaced with cardboard cutouts of fans, masked players, and calling games off of monitors. There are the great and not-so-great moments at the many stadiums, old and new, that we have witnessed, and, most of all, the relationships that have been made and developed over the years with front office personnel, owners, managers, coaches, scouts, trainers, players, and other broadcasters and media members that give us a unique perspective on "living the baseball life."

During quarantine, sometime in early May, while my wife, Jess, and our beloved dog, Reggie, were on a walk in the woods of the mountains in northern New Hampshire, an idea came to mind. Thinking out loud, I explained to Jess about this out-of-the-box thought that I had, and she strongly encouraged me to follow through. It was the basis for this book: to chronicle the day-to-day of going through this COVID-19-shortened season and all that goes with it.

I kept my daily chronicles a secret from the Dodgers and everyone else I worked with through the entire season so that no one would offer or withhold information, and people could operate around me without having to think that I was writing a book. I didn't want anyone to act or do anything differently than they normally would.

Thanks for coming with me on this ride through the 2020 baseball season, written in real-time, day-by-day, as it was happening. Hopefully, I have peeled the layers back enough to give you an idea of what it was like to broadcast games for one of the most storied franchises in all of sports during the worst pandemic in a hundred years. I hope you enjoy reading *COVID Curveball* as much as I embraced the challenge of living it and spending the time pecking away at my keyboard, doing something different, to capture the experience. I appreciate you indulging me.

November 1, 2020

This is what it has come to; TMZ reporting that they have spotted Dodgers star third baseman, Justin Turner, in the driveway of his Southern California home. Turner has yet to comment publicly on what exactly happened during and following Game 6 of the World Series. They are not sure how Turner and his wife, Kourtney, returned from Arlington, Texas, after news broke that he tested positive for COVID-19 during the deciding game of the Series, but it wasn't with the team.

This is how it ended. Now, this is how it all began.

PART 1

The Preseason

MARCH 9, 2020. SPRING HAD SPRUNG

The Dodgers' Cactus League season is in full swing and has been since February 22, when they opened Spring Training in Scottsdale against the San Francisco Giants. The big non-baseball news up until today had been the Democratic presidential debates and a strange disease with a strange name that is wreaking havoc in Wuhan, China, and Milan, Italy. As it turns out, it was already here, and would soon be crawling into the Pacific Northwest and the greater New York/New Jersey metropolitan area. New Rochelle would become ground zero for the east coast and a nursing home near Seattle for the west coast.

On this typical March Arizona morning, I sat at the kitchen table of the Westgate Entertainment Area condo I have been staying in and began preparing for that day's exhibition game against the Padres in nearby Peoria. I left the condo around half past nine in the morning, put my work bag in the passenger seat and some luggage in the back of my rented Nissan Altima. I had the rest of the weekend off, so I was planning on driving from the ballpark to Las Vegas after the game to visit with my oldest son, Matt, who had moved there a month earlier to work with Oakland's AAA Club, the Las Vegas Aviators.

I plugged the ballpark address into Waze and headed over. Little did I know that this was the weekend the sports world would be turned upside down, and COVID-19 would have its unfortunate and unwelcome coming-out party in the United States.

Prior to this morning, I had been enjoying getting reacclimated to the Dodgers' organization and personnel at Camelback Ranch in Glendale. It is one of the nicer spring training complexes I have seen.

The Dodgers entered today's game with a 9-7-1 spring training record and sent reacquired lefty Alex Wood to the mound vs. Garrett Richards. The news before the game was that Mookie Betts, the Dodgers' prized off-season acquisition, had been scratched due to a case of food poisoning. We also learned that Dave Roberts had set the starting rotation for the first regular season series against the Giants.

Nothing shocking there. Clayton Kershaw would be the Opening Day starter, followed by Walker Buehler and David Price. Price came with Betts from Boston. Having another Cy Young winner around would be a big plus for the boys in blue.

As the morning game prep went on and the clock turned into afternoon on this sunny, without-a-cloud-in-the-sky 74-degree day, I began to read reports on social media from bona fide sources regarding the coronavirus and baseball. One report said that Major League Baseball was having a 5:00 p.m. ET conference call with all thirty owners to discuss the matter, but that, at this time, the season was set to start on time on March 26.

My broadcast partner on the Dodgers Radio Network is Rick Monday, who is one of the senior broadcasters in all of baseball, and one of the absolute best at breaking down games. Rick and I chatted about this "virus thing" a little bit, but didn't make a lot out of it as neither of us knew much about it. "Social distancing" was a term not yet introduced to American nomenclature. As the game went on and the Dodgers were pouring on runs, we continued to focus on the field, not realizing what was around the corner.

The game ended at 4:37 p.m., 14–2 in favor of the Dodgers. It was three hours and twenty-six minutes, and exactly fifty different players of not-so-scintillating and partially scripted spring training baseball. There was not much to talk about concerning the Padres, except a third-inning triple by left fielder Josh Naylor that led to one of the two San Diego runs. The Dodgers banged out 16 hits and scored 11 of their 14 runs over the sixth, seventh, and eighth innings. At 4:45, I was in the car and pointed north for my journey through the desert. I stepped on the gas. At 9:00 p.m. I pulled into the Palms Hotel Residences on West Flamingo Boulevard and checked in.

MARCH 11, 2020. THE PLUG IS PULLED

Today was one of the strangest, if not the most unusual day in the history of sports. It was as though the lights were going to be shut off one at a time in a deliberately dramatic fashion.

After visiting with Matt and helping him with some car-related matters, as dads sometimes have to do, we connected with one of my best friends from Denver, Chris Fuselier. Chris owns Denver's best sports bar, Blake Street Tavern, and is an alum and athletic booster of the University of Colorado. The Pac-12 basketball tournament was in town and was being held at T-Mobile Arena, and Matt and I were going with him to sit courtside and watch the Buffaloes play Washington State. Also joining us was a former broadcast partner of mine, Mike Pritchard. Mike was the MVP of Colorado's 1990 National Championship football team and went on to have a nice career as a wide receiver in the NFL. He works now as a sports talk show host in Las Vegas.

Throughout the day, we read news on social media as the coronavirus was becoming prevalent in the US with a lot of cases in Washington: Pac-12 country. Earlier in the day, the Big East tournament at Madison Square Garden in New York halted a game at halftime between St. John's and Creighton. Then the Big Ten canceled the rest of their tournament, followed by the Big 12.

The Pac-12 decided to allow fans and let the games happen tonight with the thought that they would play with no fans the next day. With this new virus in the back of my head the whole day, I wondered what was next. Washington State beat Colorado 82–68 and set up a date with Arizona State, which they never played. We were spectators at the last major college sporting event without restricted attendance in 2020. Once inside T-Mobile Arena, we were learning more about why the Utah Jazz/Oklahoma City Thunder game had been postponed. Jazz all-star Rudy Gobert had tested positive for coronavirus. The remainder of the NBA schedule, then the NHL schedule, were shut down. It was just a matter of time for baseball.

MARCH 12, 2020. SCRAMBLE TO BUG OUT

Lunch with two good friends was the order of business, with big baseball news unknowingly soon to be on the horizon. Chris and I went to see our good friend Jay Kornegay at the Westgate SuperBook. Jay is the executive director of Race and Sports at the world's largest sports book and is considered big time in the sports wagering industry. Jay and I have known each other a long time and used to do a weekly talk show together from the old Imperial Palace Race and Sports Book in the early '90s. Occasionally, we have been known to attend NHL games together and enjoy a few beverages.

While talking over lunch, our phones became active with news about the impending baseball shutdown. There were still games finishing up in Florida, and some getting ready to begin in Arizona. As luck would have it, a lot of rain was in the greater Phoenix area and it was holding up some games. Many fans were waiting to get in or, in some cases, were already at the ballparks. The Dodgers were ready to face the A's at Camelback Ranch. Some of the rain had passed, and if a game had to be played, it could have been. With the coronavirus bearing down, "unplayable field conditions" would be the initial reason listed for the cancellation of the game that day. Camelback's main stadium is exceptionally well kept, but they had to say something since there was no rain anymore, and it was already decided that they were not going to play.

In the meantime, in Las Vegas, I received an email from the Dodgers confirming the spring training schedule had been shut down. The email also said the team would help make any travel arrangements to get me home. We had to leave Arizona as soon as we were able. At that moment, I got up from the table, said goodbye to my friends, and immediately drove the four hours and fifteen minutes back to Glendale. On the way, I was on and off the phone with the team travel agent, who got me on the red-eye that night back to Boston. I sped back to the condo, packed everything in a rush, leaving food in the refrigerator and freezer, knowing I couldn't take it with me and hoping someone else could use it and took off for the airport. Spring training was over, and the regular season was suddenly in doubt.

MARCH 13, 2020. RED-EYE AND WAIT

It was 9:00 a.m. I arrived at Logan Airport in Boston following a six-hour flight, and I was beat. I texted Jess that I was at bag claim and heading to the curb. As she pulled up, she lowered the window to the passenger-side rear door where our chocolate lab, Reggie, stuck his head out to greet me, tail wagging and a great big smile on his face. This made me forget the last twenty-four hours or so, along with the uncertainty that awaits. We headed for home to sit and wait.

MARCH 25, 2020

We've spent the last two weeks waiting and wondering what is next. Every day there were far more questions than answers. Most of the questions centered around two things: is it safe to go anywhere, and will there be a baseball season of some sort? The rest of the exhibition season had been banged, but there was nothing official regarding the regular season, and this was the year the Dodgers were planning on hosting the All-Star Game.

The unpacking from spring training was finally completed, and during the day I would turn on the television to follow the news of this virus and its spread while scouring social media in search of other news, baseball or otherwise. Social distancing, mask-wearing, hand washing, and glove-wearing were the new implementations into our daily routines. For the first time ever, I was uncomfortable going into a grocery store, doing whatever I could to stay away from people. I would ordinarily pop into the Whole Foods near our house, especially when we didn't have solid dinner plans. We could always make a decent meal out of their prepared foods section, which was wonderful. Now it was shut down, and I agreed with the reasons why.

MARCH 26, 2020. WHERE IS ALL THE TOILET PAPER?

One thing I never understood was the chase for toilet paper and the empty shelves in grocery stores. Why people thought we would run out of toilet paper is beyond me, but I didn't want to use other means to finish off my business, so we had no choice but to search for it as well. Just before leaving spring training, I did see on the news where there was a nationwide run on toilet paper. I packed all the unused rolls that I had left in my apartment, just in case. It turned out to be a good thing that I did! Eventually, we had to start our own search for the precious paper product (the original PPP). It took a while looking in a few different places, but we finally struck gold at a nearby Target after a new delivery. The store smartly had a sign up limiting people to two packages, but we only took what we needed, while watching others load up as much as they could.

The list of stores we went to got longer. We could not find Clorox wipes or any other sanitizing products at any of them. The next obvious thing to do was to log on to Amazon and try there. Nope. All out. eBay, nope. The hoarding in America was like nothing I had ever seen. It reminded me of the energy crisis from October 1973 through March 1974. My mom and I had had to wait in line at gas stations and were only allowed to get gas on certain days, depending on whether or not our license plate ended with an odd or an even number. Some gas stations limited your purchase to ten gallons. That was fun. Not really.

APRIL 1, 2020. GET OUT OF TOWN

Coronavirus cases were climbing in our area of southern New Hampshire by the end of the month of March, making their way into the state after a sharp spike emanating from the fine folks across the border in Massachusetts. In the Greater Boston area, things were bad, so bad they were right up there with the hottest of hot spots like New York and New Jersey. Data continued to roll in showing more and more cases in our county. Jess and I decided to head north to the White Mountains and self-isolate there. We found a great cabin to rent in Bretton Woods, which is a hop, skip, and a jump from Mt. Washington, the largest mountain in the Northeast.

Bretton Woods is in the southern part of Coos (pronounced Co-oss) county where there were only two cases recorded. We felt safe up there, but we saw a lot of Massachusetts license plates. New Hampshire governor Chris Sununu had signed an executive order days earlier to allow only New Hampshire residents to rent in vacation or recreation areas. We almost canceled, but since we would be in compliance, we stayed there until mid-May, each day hoping for baseball news. June felt like a lost month with all the back and forth between MLB and the Player's Association before finally settling on how to conduct a season.

JULY 1, 2020. GETTING THE CALL

Still no baseball schedule as of today, and it is still probably a few days off. Each day, from the time I was sent home from spring training on March 9 until now, I was hoping for any bit of news. I only knew there was a 60-game season and a few details about how the broadcasts would be conducted.

No travel or lodging in LA had been booked yet because I had no idea what my role was going to be. We have a three-man rotation, basically, to do play-by-play of Dodgers games on both TV and radio.

Joe Davis is the main TV announcer, and he misses about twenty-five to thirty games in a usual season for his national baseball and college football commitments on Fox. Charley Steiner is the main radio announcer and I do the play-by-play on his off days. I am also assigned the bulk of the spring training games with Rick Monday. I also did some work on the pre-game show for TV and a few other things. The Dodgers kept me busy in 2019, but I didn't know what to expect for this much shorter season.

Sitting on my back deck with Jess this afternoon, my cell phone rang. The Dodgers were calling to let me know that Charley was not working any games this season and that I would do all sixty games, specifying, "If we have sixty games you will do all of them." I would also do any exhibitions and the entire postseason. That answered a lot of my questions, but I didn't know why Charley was out. If they didn't offer the reason, I didn't think it was my business to inquire, so I left it alone and figured I would find out eventually.

Now I had the task of getting out to LA, not the shortest commute, to book a flight and a place to stay for the season. Normally, I would take the most convenient non-stop flight and book an apartment through Airbnb. In the new age of baseball during a pandemic, I thought twice. For my flight, I found one out of Boston that stopped at Washington Dulles. The reason for this is that for the longest stretch of flight, from Dulles to LAX, I would be on a bigger plane, for less time and with more potential room to spread out. Other connections I checked out had smaller planes connecting from Denver or San Francisco that had two seats on each side of the aisle.

Instead of going back to Airbnb, I booked the Westin Bonaventure in downtown LA through the team's travel site. I had stayed there last season for a while and knew that the staff would work harder to keep the hotel cleaner and more sanitized than any regular apartment building. I emailed the manager of the hotel, whom I had come to know through a mutual friend. He upgraded me to a suite and let me know that they had not been very busy and had plenty of rooms. The Westin Bonaventure is connected to a convention hall and draws a lot of its visitors through conventions and events. With no large public gatherings, I figured that I could possibly have an entire floor to myself. Bottom line, the hotel would not be crowded and would be a safe place to anchor for two or three months in an area currently considered a coronavirus hot spot.

Eventually, the plan is to move to either Southern California or Las Vegas and commute. Jess and I are leaning very hard toward the Las Vegas idea. I had lived there for twelve years in the '90s and early in the 2000s, and while there had broadcast the Padres' and Dodgers' AAA games, along with a number of other things. Vegas is a great option for us for a lot of reasons, including that my two oldest sons, Matt and Kyle, have moved back to the city where they were born and are getting themselves established there. My youngest son, Drew, a senior in Sports Management at the University of South Carolina, has expressed an interest in relocating there, too. So, family reasons, economic, and tax reasons would all play into that decision. My partner on Dodger telecasts, the great Orel Hershiser, claims Las Vegas as his home now and commutes.

Jess and I had met with our realtor in New Hampshire during the month of February to decide when to put the house on the market. Once COVID-19 hit the following month, we put everything on hold. Due to the virus, it is back to commuting to the west coast again this year. The only good thing is that I won't have to check in and out of the hotel and put stuff in storage each time we go on a road trip. There are no road trips for us in 2020.

JULY 3, 2020. ZOOM ZOOM, GET USED TO IT

Today started the "new normal" in covering baseball. Zoom. The Dodgers, after a few days of intake where players and staff were tested, held their first official workouts. Dave Roberts, the Dodgers' manager, was the first to speak to the media during the first Zoom conference, followed a few minutes later by starting pitcher Clayton Kershaw. There were no members of the media in the team's press conference room, located just outside the Dodgers clubhouse. All reporters covering the team today were located either in different, isolated parts of Dodger Stadium, at their office, or at home.

As for me, I am still in New Hampshire and have dialed up today's Zoom presser on my iPad Pro while sitting at my kitchen counter. This is what I am imagining things to be like on a daily basis during the regular season, just not from my kitchen counter. It was made known to me that we will have Zoom calls set up for us by the Dodgers media relations department with Roberts prior to each series, and with some players, due to the fact that team broadcasters are in "Tier 3" of the three-tiered personnel system implemented by Major League Baseball.

Tier 3 people are not allowed to have personal interaction with anyone in Tier 1, like the players and coaches, the people we interact with often who help us do our jobs better. Under the new health and safety regulations, no clubhouse access, no field access, no dugout access, just Zoom access. Certainly understandable. In fact, I am told the only place we can go is the assigned luxury suite that will serve as combination office and broadcast booth. The only place I would be allowed to observe any of the "Summer Camp" workouts would be from the luxury booth, and that luxury booth alone.

Back in my kitchen, Dave began his presser on my iPad wearing his Dodger blue batting practice top, white game pants, classic LA cap, and his mask pulled down and resting around his neck. Roberts explained, after the obligatory "good to be back" comments, how social distancing was a big part of camp and how the team would be spreading out players and workouts.

"We will have three waves of pitchers coming in today. About six to eight guys in each. Two waves of position players. Five to six guys in each wave there. We are staggering the workouts to social distance. Today will be a longer day than normal and we will shorten it up for tomorrow," Roberts said.

"We will start intrasquad games early next week. Clayton [Kershaw] is already built up to three-plus innings. Ross [Stripling] is up to three innings, Alex [Wood] also. So I see these guys able to go into a four-inning situation when we get going," he added.

In light of the coronavirus, Roberts was asked if everyone on the 60-man player pool, even though the Dodgers actually put fifty-one players on it to leave room to possibly add others, has shown up yet. Roberts and every other Major League manager has to choose their words carefully when answering these types of questions now.

"Not everyone is in yet today because of the staggered workouts, but guys that aren't able to start camp with us for some reason or another are not here...I can't be specific on names right now."

This is the unfortunate new manager-speak that beat reporters are going to have to hear this season, and it is not the manager's fault. Due to HIPAA laws on medical privacy, because a positive coronavirus test constitutes a medical condition that does not have anything to do with playing professional baseball, a manager is not supposed to name names. As part of the current collective bargaining agreement between the Major League Baseball Players Association and Major League Baseball's owners, players agree to sign a waiver that allows the team to release information regarding baseball-related injuries. Occasionally, we will hear that a player gets sick or has food poisoning or "flu-like" symptoms (in the old days this was a euphemism for a bad hangover) and those are openly discussed, but positive tests put the team and the manager in an awkward situation this year. Some players around baseball have just flat out given permission to the manager to say they are positive, but not everyone.

While Roberts was speaking to the press in Los Angeles and one of the team's announcers through a tablet in my kitchen, Major League Baseball was putting out its first press release regarding positive tests from the league-wide mandatory intake screening process. MLB says they conducted tests from 3,185 samples that were collected and shipped off to their lab in Utah. Of the total number of tests, there were thirty-eight positive results for COVID-19. Of those thirty-eight, thirty-one were players, with the remaining seven positives from staff members. That equated to 1.2 percent positives of all tests conducted. Also noted was that nineteen of the thirty Major League clubs had at least one player or staff member record a positive test.

It was Kershaw's time to sit in the press room and answer a round of questions. Clayton seemed to be in very good spirits and gave good, thoughtful answers. He is a veteran and understands his role, especially when he pitches. Win or lose, he stands up in front of his locker and answers questions. I appreciated that about him the few times I was in the clubhouse after games last season, asking him the first several questions for SportsNet LA's post-game show. Occasionally, I would be assigned to fill in for the Dodgers' Emmy Award-winning sideline reporter, Alanna Rizzo. No contest. She runs circles around me at that job, but when I had to post up with Kershaw after a game, he always answered the bell.

Kershaw was asked whether he had considered opting out. In January, he and his wife, Ellen, had had their third child, Cooper Ellis Kershaw. Cooper is their second son, with the middle name for Clayton's former catcher, A.J. Ellis. Older brother and sister Charlie and Cali traveled from home base in Texas with mom and dad to their Southern California residence for the season. Kershaw's family is most important to him, but he believes in the system.

"It's a trust factor. I trust Major League Baseball, the union, my teammates. I have trust that we are going to do what we have to do to play baseball...if you want to see this season through, you can't be stupid. If you want to play, that is good incentive to do things the right way," Kershaw said.

Asked about the adjustments and whether anything has been unnerving to this point, Kershaw added, "It's an adjustment for sure. Coming from Texas, you have to wear masks in stores and stuff, but not outside. When I landed here and saw people outside wearing masks just walking their dogs, that was a little unnerving."

He then reported that he was expecting to pitch five innings on Monday after building himself up while working out at home. The toughest thing for him, as well as for anyone else involved in this game, is not having a start date. What about a 60-game season? Worthy of all of the accolades of a full season, and should it have an asterisk?

"It will be different, but we are on a level playing field with everyone else. If you win it, you'll still be a champion. To say there's an asterisk, I don't think that's fair. If you win the season, it's going to feel good, no matter what."

The presumptive Opening Day starter thanked the reporters, stood up, put his mask on, and walked out of the room. Following another session with third baseman Justin Turner, day one of the "new normal" Zoom press conferences was in the books.

Today we also learned what we all already knew: that the All-Star game, to be hosted in Los Angeles for the first time in forty years, was cancelled and will be replaced with the 2022 Mid-Summer Classic instead. Atlanta is hosting next year. With the prospect of getting sixty games in during a 66-day window along with spiking COVID-19 cases in California, Arizona, and Texas among other states, it was not a shocker. MLB did the right thing in giving the Dodgers the next available All-Star Game.

JULY 4, 2020. FIRST OPT OUT

A short workout took place this morning at Dodger Stadium, and not every player was there. Dave Roberts took the virtual podium for another Zoom press conference at 10:30 a.m. He was asked about the alternate training site the team is using at the University of Southern California's Rod Dedeaux Field. Oklahoma City Dodgers (AAA) manager Travis Barbary and others from the parent club's minor league staff are overseeing the ten or so players currently working out there. Roberts did indicate that there is a date the players will have to vacate USC and will move their satellite operation to Rancho Cucamonga, home of the Dodgers' High-A affiliate in the California League. That actually never happened, and the team kept the alternates at USC for the entire season.

As the presser went on, we learned a few other things, such as the fact that the players are doing a good job policing themselves and taking the health and safety measures very seriously.

Let's not bury the lede here, though, shall we?

Asked for the second day in a row whether he expected any players to opt out of playing this season, Roberts replied in a similar way as he had done yesterday.

"At this time, no."

At this time…a bombshell was being formed that would drop in a few hours. The clock was now ticking on a decision and an announcement from a veteran player the Dodgers were going to be counting on and was considered a big off-season acquisition. By 2:00 p.m., word was out that former American League Cy Young winner David Price would be opting out of 2020. He had reported to Dodger Stadium on Wednesday like everyone else, but following further conversations with his family, he decided not to pitch and to forfeit a season's worth of service time along with a chance to play for one of the pre-season World Series favorites.

Price will be thirty-five years old on August 26. That is not exactly young by baseball standards, so missing a season, even a drastically shortened one, is effectively shortening his career. Price, in a tweet, told Dodger fans:

> *"I'm sorry I won't be playing for you this year, but look forward to representing you next year."*

It is difficult to blame anyone for opting out. We can't pretend to know the intimate details of someone else's life and what goes into making a decision like this.

I have a unique perspective, because I had also been with him during all but his last season in Boston with the Red Sox. Not exactly smooth sailing at Fenway for David. He usually acts like he doesn't know me or what I do (he probably doesn't, and it is not his job to know me) and, perhaps wrongly on my part, I hadn't put in the effort to communicate with him better. When he and I both arrived in Boston in 2016 from different places, we would have infrequent but occasional brief conversations in the clubhouse early in the season when I was attempting to establish a relationship, but after that, I don't think we spoke much other than one post-game radio interview during the 2018 postseason. We heard in our headsets that we were getting J.D. Martinez for the interview, and a few seconds later the voice on the other end quickly said, "Here's David Price." I still don't know to this day how that all went down, but the interview was good and Price gave us really good answers.

Price distanced himself from the media in Boston when he could, and in fairness to David, the media in that town can have a sharp edge to it at times. I remember a day at Fenway in 2016 when a local columnist popped into the booth to say hello to my partner and long-time Red Sox broadcaster, Joe Castiglione. Joe asked the writer, who did not visit the park that frequently, what he was working on that brought him to the park. The Red Sox had just lost six straight games, and the scribe said proudly with a smile, referring to the team's manager, John Farrell, "I smell blood in the water. That is why I showed up." It can be a mean place sometimes, and not for everybody.

During the first part of spring training, I did observe David a few times, but missed any opportunities to connect with him in person. I figured I would have plenty of time before the end of spring, but COVID-19 threw us a big curveball in the dirt and made sure that we swung and missed. It did appear as though he was much more relaxed, and from all indications, the move to play in Los Angeles was going to be the clear change of scenery that he needed. Price and Boston, in spite of winning a World Series, was not the best match. Price and LA could have been a match made in Blue Heaven in 2020, but it was not to be this year. Dodger fans should get a good chance to know him better next season.

David, or D.P., as his teammates call him, earned a lot of goodwill from Dodger fans by being that good teammate he professes to be to many he had never met. He spent two hundred thousand of his own money to financially assist the organization's minor leaguers to help with expenses during the early part of this pandemic. That, in addition to these strange circumstances, will garner him support for his opt-out decision from the front office, the clubhouse, and from many Dodger fans. He probably won't be the last Major League player to opt out either, and as I said before, under these unprecedented circumstances, you can't lay blame on anyone who does decide to sit the season out.

JULY 6, 2020. CHICO AND THE MAN

The Dodgers tried a soft streaming opening tonight before the scheduled intrasquad game. Regular batting practice on the field was streamed online with just the ambient stadium audio and no commentary. Nearly forty thousand fans tuned in online through the

Dodgers' Twitter and Facebook accounts. This is just further evidence that, in spite of what is going on around us, people are hungry for baseball. My partner on radio, Rick Monday, and I spoke by telephone, and he told me he enjoyed the sound of the ball off the bat and called it "soothing." He is also ready to get back to the ballpark.

SportsNet LA, the TV network of the Dodgers, posted the lineups during the Access SportsNet Dodgers program that usually runs before games, but also runs during prime time on non-game nights. Many of the names were regulars, some were players who we saw more of during spring training, and then there was the one-named wonder. "Chico" was listed for the "Visiting Team" as the left fielder and batting ninth against Clayton Kershaw.

Who is Chico? Francisco "Chico" Herrera is one of the Dodgers' clubhouse attendants and not a minor league prospect of any sort. He has a glove and a uniform and was just occupying a spot in the outfield with a lack of depth right now. The good-natured Dave Roberts noticed a few things about his game.

"He called off our MVP (Cody Bellinger), so we have to do pop-up communication with him. The center fielder has priority. He boxed one play when he turned a single into a triple. But, no, ah, it is good having him out here. I will say this. It is really good to see guys out here, in and out of uniform, doing more to try to be helpful any way they can."

Chico did not take any at-bats against Kershaw, although I would guess he would have relished the opportunity to stand in there against the future Hall of Famer and look foolish. I would have loved it, too, but my days of swinging a bat are long since passed. Kershaw pitched four innings, tossing 73 pitches with one strikeout. Interestingly, the only guy that Kershaw fanned was not Chico, but superstar Mookie Betts. Betts swung and missed at strike three his third time facing Kershaw. Bench coach Bob Geren was the home plate umpire, whose work, I assume jokingly, was later described by catcher Will Smith as "inconsistent."

JULY 7, 2020

As of today, seven Dodgers still have not reported to camp for one reason or another, and the manager cannot disclose why. Closer Kenley Jansen is one of the prominent absentees, and there could be a few reasons why. He had a heart issue two seasons ago, he lives in Curaçao and travel is difficult, or (hopefully not) he has COVID-19. Sixteen days remain until opening night against the Giants, and the closer is not in camp.

Gavin Lux, the up-and-coming young infielder, primarily a second baseman from Wisconsin who debuted last season, has not yet arrived. Veteran outfielder A.J. Pollock is absent. Right-handed reliever Pedro Báez, an important late-inning setup man, is also a no-show. Left-handed ground-ball specialist, Scott Alexander, is not in Summer Camp yet either. It is well documented that Alexander has diabetes, and one could speculate that he is not here due to being in a "higher risk" category. The early impression I got from several reports in June was that he was going to take part in the season.

Right-handed pitcher Tony Gonsolin from Vacaville, California, has not arrived. He would be a big contributor either as a spot starter or a long reliever. Extra catcher and solid prospect Keibert Ruiz has not been at Dodger Stadium either. There were some reports about him several days ago that stated he tested positive, but I have not seen or heard anything from the team about it at this time. Roberts says all he can about the absences, which isn't much, but he hopes to see them "sometime soon."

Many teams are either canceling workouts or pushing back the start times, due to the slow return of results from the lab in Utah that Major League Baseball is using. MLB received a strong letter from the

Players Union two days ago stating, basically, that they need to look for additional labs to handle the volume of tests. Players are tested every forty-eight hours, but are not getting results back, in most cases, before they are due to test again. There were reports today stating that some players haven't been tested every forty-eight hours, and some not for several days. There are some pretty big hiccups in the testing system right now in MLB, but no negative reports about the way the Dodgers are going about things.

At noon EST on the dot, my cell phone rings. It is the Dodgers. The voice on the other end of the phone tells me my role for the season may be changing. Charley Steiner wants to announce games but doesn't feel comfortable coming to the ballpark due to coronavirus concerns. The Dodgers, with an assist from Fox Networks, are going to attempt to install a system in Charley's home so that he can call games in real-time with no lag from the internet. Not a 100 percent done deal, I'm told, but if it happens then they are considering having me do a multitude of other things. Assignments for me would range from radio pre-game and post-game duties, some on the Dodger Talk post-game show along with some pre- and post-game TV duties, possibly some anchoring.

In less than a week, I go from doing every game during the regular season and postseason to jack-of-all-trades mode. Considering what is going on in the sports broadcasting industry, particularly baseball, I am grateful to be employed and have a season to broadcast. While I have been told that no final decisions have been made, there are lots of conversations going on regarding how broadcasting is going to work. I am reassured that I will have a significant role, possibly doing the middle innings every day, and that the club feels fortunate to have someone with my experience able to jump on in any role. I am also told to expect at least a handful of TV games to broadcast when Joe Davis goes over to fulfill his national commitments to Fox, but they have not finalized those dates yet. He wanted to let me know so that I wasn't blindsided with this information when I showed up to Dodger Stadium later this month to report for work.

If the radio setup from Charley's home functions properly, think of how many things have to go well on a Dodger Radio Network broadcast for everything to sound right, especially on a road game. Charley would be at home talking to Rick, who will be doing the games in a luxury suite at the stadium, both watching similar screens with feeds from the same game, all while keeping their fingers crossed they are seeing them at the same time. Rick will also have an empty stadium in front of him. Many times, even when announcers are in the same booth, they can step all over each other until they get to know how each other works. Doing this kind of remote radio broadcast is hard enough when you are not at the actual game, and will be even more difficult when the two announcers are not in the same room and can't just turn their heads and look at each other when needed. I think you can get away with it more on TV, like they have on the ESPN telecasts of the KBO (Korean Baseball Organization) this season, where you don't have to be as descriptive and on time. We will see how this all turns out, but I don't think that it will be perfect no matter how the broadcasts are done.

At the 2004 and 2008 Summer Olympics in Athens, Greece, and Beijing, China, I called baseball and softball off of a screen in an "off-tube" booth in the International Broadcast Center. I did Men's and Women's basketball on site, so that was much better. When you call baseball off a screen, however, it is possible to miss a lot of what is going on. You can't see where foul balls go, you can't see if a pinch hitter is on deck, you can't see when a team scrambles the bullpen and gets a reliever or two up, and it is easy to miss a pinch runner being slipped into the game. You can anticipate all of these situations, but if your eyes don't help confirm them for you, it is no good.

We will have more than one screen to call the games from, including one that will show us an "All Nine" high home plate angle, so we can see the defensive alignments. Also, we are expecting to have a bullpen camera, so we can see who is warming up.

Last night, I got a call from Mike Levy, the Dodgers' TV producer and one of the keepers of the broadcaster schedules. I had texted him earlier in the evening asking if he knew how long it would be until my first TV game, so I knew how long I had to lose the weight I gained while in quarantine. A few pounds should disappear as soon as I shave the beard I started back on March 9, the last time I shaved before a game. Anyway, he laughed about that, and I did too, but just for show.

One good piece of intel I got from Levy was about the artificial crowd noise that will be used. Apparently, a Grammy Award-winning audio engineer was negotiating with the ball club to finalize arrangements for his team to provide the ambience at Dodger Stadium. The report was, after it was tested out, the players loved it. Mike told me that if all went well, we will have the crowd noise in our headphones for both radio and TV. That was a big relief. In my opinion, it will be so much better to hear crowd noise and the beautiful "hum" of the ballpark between pitches, than talking over the strange sound of an empty stadium.

JULY 13, 2020. ALL HAIL BASEBALL

T-minus three days until I rejoin the Dodgers in Los Angeles. To this point, every bit of work that I have done to prepare for the season has been remotely, including watching the intrasquad games and press conferences. With just a little time before I report out west, it was possible to sneak in one more quick trip into the White Mountains of New Hampshire. We have learned to appreciate all that the area has to offer, so I quickly put together a two-day trip. Jess and I were accompanied by my twenty-one-year-old son, Drew, along with our trusty sidekick, Reggie, a go-everywhere chocolate lab.

Drew is up for the abbreviated summer and had about forty-eight hours off from his summer job as a jack of all trades with the Nashua Silver Knights of the Futures League. He had never been that far north in New Hampshire, so I thought it would be good for him to experience it. After getting up there last night, we took our time in the morning before we headed out for an upward hike that would have us reach the summit of two mountains. Drew didn't know what to expect and how challenging some of these mountain trips that Jess and I take can be.

We decided on Mt. Starr King and Mt. Waumbeck, located in Jefferson, NH. Neither of us had been there before, although I was pretty familiar with the area. There is a family hunting camp affectionately known, to those of us who get to experience it, as Lumbago Acres. I have been going to this camp since I was a kid that is nestled into a 140-acre plot of birch trees and hardwood timber that was only about a ten-minute drive from the turnoff for the mountain trailhead.

The four of us got going and began our ascent up the steep, rocky trail of Mt. Starr King. The elevation gain for us was over thirty-eight hundred feet. We started at twelve hundred feet and the top of Mt. Waumbeck summits at 4,006 feet. It was a tough climb to the Mt. Starr King summit, which was just under four thousand feet, and it was only a mile or so from there to the Mt. Waumbeck summit. At the top of Mt. Starr King, we stopped for a bit, looked at the bright blue skies, and checked our weather app on the phone to make sure no unexpected weather would sneak in overhead, which it sometimes can in that part of the country. All clear.

The rumble of thunder was suddenly audible now in the distance as we began the trek over to the next summit. The closer we got to the summit, the darker the skies were quickly becoming, and the claps of thunder were not so much in the distance anymore. The plan was to stop at the summit and break out the lunch I had carried in my day pack and rest awhile before starting our descent. That plan was changed, and fast. The moment we reached the top of the mountain, the wind picked up greatly and the temperature dropped about fifteen degrees. A light rain began to sprinkle, and we knew that was not the end of it. Not even close.

We decided we could not stick around and quickly began our way down, and as soon as we pointed ourselves from whence we came, the skies opened up. I was already pretty wet with sweat and was soon to be completely soaked from head to toe, but the worst was to come.

Almost remarkably, I had four bars of cell service on this mountain summit, and just as the skies opened, my phone rang. It was Erik Sherman, one of my best friends, and a former baseball teammate at Emerson College. Erik just happens to be a *New York Times* bestselling author of books on baseball, and at the time of this writing, has one book in the can ready for a 2021 publication, and is working on another with a strong Dodgers theme. I didn't answer, but he sent a text that showed up on my Apple Watch that said it was a good idea to do the book you are currently reading, and his agent agreed.

Literally fifteen seconds later, my radio partner, Rick Monday, was calling, as my watch indicated. Simultaneously with Rick's call, hail began to fall, then began to roar out of the sky as though it had a problem with us. Somehow, and I still have no idea how, my phone must have answered because I heard Rick's booming voice. He hung up and called again. In the meantime, good-size sky rocks from the clouds were pelting us at an alarming speed while we tried to navigate around huge shin-high puddles that had not been there just fifteen minutes earlier. My son, Drew, took his twenty-one-year-old legs and plowed way ahead of us, well out of sight. Jess just put her head down and kept moving fast in front of me. Our dog, Reggie, was weathering this alright because, well, he is a Labrador retriever and they love this kind of stuff.

So next, I felt the vibration on my Apple Watch indicating a text. It had one word in the text from Rick: "Absolutely." I had no idea what that meant, but I would find out later. I just kept on going, completely soaked through with my heart pounding out of my chest and Armageddon going on all around us. A mile after descending the summit of Mt. Waumbeck, we got back to the Mt. Starr King summit. The rocket hail had subsided, but it was still raining sheets and the cool wind was gusting. I looked down at my forearms briefly to see the red marks the half-inch-to-inch hailstones had left on me. I have been in extreme weather of all kinds many times before, but for a few moments, it felt like the actual sky was falling. The weather statement we saw afterward showed the wind was recorded as gusting better than fifty miles per hour.

When the pouring finally slowed to regular old rain, I got another baseball-related text. It was Colorado Rockies radio announcer Jack Corrigan, asking if I could do a Dodger preview on the Rockies flagship radio station later in the week. I had to answer him later because I was in no condition to talk shop at that point. I also noticed a return text I had somehow sent to Rick that said, "Can I call you later?" My only thought is that a piece of hail hit my watch just right and sent him an automatic response. Later in the evening back at our place in Bretton Woods, I called Rick back and he asked me what the hell was going on. He said when the phone picked up it sounded like the "end of the world." While it temporarily seemed like it, it wasn't, but the physical challenge of getting down this mountain while soaked through still lay ahead. When I arrived at the car after a two-hour trek down and my legs barely able to hold me up, my thought was how overdue I was getting back to the ballpark.

JULY 14, 2020. TESTING, TESTING...IS THIS THING ON?

T-minus two days to travel to LA, and the reports are going from bad to worse in Southern California regarding the spread of the coronavirus. California Governor Gavin Newsom issued orders for certain businesses in the state to go backward. Back to outdoor dining only; hair salons, gyms, and bars were to close again. Newsome happens to be the nephew of the speaker of the House of Representatives, California congresswoman, Nancy Pelosi.

Los Angeles mayor Eric Garcetti, who, like many, is a big Dodger fan, also had to issue further orders to help protect LA and LA County. One of the new rules was that if a person was exposed to someone with COVID-19, even if they had a negative test, that person would be required to quarantine for fourteen days. From the baseball perspective, this was something that could be problematic. With this rule, it was determined that anyone who had not been tested could not enter Dodger Stadium, even if they worked there. Someone like me, perhaps.

I was notified via email late in the afternoon, east coast time, that I needed a test. The lab that was doing the testing was only there this week for us Tier 3 personnel at certain times, and my currently scheduled flight would have me landing at LAX a half hour before the final test would be issued for this round. If I didn't get a test, then there was a chance I would not be allowed into Dodger Stadium, by City and County order, until well after Opening Day on the 23rd, which for a Major League broadcaster, you can understand how that would be an issue.

My first call was to the local testing clinic in my town to see about getting a private test before I got to LA. The clinic said they would be happy to test me, but that my results would not be available for seven to ten days at least. That wouldn't do, so the only option I could think of was to ask the team to change my travel so that I could get in tomorrow night and make the final round of testing on Thursday. I hadn't packed a thing yet for what would be a trip that could last up to three months if the Dodgers went back to the World Series.

The Dodgers roster got some needed help today when veteran outfielder A.J. Pollock finally reported to camp. Still no public reason as to why, but in this time of baseball amid a pandemic, there could be any number of reasons. The main thing is that he is here. The bad news is for Chico Herrera, the suddenly famous clubbie who robbed Mookie Betts of extra bases and turned it into a double play from left field. The legend of Chico will have to live on via some T-shirts that have been made to commemorate his short-lived baseball fame.

Also showing up was left-handed reliever Scott Alexander. Alexander did some throwing and is getting himself ready for the opener that is now nine days away as best as he can. Alexander would be someone in a "high risk" group as he is a diabetic, so the Dodgers will be watching him closely.

Kenley Jansen took off his mask, came out of the bullpen, and threw darts during tonight's intrasquad game. He got three outs on seven pitches, retiring Mookie, Corey Seager (three-pitch strikeout), and Justin Turner. Because he didn't get enough work in, another hitter was sent up to face him. Cody Bellinger swung at the first pitch and popped out. Four outs on eight pitches is pretty good, especially for a guy who just recovered from coronavirus! Kenley cut off his dreadlocks and looks in really good shape. His cutter looked sharp as well, as the toughest part of the Dodgers batting order can attest to. I am looking forward to his next outing.

JULY 15, 2020. TRAVEL DAY

It is morning, and I am still finishing up my packing for the long trip in front of me. Due to the fact that things are so fluid on the team's broadcasting front, I still have no idea what my schedule will be and when my first game is. I have to pack some things to wear for television games and possible pre-game shows. Strategic packing takes two full suitcases, a roller bag, and my regular work bag. Ready to go. I have not been on a plane since March 12, when I left spring training.

Jess, Reggie (our very good dog, in case you forgot), and I piled in the car and made our way to Logan Airport in Boston at 1:15 p.m. to catch a 3:45 p.m. flight. The traffic was lighter than usual on the way down since most, presumably, are working from home and staying off the roads. Once we said our goodbyes, it was time to mask up for the rest of the day and evening.

Already having checked in online, I wheeled my luggage to United Airlines Priority Access bag drop. The attendant noticed my Dodgers luggage tags with my name on them and said he remembered me from my days broadcasting Red Sox games. I thought that was funny in a way since no one ever recognized me in Boston from just being on radio only. In Pittsburgh, I did a lot of TV too, so I got recognized there and still do, but not in Boston. I thought I was invisible in that town. Anyway, he was nice and asked all about my move to the Dodgers and how the team was going to be. Turns out, he did some work with both the Red Sox and Dodgers charter planes for United during the 2018 World Series. Small world.

Next, I went to TSA Pre-Check where, without another soul in line, I breezed through. It must have taken less than a minute from the time I showed my ID until I was on the other side of security. That doesn't happen often. When walking to the gate, I observed most everyone with masks on, not many restaurants or shops open, and a quiet, more subdued mood prevailed. People were sitting spread apart at Gate B30. When I got on the plane, I was handed a packet of 70 percent isopropyl alcohol wipes. Nobody in the row behind me and no one at all in the middle seats. One of the flight attendants handed me a plastic bag containing an eight-ounce bottle of water, a small bag of pretzels, and the airline staple; the Biscoff cookie. Still "Europe's favorite cookie with coffee." I wouldn't really know since Americans are not currently allowed to travel to Europe!

The flight was probably the most quiet flight I have ever been on, and I've had my share of the friendly skies over the years. There was only one reminder announcement about wearing the masks about three hours into the flight. I guess someone had taken theirs off. After landing and collecting my bags, I made my way to the curb to meet my rental car, which was being delivered to me. I knew I was back in LA once the doors opened and I took my first step outside. It felt good to be back.

JULY 16, 2020. TESTING DAY AT DODGER STADIUM

My COVID-19 test was scheduled for 11:25 a.m. I cannot go into the stadium until I receive the results. It might be a couple of days. Who knows? I pulled into a spot in Lot P, the designated area for Tier 3 personnel. Rick Krajewski, our statistician and researcher on telecasts, happened to be parked to my left. He didn't know any more than I did in terms of when we might get a result.

Outfielder A.J. Pollock is in Summer Camp now and seems ready to go. He was considering sitting out, and for good reasons. His daughter, Maddie, had been born three months prematurely, weighing a little over a pound. I knew exactly how he was feeling after having gone through it twenty-four years earlier with my middle son, Kyle, who had been born almost as early as that. I can tell you how much that weighs on the mind of a parent—the constant questions, the wondering about its effect on their development. It is downright frightening and terribly stressful. Kyle turned out just fine and his development was normal.

Along with the premature birth, there was the not-so-minor detail that Pollock had tested positive for COVID-19. He had some symptoms but recovered quickly enough. Being positive and now having his wife and daughter, especially, in a high-risk category, he was ready to check out for the season and not take any risks. A.J.'s wife, Kate, had been a lacrosse player at Notre Dame, where she met the star of the Fighting Irish's baseball team. Kate also had a stint with the national team of Great Britain. As an athlete, she understood the need for her husband to compete. She told him there was no way he could sit on the couch and watch his teammates win a World Series without him, so he should get out there and play.

"It is strange," Pollock told SportsNet LA. "I've got Kate back in Arizona—she's still grinding pretty hard right now. She's at the hospital maybe ten hours a day. That part, mentally, is hard, knowing she's there. It's a nice escape for me but tough thinking what my wife is going through."

JULY 17, 2020

My COVID-19 test results, I was told, should be available today. Nothing. Nothing in the morning, nothing in the afternoon. I continued to check my phone throughout the evening like an expectant father. It became obsessive, looking at my phone, checking my texts, emails, and spam folder over and over. I stayed put in the hotel, just in case. Now I needed to know if I was positive, asymptomatic, or negative. Peace of mind was in order. It was midnight, lights out, still no word. Maybe tomorrow.

In the meantime, I still assumed that I would be broadcasting the exhibition game in two days. After all, that is what I'd been told a few weeks ago, but the broadcast schedule has been as fluid as the Pacific Ocean. I learned through a chain of emails that I was to do a daily five-minute segment early on the pre-game and late on the post-game. At least I knew now that I had something to do that could be scheduled and planned. I was glad to find out that I was included in some aspect of the broadcast.

I appreciate the Dodgers organization for not furloughing anyone during the pandemic and realize that this season will not be normal at all. We did have to accept sizable pay cuts, but it was far better to accept the haircut than losing my hair entirely. The Dodgers' ownership and executive team deserve a lot of credit for finding a way to keep everyone and showing they value their employees.

Another Dodgers intrasquad game tonight, and I couldn't go and watch in person. I stayed in and watched it on TV, hoping to get as much out of it as I can.

JULY 18, 2020. NEGATORY, GOOD BUDDY

Still no results. About mid-day, I text Rick Krajewski, our stat maven, to see if he has received his results. He says he got his the morning after, in less than twenty-four hours. I'm closing in on seventy-two hours. I notify our radio producer, Duane McDonald, that I don't have the results yet and might not be allowed into the stadium for tomorrow's exhibition game with the Diamondbacks. I get a text from the broadcasting department a short time later asking if I've received my results. When I tell them no, they get a hold of Human Resources and the investigation is on. Toward the end of the day, they find a test for N-e-v-e-r-e-y-y, with my date of birth. Apparently someone, somehow, mistook two *T*s for two *Y*s. That delayed everything by two days.

Negative, by the way. Even though that is the result I expected, it is a relief to actually know. Next test is Tuesday the 21st at 11:10 a.m. I am in a testing group identified at "Frequency One," which basically means I will be tested about once a week. It is comforting to know that the people I will be around all the time are in the same group.

JULY 19, 2020. GAME DAY

At 3:10 p.m., I drove down Vin Scully Avenue to Sunset Gate A. At the guard gate, I was asked if I was experiencing any symptoms and if I had been around anyone showing symptoms or was positive. No to all. The thermometer was placed up to my forehead and I registered a low 97.7. I chalked that up to having the air conditioning on high in the car for the short drive from the hotel to the ballpark.

At 3:30, I recorded my first pre-game segment of the season with Tim Cates, the host on AM 570, which is the Dodgers flagship radio station. At 3:35, I was finished until the fifth segment of the post-game show. It was about this time that I realized that I had left my dinner at the hotel. One of the other new features of this season is that the team cannot provide food for us as they normally would. I left the park, drove back to the hotel, grabbed my food from my twenty-second-floor room, drove back to the park, and walked back into the stadium. This took about twenty minutes, unheard of in Los Angeles. There was no traffic coming or going. I experienced the quickest getaway after the game too. If there is one good thing about having no fans at Dodger Stadium, that is it. I would take the traffic any time.

The Arizona Diamondbacks were down on the field, many watching the Dodgers take batting practice, and we were a short time away from what would look like an actual game, one the Dodgers would win 9–2. It was good to finally see some baseball with one team playing a different team.

JULY 20, 2020

The Dodgers and D-backs went at it again. This one was over early, as Mookie Betts's three-run homer in the second inning would be more than enough. The boys in blue rolled to a 12–1 win. Chris Taylor contributed with a three-run shot of his own in the fifth inning. Tonight was pretty uneventful other than Gavin Lux being optioned. Lux was told before the game that he would not be on the Opening Day roster, and when he took the field, his play reflected that. He committed a throwing error on his first defensive chance and was shaky on a couple of other plays. It was announced the next day that he would be getting his at-bats at the alternate practice site at USC.

JULY 21, 2020

I have been in town for a week, and I had my second COVID-19 test at Dodger Stadium this morning. Parked in front of me was the Spanish-language father-son radio tandem of Baseball Hall of Famer Jaime Jarrin and his son, Jorge. They are some of the nicest people I have met out here. When I first got to the Dodgers in 2019 after a three-year stint with the Red Sox, the Jarrins were immediately welcoming when we first met at spring training, and I have enjoyed their company ever since. I have had the pleasure of dining with them a number of times and I occasionally would share a row on the team's charter flights with Jorge. Jaime is starting his sixty-second season broadcasting Dodger Baseball. Incredible. On some off nights last season, I sat in their booth with headphones on listening to him call the game in Spanish. I don't speak or understand a lot of the language, but it was like listening to a finely tuned orchestra playing a Top 40 hit. It sounds so beautiful.

Tonight is the last of three exhibition games before the start of the truncated 2020 season, and the Angels have come up from Anaheim. Chris Taylor hit another three-run home run, his fourth of the combined spring and summer trainings, and the Dodgers prevailed 6–4. They would outscore their opponents during the three-game stretch 27–7, in what appeared to be a sign of what many think is to come during the regular season. For the third night in a row, I sat in the front row of suite 215, which is the home of the Dodgers radio for this crazy season, still with no game assignments. From my new perch, I looked down on the solid white backing of the cardboard fan cutouts that arrive early and stay late. In fact, they don't move at all. Each night I have come to the park there are more added, but I still can only see the backsides of them, and they all look identical to me.

Rick Monday drove cross-country from his home in Vero Beach, Florida, to avoid flying on a commercial plane and just arrived in Los Angeles today, so he still hasn't worked any games since he worked with me on March 9 in Peoria, Arizona, in a game against the Padres. He doesn't need the work, though. He is probably the most prepared and intuitive analyst that I have worked with on a Major League game. Former Red Sox, Cubs, and Dodgers All-Star infielder, Nomar Garciaparra has been filling in for Rick on the radio side. Nomar is a TV studio analyst and does color on selected Dodger telecasts on SportsNet LA. I have worked with Nomar a number of times, and he does a great job and is fun to be around and he knows the game inside and out. I also haven't met too many people who know wine like Nomar does.

JULY 22, 2020. PAY DAY FOR MOOKIE

I woke up this morning to two things. First, a text informing me that yesterday's COVID-19 test was, thankfully, negative. Again. Secondly, and even more eye-opening, was the news that was traveling around social media about the Dodgers' new right fielder.

Today was a huge day for the Dodgers. Today was a huge day for Mookie Betts. Today was a huge day for Dodger fans everywhere. Today was a sad day for Red Sox Nation as any chance Boston might have had to make a play for their favorite baseball son to return to Fenway is now history.

The Dodgers had made the off-season splash they were looking for when they acquired 2018 American League Most Valuable Player Mookie Betts, along with former Cy Young winner David Price. Once the COVID-19 shutdown occurred in March, the prospects of even having any kind of a season were unknown for quite a long time. As the fight continued between MLB and the Players Union over a number of issues, there was serious doubt if Mookie would ever even play for the Dodgers. If the season was banged, he would be a free agent in November and would be on the open market for the Dodgers to bid on him like everyone else.

Dodgers President of Baseball Operations Andrew Friedman was on a mission. He fell totally and hopelessly in love with Mookie a long time ago and had made overtures to Boston in the past about him. Friedman's patience paid off when he was finally able to pull off the deal to get him, even though the original deal was held up by a bad medical report by the Red Sox doctors on another piece of the trade. It was structured as a three-team deal with Minnesota. The Twins were going to take Dodgers starter Kenta Maeda, and the Twins would send hard-throwing right-hander Brusdar Graterol to the Sox. Boston, interested in Graterol as a starter and not a reliever, felt his medicals didn't pass muster and used that as a reason to cancel the deal.

The creative Friedman and his staff had Graterol's medicals examined by the Dodgers doctors and everything came back fine. Friedman restructured the whole thing and made a separate deal with Minnesota sending Maeda there for Graterol and former Dodger prospect Luke Raley, an outfielder with a pretty good bat. Friedman and the Red Sox then sent outfielder Alex Verdugo, along with two prospects, shortstop Jeter Downs and catcher Connor Wong, to Boston in exchange for Betts and Price, with the Red Sox having to pay half of Price's remaining salary, known in the industry as "cash considerations." Can you imagine a shortstop in Boston named Jeter in the future?

The Price was right for Boston, who got out of at least half of the $96 million still owed to the left-handed pitcher. Price, who had an opt-out clause, decided to stay put and pitch in Beantown for what turned out to be one more season.

The real prize, however, was Betts, the one guy Friedman wanted all along. The Red Sox had every chance to re-sign Mookie, but after he turned down a $300 million extension, the team said they would take him to arbitration. This probably didn't sit too well with Betts. Before the hearing, he and the Red Sox settled on a deal for $27 million, the most any player has ever received in his final year of arbitration eligibility. Nolan Arenado had received $26 million the year before, from the Rockies.

At 11:00 a.m., the Dodgers held an already-scheduled company-wide Zoom meeting to talk about Opening Day. The call opened with Dodgers president Stan Kasten letting us all know that the rumors on social media were true and that later today there would be an announcement regarding a long-term extension for Markus Lynn Betts. Stan was all smiles. Just a few hours later, the team made it official, announcing a twelve-year, $365 million deal. Holy smokes! Betts had broken the bank during a pandemic, while the Dodgers made a statement that they are in it to win it for years to come. Friedman captured his man, put the vice grips on him, and had no intention of letting him go.

At a 2:30 press conference (on Zoom, of course), Betts told us that he was "here to win some rings and bring rings back to LA.

"This is what I've been working for my whole life", he said. "I know the Dodgers are going to be good for a long time. I love being here, everything about being here. This organization is a well-oiled machine."

Los Angeles is now beginning what should be a long and storied love affair with Mookie Betts. I only wish there could be fifty-thousand fans at Dodger Stadium on Opening Night against the Giants tomorrow to greet him. The piped-in ovation won't be anything like the real thing.

PART 2

The Season

The Season

JULY 23, 2020. OPENING DAY/NIGHT AT DODGER STADIUM

Opening Day always feels like the first day of school. I always look forward to it and am very much looking forward to Opening Day 2021, assuming the coronavirus is in control by then and the ballparks can be fully opened up. This Opening Day was different, however.

Early in the day, it seemed like any other. Nothing unusual, except understanding no one can go anywhere without wearing a mask. Opening Day is always best when it is an afternoon game. All the pomp and circumstance, the flyover, the anticipation of beginning the 162-game journey. The celebration of our national pastime and what it means is always well planned and is just so different than the atmosphere for the remaining 161 games, or in this case, fifty-nine. We hope. There is a certain feeling you get on that day, but today it was hard to fake it. In 2020, it was just Thursday.

As the clock moved to the midafternoon, the Dodgers put out a press release announcing unexpected news. Clayton Kershaw would not start due to tightness in his back. Kershaw had been in the weight room two days prior doing his regular routine and tweaked something. With no reporters or broadcasters able to mill around in the clubhouse, dugout, or field, the Dodgers had a much easier time concealing this news until a few hours before the matchup with the rival San Francisco Giants. The Opening Day start for Kershaw would have been his ninth, which in today's game is nearly unheard of.

No Kershaw, no problem. This Dodgers roster is one of the deepest in the game. Twenty-two-year-old Dustin May would get the nod and was notified clandestinely the day before, so he would be ready to go. May, the tall, ginger-headed flame thrower, would become the first rookie to make an Opening Day start for the Dodgers since 1981, when Fernando Valenzuela did so. Valenzuela, then just twenty years old, was sent to the hill to face the Houston Astros in place of the injured Jerry Reuss, and the once-in-a-lifetime Fernandomania phenomenon was born.

This wasn't anything like Fernando's coming-out party, but May certainly held his own going opposite veteran right-hander Johnny Cueto. May tossed four and a third innings, allowing seven hits and one run while striking out four. Not bad for a guy who had been optioned out to the team's alternate camp at USC just a couple of days earlier.

The Dodgers toyed with the undermanned Giants like they were a cat pawing at a helpless mouse, going on to win 8–1 to take the first game of the season. The game was nationally televised on ESPN, though the announcers for the four-letter network were not on site. In the radio booth, Charley and Rick worked together for the first time since a couple of early spring training games in late February.

Charley was set up at home in his command center/living room in Brentwood while Rick, our producer/engineer Duane McDonald, and I were in the booth. After a brief pre-game segment, I didn't have another responsibility until a segment on the post-game show. I sat in the front row of our suite, socially distanced from everyone. Rick was set up just inside the booth along the bar table behind the two rows of seats, while Duane was set up well behind Rick, completely inside the suite and not facing the field. That seat in the front row would become my seat for the entire shortened season.

With empty stands and an empty parking lot (I don't think you can find a bigger lot in baseball), Dodger Stadium sits in the middle of 365 sprawling acres. The reason I mention this is that during one of the late innings, something caught my attention. Out of the corner of my left eye, I noticed some movement near the upper deck on the third base side. Quickly, I turned my head to look and spotted a silver mylar balloon floating over the roof as though it didn't have a care in the world. It continued its slow, downward trajectory and ended up on the ground near second base. This was the COVID-19 season's version of a beach ball being accidentally tossed onto the field from the grandstand. Come to find out the next day, some dude on Instagram, who is, of course, a Dodger fan, mentioned that it was his balloon and he let it go in honor of his recently deceased mother with no idea how far it would travel, and he never imagined it would head in the direction of Dodger Stadium, never mind landing in the middle of the infield. Makes you think.

Rick Monday is one of the more interesting guys you will ever come across in the game. Smart, prepared, and never at a loss for a story about baseball. Those stories are really good, too. Monday lives in Vero Beach, Florida, and spends the season in a hotel in downtown LA—usually. A renovation and the COVID-19 crisis affected his normal baseball season residence, and he needed to find a place to stay. He found the friend of a friend who had an RV sitting in storage, made a deal with the owner, and set up his temporary residence. Rick parked the RV right at Dodger Stadium in Lot E, a little sliver of a parking lot on the left-field side that is nestled under a bunch of trees and is only a short staircase commute from work.

The Dodgers were great about Monday living on campus, so to speak. Upon his arrival, workers ran electricity, water, and an internet cable to the RV. It is quite the setup considering the parking lot is a very quiet place this year, except for a nearby owl and some occasional coyotes. Rick invited me out to see his tricked-out camper after the game and hang out for a while. As I backed my car into the lot, he took out two folding chairs and placed them under a large awning attached to the RV. We had some laughs until a little after midnight. I have a feeling there may be some more nights at "Mo's Bar and Grill" in Lot E.

JULY 24, 2020. GAME 2. MAD MAX GOES YARD

97.7. This is not an FM radio frequency. This was my temperature again this afternoon as I passed through Gate A and drove to Lot D to park for the evening. Today seemed remarkably like yesterday. Usually, the day after Opening Day feels like just a regular season game, as this one did, but it was just Game 2 as yesterday was basically just Game 1.

The Dodgers would throttle the Giants again 9–1 behind a solid pitching performance by right-hander Ross Stripling. "Chicken Strip" tossed seven innings, scattering four hits while striking out seven. Good for him. Stripling is a good dude. He played at Texas A&M before getting drafted by the Dodgers in the fifth round of the 2012 draft. He also happens to be a licensed, practicing stockbroker and the creator and host of a popular podcast called the *Big Swing Podcast*. Still waiting for my invite to be on it…I say while looking at my watch…tick tick tick.

First baseman Max Muncy hit two bombs for his fifth career multi-HR game. Muncy added a double, a walk, and three runs scored for good measure. He was a one-man gang against the San Francisco contingent on this night. Third baseman Justin Turner contributed with three hits and two RBIs. All-world outfielder Mookie Betts was not off to a great start offensively, having gone 0-3 with the bases loaded over his first two games as a Dodger. While some fans would start wondering if the Dodgers had made a mistake in signing Betts to a long-term mega-deal, I am here to tell you that I would not worry a bit. You will see. The team was 2-0 with two games to go in this four-game series, which had many looking ahead to a sweep of the rebuilding Giants. An age-old axiom in baseball is to never look past the next day. That axiom was just about to come into play.

The Season

JULY 25, 2020. GAME 3. TOOTBLAN

There is an abbreviation in baseball for a bad base running play. TOOTBLAN. When you see it, you understand it.

TOOTBLAN means Thrown Out On The Bases Like A Nincompoop, which describes the Dodgers' performance on multiple occasions tonight against the Giants. Justin Turner got doubled off of second when he misread a ball off the bat of Cory Seager. Joc Pederson got doubled off of first when Kiké Hernández flied out to center field. Just prior to that, Chris Taylor attempted to go from second to third on Pederson's base hit when he had absolutely no chance to make it. Another baseball axiom applied here: never make the first out of an inning at third base. The Dodgers ran themselves into outs and gave this game away.

A late-inning comeback fell short. Catcher Will Smith hit one into the new home run seats behind the left center field wall for his first long ball of the season to bring the Dodgers within a run. His ball hit one of the cardboard cutouts right in the head and snapped it almost all the way off at the neck. It turned out the kid whose photo it was had it pointed out to him by a number of friends who were watching the game. He posted on social media asking for the ball and a response from Smith. The likable Smith responded: "Sorry I took your head off. Shoot me a DM and I'll hook it up for you."

The Giants won 5–4 and dropped the Dodgers to 2-1. The focus now would be to shower this game off and come back tomorrow to win the series.

In the radio broadcast booth, we dealt with a timing problem. Due to the fact this was a Fox television feed, it was getting to Charley Steiner's home studio monitors much later than the live action. Technically speaking, the national video feeds take extra steps to get to us, more than the local TV feed we from SportsNet LA. The Friday night game telecast by SportsNet LA only had a second-and-a-half delay, while the delay tonight was between seven and eight seconds.

On the air, listeners can hear the pop of the catcher's mitt, and bat on ball contact. Rick Monday was at the game seeing it live, and Charley was at home seeing it after that long delay. When a batter put the ball in play, the listener would hear the contact, the artificial crowd reaction complete with organ music, followed by the public address announcer introducing the next batter, just as Charley was starting to call the play. If a pitcher threw a pitch that was taken by a batter, you could hear the pop of the catcher's mitt but the pitcher would be almost ready to start his windup for the next pitch by the time Charley was calling it. The sounds of the stadium and the play-by-play were not matching at all. Not his fault. He can only work with the tools provided for him. It was difficult on Rick to provide on-time analysis when the next pitch or play is happening and he has to comment on the last thing he saw.

Duane was suddenly standing to my right sometime during the fifth inning. "I've been told to tell you that you're doing the game tomorrow night," he said.

This whole thing exposes a new problem with the technical side of things, and I am anticipating it will be resolved one way or another, possibly. In the meantime, I remain on standby.

JULY 26, 2020. GAME 4. BACK IN THE SADDLE

Putting stories together and preparing for a broadcast is something I enjoy, and I spent a lot of today doing just that before the final game of the opening series with the Giants, but their new-school manager, Gabe Kapler, makes it difficult to prepare for the Giants when it comes to starting pitching. He isn't listing his probables at this point in the season, so we had TBA listed for each game of the series. Kapler apparently believes that withholding the name of the starting pitcher and starting lineup gives his team a competitive edge.

Each team's broadcasters, however, need the info to properly prepare for the telecast.

Even without the Giants' info, I put a lot of stuff together for the game before jumping on a Zoom presser with Will Smith at 2:30, and manager Dave Roberts at 3:00. All these conversations would usually be done at the ballpark in any regular baseball season, but I do it from my hotel suite, then jump in the car and take the short ride to Dodger Stadium.

Duane set me up so I could do the broadcast from my seat in the front row of the luxury suite, safely distanced from everyone else. When we went on the air right after the national anthem, the game portion of the broadcast started with the voice of the great Vin Scully saying his famous line, "It's time for Dodger baseball!"

Rick followed with a big, booming, "Live! From Dodger Stadium in Los Angeles, it's the fourth and final game of the opening home stand in 2020 as the Dodgers host the San Francisco Giants. Hi, everybody, I'm Rick Monday along with Tim Neverett…"

It felt good to be back, working the in profession that I like best. I had not done this in more than four months, so I expected a little rust would have to be banged off. After an inning or two, it felt better. It felt natural again.

Now, I am in the front row of the suite, and Rick is sitting three rows back at a bar table. We can't see each other during the broadcast, although I guess he could see the back of my head if he wanted to. We didn't look at each other while on the air during the entire broadcast, and we were far apart, but we were in the same venue seeing a live game in real-time and not depending on a video feed. Our timing was good, and we picked up where we left off in the way that we communicate during a game without stepping on each other. I like to give him lots of room on the broadcasts because he has so much to offer the listeners.

During the early portion of the game, it was noticeably quieter in the ballpark than it had been over the first three games. Apparently, the players thought the artificial crowd noise had been too loud and asked for it to be turned down. I found that I had been relying on the piped-in crowd to mentally fool myself into thinking that there were more than cardboard fans in the seats. The atmosphere when calling the game was different at first, but once I got going, it was still baseball and still special.

While I was happy to be doing what I love to do, there was no way to predict the way this game would go. Baseball is hard to impossible to predict. The Dodgers laid an egg, losing this game 3–1 and settling for a disappointing season-opening split with a team that, frankly, is not very good right now. The Giants have a lot of work to do to improve, and they should in the future, but they are not yet ready for prime time. The Dodgers somehow couldn't manage a run against a well-used bullpen in a lackluster offensive performance, leaving the field with their tails between their legs, their record even at 2-2 in front of a series with the hated Houston Astros.

JULY 27, 2020. FIRST TRAVEL DAY

Today is an off day for some, and a travel day for Tier 1 and some Tier 2 personnel. That means the team and staff. The broadcasters don't go anywhere this year. The team had a different travel experience in the age of coronavirus. Players were handed bagged, prepared meals when they got on the plane instead of the usual fare that is ordered and served. The Dodgers had to confirm that the flight attendants had been tested for COVID-19 and were negative. Players entered the plane wearing masks and were seated further apart than normal.

Although the traveling party is much smaller this season, most teams are flying bigger aircraft, like 757s, so that there is a lot of room to social distance. As the players were boarding the plane and settling in, they were learning of the positive COVID-19 tests that were ravaging the Miami Marlins roster and staff and causing major concern over whether this season could be completed. In light of the Marlins news, the Dodgers sent out a group text to everyone traveling reminding them that they were traveling into a coronavirus hot spot and to be mindful of what is going on. In the Marlins' case, it was reported that at least one player, maybe more, decided to relax team and league safety protocols. The Marlins, Phillies, Yankees, and Nationals all missed out on playing games and had to either pause for a few days or rearrange their schedules on short notice, all because someone didn't adhere to MLB's health and safety mandates.

The team arrived at the hotel in downtown Houston about seven in the evening and checked in. The players, many carrying video game systems that they would hook up to the hotel TV and some carrying their own monitors, knew they had to stay in. No going out this season. Hotel, ballpark, hotel. Room service for one or two meals will be normal with individual meals being provided mid-day in the same conference room they will conduct their COVID-19 tests in, which are taken every forty-eight hours.

"We are doing what we can to make this season happen and be able to play. Wearing masks and gloves on the plane is one thing. Don't use the remote control or pick up the phone at the hotel is another," Joc Pederson said. "We have to take every precaution to be safe. I can understand why some players would sit out due to health concerns. Some people think this thing is fake, but it is definitely real. We have to hold everyone accountable. There have been some tough conversations that have been had. Sometimes we get lackadaisical due to our success with a low testing rate, so we have to be careful."

So far, so good with the Dodgers and most teams. Major League Baseball released testing numbers today that were very good. There have been more than 6,400 tests conducted since Friday, July 24, and during this period of time, the Marlins have been the only team with positive cases. If you go back to the beginning of Spring Training 2.0 through July 23, ninety-nine of the 32,640 samples have turned up positive. That is a percentage of 0.3 percent.

JULY 28, 2020. GAME 5. JOE KELLY FIGHT CLUB

A large number of Dodger fans, and perhaps some current and former players, wanted some fireworks tonight in Houston. The Astros cheated during the 2017 season when they won the World Series over the Dodgers, and people are still furious about it. With good reason. When the news broke in November in a story in *The Athletic* by Ken Rosenthal and Evan Drellich, the baseball world was turned upside down. The Dodger faithful were angrier than anyone else, multiplied by a hundred.

In 2017, it was the Red Sox who were eliminated by the Astros in the American League Division Series, as they got a taste of the trash-can-banging methods Houston employed. Game 2 of that series saw Chris Sale, Boston's ace left-hander, get absolutely lit up. Astros diminutive second baseman José Altuve would hit the first of his three home runs that night, going back-to-back with third baseman Alex Bregman to lead off the home half of the first inning. Other than that, Mrs. Lincoln, how was the play?

The lanky southpaw gave up seven runs on nine hits before he could blink. The Astros pretty much laid off of Sale's usually devastating slider all night by design and with a lot of help in real-time. I called that game for the Red Sox Radio Network and it was one of the only times I have ever thought during a game that either the Astros hitters knew exactly what was coming or Sale, all of a sudden, was tipping his pitches badly. I was leaning toward the former. That game should have been a classic pitchers' duel between Sale and Justin Verlander, who joined the team following the non-waiver trade deadline on August 31 in a blockbuster deal. Somehow, an eleventh-hour trade was worked out with the Detroit Tigers for the instant staff ace, a move that turned out to be a shocker to teams.

Joe Kelly relieved the beleaguered Sale and gave up a couple of hits in his one inning of work before the Red Sox fell 8–2. Kelly would be credited with the lone Sox win in Game 3 back at Fenway, a 10–3 decision. Boston would be eliminated in the following game, and it cost John Farrell his job despite winning three straight division titles.

Former Dodger infielder Alex Cora took over the reins in 2018, coming over from a stint as Houston's bench coach in 2017. He had an incredible debut that culminated with a World Series win over his former team. During that season, the evening of the 11th of April was a chilly, raw night in the Back Bay, and the Red Sox's hated rivals, the New York Yankees, were in town. Earlier in the game, there was a play at second base in which Tyler Austin slid hard and took a piece out of popular Boston infielder Brock Holt. Holt took exception to the slide and words were exchanged. When Joe Kelly took the mound in the seventh inning, Austin stepped into the batter's box and was promptly drilled in the ribs by a fastball. They stared each other down, then chirped at each other, with Kelly challenging him.

"Come on—let's go," Kelly barked. The gloves came off and the benches emptied. Due to the hard-edge nastiness, mostly by the fans, in the Red Sox-Yankees rivalry, Kelly became an instant hero in New England. Pitcher Rick Porcello, the team's T-shirt master, showed up to Fenway the next day and handed out "Joe Kelly Fight Club" shirts. Some players wore those T-shirts on the field for early work the next day. Copies of the shirts ended up online and became a bestseller. The hashtag #joekellyfightclub trended on Twitter. There were bumper stickers too. One was slapped onto a stop sign in my neighborhood. The T-shirt is still seen around the greater Boston area.

In 2018, Kelly and the Red Sox would get another crack at the Astros, this time for the American League pennant. It would be different this time. No one in the press had uncovered the Astros cheating scandal yet, and there is no telling how much they employed it during this season. I distinctly remember being in Cora's office before the first game at Minute Maid Park when it was my turn to record the manager's pre-game radio interview. I asked Alex, off the air, about facing his old team, and were there any advantages in a series like this for him knowing what they like to do? Cora chuckled a little bit and told me he was very familiar with what the other team does and they knew that he knew. I thought he was talking about general baseball stuff and had no idea, at the time, what he really meant. If we had only known then what would eventually be reported in November of 2019. When I read the story in *The Athletic*, it dawned on me what he might have meant by that. I told my wife about it and said that Alex was probably right in the middle of this thing, which proved to be true, along with Carlos Beltrán. I told her, if this was all true, it would cost him his job with Boston, which it originally did. It also cost Beltrán his job as manager of the Mets, long before he ever put on the uniform.

The 2018 Red Sox were investigated for sign stealing. That investigation uncovered that some players were getting some signs from their replay coordinator and relaying them through a player in the dugout to a runner at second base. The runner at second would then relay the sign to the hitter. It was not exactly real-time relaying in a lot of cases, and not every player took advantage of the information. MLB ruled that while they did break the rules, it was not nearly as egregious as what the Astros did. They suspended the replay coordinator for a couple of seasons. No players or coaches were punished.

Fast forward to tonight in Houston. Bad blood to begin with, but the Dodger skipper told us broadcasters during a private Zoom call this morning that he was more interested in winning a ballgame than anything else.

"It opened up a wound, but time has passed," Roberts told us. "I don't see past experiences as motivation to win a baseball game. If anything happens there won't be any intent. We are expecting to play a clean baseball game and try to win."

In the sixth inning, with the Dodgers leading 5–2, Joe Kelly was called upon to hold the lead for an inning as the bullpen was working behind starter Walker Buehler, who made his season debut on his twenty-sixth birthday. Kelly at times can be what is known as "effectively wild," and he certainly was at least that on this night. Kelly got Altuve to fly out to left for the first out. Alex Bregman, who Kelly had plunked in Game 1 of the 2018 ALCS, went to 3-0 before ducking a fastball thrown behind his head. Ball four. Kelly yawned. Knowing the history, I was surprised that home plate umpire Alfonso Márquez didn't toss Kelly or, at least, issue a warning. Warnings would come later. The tension was building, and it seemed an incident was imminent.

Michael Brantley charged hard down the first baseline with Kelly covering on a possible double play grounder to first baseman Max Muncy. Kelly didn't get his foot down where he wanted to, drifting toward the middle of the bag while catching the return throw from shortstop Cory Seager. Brantley couldn't adjust his route and spiked him on the way by. Kelly stood there a moment longer than normal. As he did, you could hear a voice coming from the Astros' dugout, "Get back on the mound, m*********r!" It sounded remarkably like the voice of Houston manager and former Dodger Dusty Baker. I am not outright accusing him, but I listened back to the highlight a couple of times after the game and Dusty is my number one suspect. In the empty ballpark, trash talk like that is easy to hear.

With two outs, Houston shortstop Carlos Correa, who homered earlier, was up. Kelly was using his curveball inside, and it wasn't breaking much. The cement mixer pushed Correa off the plate and nearly took a button off of his jersey. The next pitch was a breaking ball that came close to Correa's head. Scary pitch. Sometimes it seems like Kelly has no idea where his pitches will end up, which makes for some uncomfortable at-bats. The Astros looked uncomfortable against Kelly. Joe then broke off another deuce down and away out of the zone and struck Correa out. Correa didn't like the previous pitch, and he and Kelly began some socially distanced jawing, with Kelly making some faces at the Astros shortstop which helped to escalate an already tense situation.

"Nice swing, b***h," said Kelly. Correa took further exception and the benches emptied, but the players were being extra careful given the serious punitive action possible for any incitement of incidents such as these in the year of COVID-19.

Dodger fans who had not taken to Kelly in 2019, given his mediocre season, were now singing his praises. Kelly's episode tonight overshadowed a great outing by lefty Caleb Ferguson, who punched out the side in the seventh on thirteen pitches, while Blake Treinen's nasty two-seamer set up Kenley Jansen to close it out. I am sure the "Nice Swing, B***h" T-shirts are being printed up all over Southern California as I write this.

Following the game, Baker took exception to Kelly's errant pitches to Bregman and Correa.

"You don't throw at a guy's head," he said. "That's dirty baseball."

Lance McCullers, one of the Astros' starting pitchers, piled on. "Joe Kelly threw a ball behind Bregman's head on 3-0 on purpose. Not only did he take it upon himself to send a message, but he wasn't even a part of that team. We knew coming into the game he likes to go off-script. What he did was unprofessional."

When asked about the purpose pitch to Bregman, Kelly deadpanned, "It wasn't my best pitch. It was ball four." On the chin music to Correa, he said, "I guess he didn't like my curveball or something."

JULY 29, 2020. GAME 6. GHOST RIDERS IN THE SKY

Major League Baseball acted faster than I can remember, and Kelly became the talk of the baseball world when MLB slapped him with an eight-game suspension. Dave Roberts received one game and is sitting out tonight. Kelly appealed his suspension, and was available out of the bullpen, but did not appear in tonight's thirteen-inning, four-hour-and-forty-four-minute Dodger win over the Astros.

Throwing a baseball in the direction of a batter's head is not the best way to go about sending a message, and MLB agrees. That being said, in a 60-game season, eight games is pretty harsh, the equivalent to a 22-game suspension in a normal 162-game season. That is how Kelly saw it. I am guessing in a few days I will be writing that after appeal he will have it shortened to five or six games.

Dusty Baker got hit with a fine. No player for the Astros was punished. Seems to be a theme if you ask some people around the game. Word is that MLB has been working on legislating punishments to players who take part in electronic sign stealing, and we are expecting some sort of an announcement on that in the near future.

In anticipation of tonight's game, there were many questions concerning the expectation of retaliation. Roberts was confident that if anything happened, "the umpires will handle it."

One side story of the Kelly/Bregman/Correa saga that can't be ignored is how upset Major League Baseball was with the players clearing the benches and disregarding the social distancing protocols that they have in place. Roberts, before the game, reminded Dodger players of the protocols in place regarding such situations and told them they are not allowed to leave the dugouts. Naturally, in the heat of the moment, players are going to react the way they are going to react. Their instincts take over. It will be a hard adjustment, but the players have to find a way.

Another day, another person from the Marlins tested positive. What a mess. It serves as a sharp reminder to every other player and staff member that during these challenging times, you have to be better in every way if you want to play—especially if you want to win.

Ross Stripling, who lives in Houston and whose home is a ten- to fifteen-minute drive from Minute Maid Park, was allowed to leave the team hotel and stay at home. He, however, turned down multiple opportunities to see family and friends and kept himself as safe as possible for the sake of his teammates and the game. He is a player who realizes that sacrifice is necessary if you want to see this season to its completion. Good for Strip.

Dustin May had the start tonight but only lasted three and a third innings. His outing wasn't bad, but bench coach and acting manager Bob Geren had to come out and get him due to the game situation. May only gave up a run on three hits, but with Houston threatening to erase a 1–1 tie, the bullpen was called into action. New lefty Jake McGee led the parade of eight different pitchers with a scoreless inning. The pen men didn't give up an earned run the rest of the way. The only other run to score was a "placed runner" in the bottom of the eleventh, which does not count against the pitcher on the hill.

This was the first game the Dodgers had played with the new extra-innings rule. If you are someone who likes to stump people with random and innocuous trivia, Justin Turner was sent out to second base to start the top of the tenth inning as the first extra-innings "placed runner" in Dodger history. In fact, Turner was "placed" again in the twelfth inning. Kiké Hernández was also "placed" twice, once in the eleventh and then again in the thirteenth and final inning. Per the rule, the batter who made the last out during the prior inning becomes the "placed" runner for the following inning. It just so happened that Turner and Hernández made the final outs of the prior respective innings.

Mookie Betts in the eleventh had his first "Mookie Moment" as a Dodger when he hammered a double off the top of the bullpen wall, just a few feet from a home run, scoring Hernández and giving the

Dodgers a 2–1 lead. When I was announcing the Red Sox games and Betts did something really big in the game, I would describe it as a "Mookie Moment." I am looking forward to doing more of that.

One of the biggest Mookie Moments for me was on July 27, 2018, in a game against the Minnesota Twins. That was one of the worst days of my life, however. In the early morning hours, my dad, Bill, suddenly passed away. Around half past three in the morning, while my family was gathered at the hospital around my dad's body in a private room, my mother, Sheila, looked at me and asked me if I was going to go to work that night. I told her, "No, probably not."

She said, "You should go to work, you need to go to work tonight." I will never forget that. I went to work. I'll always appreciate my great friend, Erik Sherman, who, when he found out my dad had passed, got in his car and drove six hours from his home in New Rochelle, New York, to my house in Nashua, New Hampshire, in time to drive to Fenway with me. He sat in the booth the whole night.

The last place in the world I wanted to be was at the ballpark. I fought through the day and into the evening. It didn't get much easier. Prior to the game, I was in Alex Cora's office and he closed the door. He told me he had heard what happened, hugged me, patted my back, and said how sorry he was to hear the news, before sharing the story of how he lost his dad when he was only thirteen and how difficult that was for him and his brother, Joey.

Shortly thereafter, on the field during batting practice, I was looking around for the cleanest BP ball I could find. I never take a ball from the field, but I wanted one from Fenway to put in my dad's casket. Cora saw me with the ball and asked about it. When I explained what I was doing, Cora said, "Let me see that ball." He threw it down the right field line into the outfield. "You don't want that ball," he said. "Send someone down to my office and I will make sure you have a brand-new pearl for him." I will always appreciate how he responded to me and what he did.

My mom signed the sweet spot. My two sisters, Nancy and Kathy, my brother, B.J., and I also signed it. I placed it near my dad's head, and it rests with him now.

That night, the game went to the tenth tied at three runs apiece. The Twins would send right-hander Matt Belisle out to the mound after third baseman Rafael Devers hit a game-tying home run in the bottom of the 9th to force extra frames. Mookie made it short and sweet, hammering a 0–1 Belisle pitch over the Green Monster to end the game and record his first career walk-off home run. On the broadcast I yelled with as much emotion as I could muster that was coming from different places, "Mookie hammers one…we're going home!" Some people complimented me on that call, but they had no idea that my intentions had nothing to do with baseball. Getting home was all I could think about.

The next day, before the game, Sherman and I were on the field. I saw Mookie near the top step of the first base dugout. He told me he was sorry to hear about my dad and asked if there was anything he could do. I usually don't ask players for much but took him up on it. I told him it would mean a lot if I could have a picture with him holding the bat that he used to hit that walk-off homer. He said, "Sure, I'll be right back." He went into the bat room behind the dugout, came back out by the batting cage, and handed me the bat. Sherman took the picture, which was framed, and went above my mom's couch. She took a picture with my kids in it down to put the picture of her favorite player and her youngest son up. There was a lot of meaning in that picture for my family. To me, a small gesture from Betts turned out to be the greatest personal "Mookie Moment." I hope there will be plenty more on the field for him to come.

In tonight's game, Edwin Rios smashed the first lead-off two-run homer I have ever seen in the top of the thirteenth inning to give the Dodgers a 4–2 win. On to Arizona for four.

JULY 30, 2020. GAME 7

COVID-19 test number three for me today. The process is pretty easy for us. Show up, get handed a test kit, swab your mouth for twenty seconds and drop it in the vial. Seal the bag and drop it in a bucket on your way out. I was there for probably five minutes tops. Next test will be in a week or so.

The Dodgers continue to do a great job in testing the people who need to work at the ballpark, and I will say that I feel much safer at Dodger Stadium than I do anywhere else in Los Angeles. When shopping for food, I cannot get in and out of the grocery store fast enough. When walking to a store downtown, I will cross the street just to avoid other people and keep space between us.

The Marlins had another positive test and more games postponed. This is really a mess and could turn out to be very problematic as they try to fill out some kind of roster. The Phillies closed down their stadium today due to a coach and clubhouse guy testing positive. No players are positive for now.

The road trip is off to a good start after winning both games in Houston. Tonight is the first matchup against the Diamondbacks at Chase Field with lefty Robbie Ray going against Ross Stripling. The Dodgers didn't get to the team hotel in the Phoenix area until about two in the morning following that 13-inning marathon in Houston, but travel like that is pretty common in the big leagues, so no big deal.

The outside temperature in Phoenix is a smoking hot 117 degrees. Good thing for the roof. Last year, the Diamondbacks replaced their grass with an artificial surface and found that by leaving the roof closed on the hot days and running the air conditioning to a steady, room temperature 77 degrees, they save energy and money. It was a decision that made a lot of sense. Previously, they opened the roof during the day to the let the natural grass grow and would have to blast the air conditioning at an enormously high level just to have the stadium cool enough by game time.

Back in 2007, I was a victim of the open roof. I was filling in on play-by-play for the Colorado Rockies one weekend, and the first day of the series I was in the Rockies' dugout on the first base side. There was a fiberglass bench just behind the railing and it had been baking all afternoon under a cloudless Arizona sky. Wearing thin linen pants might not have been the best idea. Sitting on that bench was like sitting on a hot stovetop. I burned myself right through my pants! A valuable lesson was learned that afternoon. Don't sit on anything that has been in the sun in the summer until the sun goes down. The burn hurt for several days.

Three home runs and solid pitching was the basic story of the Dodgers 6–3 win. Former Diamondback A.J. Pollock hit his first of the season; Corey Seager and Max Muncy added two more. Stripling had another solid start, going five and a third innings, allowing three earned runs on just four hits, and earned his second win of the season. The Dodgers were now 5-2 and had won three in a row to start the road trip.

JULY 31, 2020. GAME 8

Today should have been the Major League non-waiver trading deadline. This is one of the most important dates on the Big League calendar. The weirdness of the 2020 season continues.

Another Marlin and two Cardinals tested positive today. The Marlins and Phillies are already shut down and the schedule of games in the east is in disarray, so much so that MLB decided to make doubleheaders into two seven-inning games, just so there is a chance to make up all the games missed and not burn up all the pitching.

The Cardinals' situation is disturbing. They are in Milwaukee and set to play the Brewers. Those games were postponed until further notice. This is the first COVID-19 problem in the NL Central.

The Season

Commissioner Rob Manfred and staff have to be upset with the Marlins. The investigation into their situation apparently found the team being lax in the enforcement of the health and safety protocols. They also found out that a number of players went out while finishing their exhibition games in Atlanta, and that there were players hanging out in the hotel bar. Not good at all.

Manfred talked with MLBPA Chief Tony Clark and sent a strong message. "Get your players in line now or we risk having to shut the season down." Think of how much money would be lost if the season had to be canned. It could be a devastating blow to the industry.

I don't blame Manfred one bit for the threat. I'm hoping there are no more outbreaks and this crazy season can go on. Only seven games have been played and it took a Herculean effort by teams and players just to get to this point. I have been asked a number of times whether I think the season will be played in full and I always say that I am pretty confident it will be. That is my expectation, but today was the first day I have really had some doubts.

The Dodgers re-emphasized the rules and made some of their own today, to go above and beyond MLB's protocols. No offensive coaches in the dugout when the team is in the field, and no defensive coaches in the dugout when the team is at bat. Masks are now part of the equipment and must be worn in the dugout at all times and are encouraged on the field. Players who are not in the game cannot sit in the dugout, and no more high fives or handshakes. No touching, period.

Justin Turner texted many of us who cover the team and asked if we could put the word out as to what the Dodgers players decided to do to try and make things even safer. This team wants to play and they want to win, and by going above and beyond, they are showing just how much. Turner is a really good guy. I remember my first day at Camelback Ranch in February of 2019. While walking down the main hallway just outside the clubhouse, the always-affable Turner was walking right toward me. We stopped and talked, and he told that me that if I ever needed anything to make sure and come see him. Most players are good people, but this was the first time I had a player extend this generous offer.

To this point, the Dodger bullpen had been nails. As a group, they had tossed thirty-five and two-thirds effective innings with a 1.02 ERA and an opponent batting average of just .138. It is always just a matter of time. When a team's pen is on a great stretch, it can be the equivalent of a ticking time bomb. You never know when the blowup is going to happen. Unfortunately, tonight was the night.

Corey Seager and Mookie Betts had homered, Seager for the third straight game, and Betts with his first Dodger homer, the 140th of his career. Betts would go three for five and made one of the best throws from right field I have ever seen. Most of the great throws I have seen from right field in my career have been from Betts.

The exciting Ketel Marte was Arizona's first batter of the game. He pulled a Tony Gonsolin pitch to the right field corner and put on a display of his speed getting from home to second in a flash. Marte did not stop at second, figuring he had a triple. Instead of just cutting the ball off, spinning, and throwing to the infield like most outfielders would do, Betts circled behind the ball, grabbed it, and shot a bullet out of his rifle-like arm 305 feet *in the air* to Seager, who was covering on the play. Seager slapped the tag on a sliding Marte and the Diamondback star, as well as most of their dugout, hung their jaws in disbelief. Probably the one guy not shocked was Arizona manager Torey Lovullo. Torey was the bench coach in Boston, and interim skipper for a short time when John Farrell had to leave the team for cancer treatments in 2015. He knows Betts well, and I am sure that while he didn't like his leadoff hitter making the first out of the first inning at third base, breaking one of the cardinal rules of base running, he could appreciate Mookie's defensive gem.

The lead was handed off to right-hander Blake Treinen in the eighth, as the Dodgers were up 3–1. His two-seamer is just plain nasty, but he seemed to have some issues controlling both that and his four-seamer. Marte hit a ground ball that kicked off the right side of the mound and Justin Turner, playing up the middle in a shift, had the ball take a hop on him and was charged with an error. Treinen then walked Kole Calhoun. After a groundout by Starling Marte that was too slowly hit to record a double play, Dave Roberts rolled the dice with Eduardo Escobar coming up. Escobar is one of the best switch hitters in the game but was only hitting .133 to start the season. Roberts decided to intentionally walk Escobar, which goes against the axiom of never intentionally putting the go-ahead run on base. In this case, Christian Walker, who in a short period of time has come up with some big hits against LA, was the batter Roberts determined he would rather face in this situation. If you were thinking about whether or not he was a better matchup based on past meetings, that wasn't the case because Treinen hadn't faced either Escobar or Walker before. The only thing I could think of was getting the right-handed hitter vs. right-handed pitcher matchup.

"For me, on the road, guys on second and third, open base, I just liked the matchup with Blake versus Walker more," Roberts said trying to explain his decision after the loss. "I really did. Whatever book, to put the winning run on base, it's different for me when I'm on the road and not trying to play to tie. I'm trying to play to win that game and get that hitter out. It just didn't work out."

Walker clubbed one into deep right center field and the tremendous backspin on the ball kept it from being caught by Betts, who took a slightly off route to try and snare the ball in the air. The ball went over Betts's glove to the wall and cleared the bases. It was a bad loss, 5–3. The Dodger bats, especially Cody Bellinger's, were not too hot. Bellinger took an 0 for 5, while the team struck out a whopping 15 times.

"Sometimes you win, sometimes you lose, sometimes you get rained out."—Crash Davis in *Bull Durham*.

AUGUST 1, 2020. GAME 9. IT'S A NEW MONTH

The Cardinals have a couple of more positive cases and are still holed up in the team hotel in Milwaukee, with no game allowed with the Brewers today. The biggest news of the day, as far as this series goes, is that Brewers center fielder Lorenzo Cain announced he was opting out of the rest of the season. This is one of the more prominent players to opt-out and shows just how concerned players are at this time.

The Phillies and Blue Jays doubleheader (two seven-inning games) has been postponed, as has the game between the Nationals and the Marlins, all due to coronavirus concerns. All these games will be difficult to make up. It is unlikely now that all thirty teams will play 60 games. The Marlins are hoping to play on Tuesday.

Tonight, the Dodgers were playing the third game of a four-game set against the Diamondbacks, and it was time for me to get back to work. It is very enjoyable to work alongside Dodger great Orel Hershiser. Joe Davis is off doing a network game for Fox, so tag, I am it. Games to call for me this year are few and far between due to the truncated schedule, so any game I get assigned is a game I get up for. Orel is easy to work with. I can throw anything at him and he has something to offer. He understands TV and the nuances that go with it, so that makes it much easier for the crew.

The game is at Chase Field in Phoenix, while we are in the TV booth at Dodger Stadium. We have one monitor mounted high and to my left that is split into four boxes. This is called the "multi-view." It shows the "all-nine" look, a high-behind-home-plate look so we can see all nine defenders and how they are aligned. There are two boxes showing each bullpen and another that is locked down on the stadium scoreboard so that we can always see a running line score and be able to take advantage of anything else in view, such as mound visits remaining (MVR) or pitch speed.

We have another two main program monitors that are positioned like a *V* with one angling toward each one of us. There is another monitor positioned just to my left that the crew in the truck uses to put up commercial copy, eliminating the need for paper or cards. One more monitor is placed above the *V* monitors and has a larger "all-nine" look on it.

Working behind us are Boyd Robertson and Brian Hagan. Boyd has been the stage manager on Dodger telecasts for many years and was a big help to Vin Scully, especially since Vin worked alone on the air. Brian was Vin's booth statistician for years and does a lot of that kind of work with the Lakers and Kings as well. During a normal season, he will work home games in the Dodger radio booth. We couldn't be in better hands.

The second time Diamondbacks center fielder Starling Marte came up to hit, I brought up the story that he is one of only thirty players in MLB history to hit a home run on the first pitch he ever saw as a big leaguer. I know; I was there and called it on TV in 2012. It was against Houston when they were still in the National League (remember that?). In Marte's first game, he was the lead-off hitter and hit the first pitch he saw out of the ballpark. It was delivered from a young Astros lefty named Dallas Keuchel.

On the telecast after telling the story, I mentioned that he was the second to last to pull off the feat and that the last to do it was Welington Castillo of the Cubs in 2015. Only problem was, it was not Castillo, but Willson Contreras. I got stuck on the *W* and the *C* first and last name. Two seconds after I said it, I am thinking, *Shoot, I goofed*, but kept going as time and situation in the game didn't allow me a natural break to fix it. I let it go. Not a soul said a word. Not even anyone on Twitter chimed in as I checked after the game. When Justin Turner hit his first-inning triple, I did not see him advance to third base on the main monitor I was watching and initially called it a double. The next shot I saw was him standing at third base, so I corrected it. Other than those two goof-ups, things seemed to go pretty well, seeing as though I had not done any TV at all since early March at spring training. Again, nothing on Twitter mentioning the slip-up on the double that was a triple.

Twitter trolls love to pounce on people doing live TV who might make an error or sometimes are perceived to make an error. Twitter is a funny thing when it comes to doing a TV game, and I usually get some good laughs at what people say, especially those with extreme keyboard courage. Last year, my first with the Dodgers, but far from my first doing Major League Baseball, I used to get the "who the heck is this guy?" tweets, which I fully expected, but I did not get a single one of those during or after tonight's game. That's a good sign. Can you imagine if people would only tweet something that they would say to someone face-to-face rather than hiding behind a digital wall? Things might be much more pleasant in the social media world. I scrolled through the mentions when the game was over and there were mostly positive notes from viewers, which I appreciated, but there are always some beauties.

One said they saw me quickly on camera and thought it was Joe Davis and he got fat. That made me laugh. I have twenty-four years on Joe, so my metabolism is a lot slower than his, and for the record, I had lost nearly fifteen pounds since I arrived in LA on July 15 and plan on shedding ten more. I was relieved he didn't say I looked old! Social media is a great platform and highly useful, but there are a lot of folks out there who, unfortunately, use it unwisely.

Calling games off of a monitor is not the most efficient way to do it, especially if you are in a completely different location than the event. We have to do what we have to do this year. As I mentioned earlier, I have had extensive experience calling multiple events off of TV screens at four different Olympics, so it wasn't new to me. Our setup at Dodger Stadium, however, utilized more video resources than I had had when doing the Olympics, which makes it a little easier, but it is still difficult to call a home run with conviction when you can't see the ball the whole way off the bat. The ball disappears when the director cuts from the contact shot to another shot and you have to try to find it again while watching the fielders, if you can see them. While the TV production crews are doing a great but difficult job, we are at their mercy.

Even with all the monitors, I still found myself, out of force of habit or muscle memory perhaps, looking down at the empty Dodger Stadium field. Every time I did, all that could be seen were two blue circular tarps, one covering the pitcher's mound, the other covering home plate. The only other thing out there was a watering hose draped over the tarp on the mound.

During the middle innings, someone decided they had to test the public address system. Whoever it was probably was not aware that the live game broadcast was emanating from the stadium just a few booths over. We could hear it clear as day in the background, but to the viewer at home, it probably sounded like something coming from Chase Field. I ignored it on the air figuring it would just blend in with whatever ambient noise was being mixed into the overall show. I guess it did just that because I never heard anything about it during or after the game.

Edwin Rios, Matt Beaty, and Chris Taylor all hit home runs, with Rios's dinger recorded at 434 feet. He got cheated. It hit a vertical steel beam that supports the huge scoreboard at Chase Field. If there was no beam there, I am sure that Statcast would have registered a longer distance. Cody Bellinger sat this one out due to his struggles at the plate and got to watch his teammates rake. He will certainly have his share of good nights to come. The Dodgers won 11–2 and took the lead in the series.

AUGUST 2, 2020. GAME 10. KERSHAW'S RETURN

Clayton Kershaw's back is feeling fine, and he was activated from the IL today to make his first start of the season. He looked more than fine as he retired the first ten Diamondbacks, striking out four of them. His fastball had a little more uptick to it and sat about 92–93 mph when last year it was typically 89–90. His slider was deep and had good tilt to it, and his curveball was fantastic. Of the eighty-one pitches needed to get through five and two-thirds innings, Kershaw threw thirty-eight fastballs, thirty-four sliders, and nine well-placed curveballs. He allowed only three hits and was upset at each one of them. He allowed no runs and whiffed 6. When Dave Roberts came out to replace him with Pedro Báez, he left the field with a smile. Mission accomplished. Kershaw is back.

Bellinger returned to the lineup and hit the first pitch right-hander Merrill Kelly threw him into the Dodgers bullpen in the right field corner. It was a frozen rope and a two-run shot. With one out in the fifth, Mookie Betts was up with no one on. He took an uncomfortable-looking swing and looked at his left hand. He shook it slightly and then dug back in. The next offering by Kelly was driven deep to the opposite field and splashed down in the swimming pool, to make it 3–0. Pool party at Mookie's house! The bullpen threw up donuts the rest of the way to preserve the final score.

The road trip has been very good so far, with a record of 5-1. The team is now 7-3. If a team were to win 7 of every 10, it would be a monumental 42 wins. The Dodgers went an MLB-best 41-19 after 60 games last year, but 42 victories will be really hard to achieve, especially this year. On to San Diego, for three games and the completion of what will be the longest road trip of the season.

AUGUST 3, 2020. GAME 11. MISSING SAN DIEGO

COVID-19 test number four. The team has this testing thing down to a science, if you will pardon the pun.

No new coronavirus cases for the Marlins today, and they were scheduled to play the Orioles in Baltimore. The game was delayed, not for rain, which is common in Baltimore in the summer, but because some of the Marlins' tests came back inconclusive. Those players had to be tested all over again, and the starting pitchers were held up from going out to warm up until the results were known. Eventually, they all came back negative and the game went on. The Cardinals are still shut down.

San Diego might be my favorite road city. I have gone to San Diego each year for one thing or another since around 1996. Over the years, I have broadcast minor league hockey, as well as a lot of college football, basketball, and baseball involving San Diego State and, of course, many Major League Baseball games. Whenever the MLB schedule would be released each year, I used to immediately check to see when we would be there and whether there was an off day. I am certain that I am not the only broadcaster who took part in this annual tradition.

One of the things I always look forward to is indulging in one of my guilty pleasures in that town. Baseball people know the KC Barbecue joint across the street from the Manchester Grand Hyatt. It is also known as the "Top Gun" bar because, as the place claims, the "sleazy bar scene" from the movie was filmed there. It has been good marketing for them, as I often see people coming inside just to take pictures. My favorite bad menu item is the Mac and Cheese with Hot Links. I can taste it while pecking at my keyboard right now. There is nothing gourmet or fancy about it, and it is served in a paper bowl, but it is so good after a game with a couple of barley and hops sodas. I just pretend that it is good for me. It is not uncommon to see umpires in there. Veteran Joe West has been known to inform patrons about the country music CDs he has recorded.

Last year, Jess and I took the train from downtown LA to San Diego and the ride was beautiful. The Pacific Surfliner hugs the coast for most of the two-hour-plus ride and offers some spectacular views of the Pacific coastline. It lets you off right in downtown, and only a few blocks from the team hotel and Petco Park. We are looking forward to doing that again sometime, hopefully in 2021.

Tonight's game was between two young headline-making pitchers, Chris Paddack and Walker Buehler. It was set up to be a heavyweight fight of a pitchers' duel but didn't exactly turn out that way.

The first pitch out of Paddack's right hand at 6:11 p.m. was drilled by Joc Pederson over the right center field wall for some instant offense and a 1–0 lead. It was his first leadoff home run of the season, in his first at-bat leading off a game. Pederson hit 9 leadoff dingers in 2019, breaking his own single-season team record of 8, and has 21 in his career now, still chasing Davey Lopes for the Dodger record of 28.

In the bottom of the first, the Padres' second batter, Trent Grisham, hit the first pitch from Buehler out to tie it up. Three more home runs would be hit as Cody Bellinger hit his second of the season, while Fernando Tatís Jr. and Wil Myers each went yard for the Padres. San Diego would prevail 5–4 in the series opener, and pull into a tie in the standings with the Dodgers at 7–4.

AUGUST 4, 2020. GAME 12

Woke up to a text with my COVID-19 test results. Negative. Again. I have been living the bubble life this season, with the vast majority of my time spent in the hotel. I drive to get groceries and don't walk around downtown. I shop at the same market in Silver Lake and go to a CVS near the ballpark. Other than Dodger Stadium, those are the only places I go. I am not taking any chances, although I am getting a bit of cabin fever and will probably plan an outdoor activity for Thursday's off day, probably a short hike at Runyon Canyon in the Hollywood Hills with all the beautiful people.

The players have to now adhere to stricter protocols when on the road, with food brought to them. Departing the hotel for any reason other than going to the ballpark has gone from highly discouraged to forbidden. For this 2020 baseball season to be played to its conclusion, a lot of people around the game, players, staff, and broadcasters included, have to make these short-term adjustments in their lives. None of us involved are front-line workers. We are lucky enough to work in baseball. It is not life or death, but entertainment. We have nothing to complain about.

The Marlins played two seven-inning games with the Orioles last night and won both with a patchwork roster. The Cardinals will hopefully return to playing next week. All other teams are reporting no positive tests. Let's hope it stays that way.

Dustin May made his third start of the season and gave Dodger fans a glimpse of the future while putting the rest of MLB on notice. In the bottom of the first inning with two outs, May faced Padres third baseman Manny Machado. May, who likes the nickname "Code Red," which is stitched into his glove, released the kraken. I have seen some two-seam specialists with great movement in the past, but I do not ever remember seeing any like the one May delivered to Machado. With two strikes, May fired a 99 mph sinker that he started over the outer third of the plate and ended up forcing Machado to jackknife out of the way. It broke almost two feet and had major screwball action. It was jaw-dropping. It caught a lot of the plate as it whistled diagonally over it, and Machado was rung up for strike three by Mike Muchlinski. The video of this pitch went viral and almost broke the Internet.

Dustin May said after the game that his phone blew up with mentions like he had never seen before. He earned it. But his performance on this night was about more than one physics-defying pitch. His velocity continues to hover around 100 on the hard stuff, and he had great command of his cutter, too. If he can develop a good off-speed pitch, maybe advance his curveball or learn a changeup, it could be a knee-buckler. He only threw 5 curveballs to go against 44 two-seamers and 33 cutters. One major improvement for him was his first-pitch strike percentage, as he pumped in a strike on the first pitch to nineteen of the 22 hitters he faced. I am looking to see Dustin in about two more seasons. He could be an absolute front-of-the-rotation beast. This COVID-19 season is giving him an opportunity to figure it out. With the bullpen hanging zeros behind him, May got his first win of the season. The Dodgers would win the game 5–2 to even up the series.

AUGUST 5, 2020. GAME 13. AMAZING FINISH

Today, we are hearing that Rob Manfred has been generally happy with the following of health and safety protocols by teams since the Marlins and Cardinals outbreaks. In addition to the already-stringent protocols, players will now be required to wear masks in the dugout at all times. The Dodgers began this practice last week on their own, but sometimes players forget, and MLB sent a reminder.

Normally this time of year, about 115 games or so would have been completed, and a number of teams would be all but eliminated from postseason contention. These would usually be the start of the "Dog Days" of the season. I never was exactly sure why this time of the season was referred to in that way, and am hopeful it is not a derogatory term toward dogs. Dogs are actually better than people in a lot of ways and, in my opinion, anything referring to dogs should be positive. In this self-imposed partial quarantine here in Los Angeles, I am missing a lot of things, including my dog, if you can't tell.

The Season

Instead of teams just beginning to play out the string at this time of year, one positive aspect about 2020 baseball on August 5 is that everyone is still in it and playing for something. Everyone, except maybe for my former team, the Pittsburgh Pirates. My Buccos are 2-10 out of the gate and unfortunately for my friends there, I doubt it is going to improve much. No "Buctober" this year, even with expanded playoffs.

Twenty-nine teams are realistically in a pennant race and each game is super important. One win this year equals 2.7 wins in a normal season. A single loss is like 2.7 losses. Many games now, even without fans in the stands, can have a postseason feel as you sometimes hang on every pitch, especially in the late innings. Tonight's series finale in San Diego was like that.

In the second inning, Joc Pederson crushed a Garrett Richards hanging curve after Chris Taylor tripled for a quick 2–0 lead. The Dodgers would make it 4–0 in the fifth on RBI hits by Will Smith and Kiké Hernández.

Fernando Tatís Jr. destroyed a Ross Stripling offering and showed off the best bat flip this season so far to make it 4–2. Not sure how the Dodgers felt about Tatís Jr.'s response, but no one outwardly seemed to take exception to it. Players are evolving into the "new school" more and more these days anyway, so I guess no one cared.

In the ninth, closer Kenley Jansen was performing a high-wire act without a net. He walked Tatís Jr. with one out and then gave up back-to-back singles to Trent Grisham and Tommy Pham, allowing Tatís Jr. to score. With the tying run at third and the winning run at first, Machado was up and could cap off a big comeback for the Friars. Machado lined the first pitch from Jansen to left field that was caught by Taylor for the second out. Grisham tagged up and was heading home to tie the game, but Taylor unleashed a rocket to the plate that was measured at 93.3 mph. It was a one-hop perfect throw to Smith, who had lined himself up correctly out in front of the plate so as not to violate rule 7.13 (the Posey rule) and avoid a collision. He made the catch and quick sweep tag in the same motion, touching Grisham on the back first, and then his left arm on the follow-through. Game over.

What a way to end a game, a series, and a road trip! The Padres challenged the call at the plate because...why not? They had one to use and didn't want to leave it in their back pocket, but the play wasn't that close. The Dodgers would hang on and win in thrilling fashion 7–6 to take two of three against the much-improved Padres and finish their road trip seven and two. Machado led the Majors in grounding into double plays in 2019 with 24, but he probably never thought he would hit into a game-ending double play like the one Taylor and Smith just pulled off.

As a TV director I used to work with, Jeff Mitchell, used to say all the time, "Big League Ball, baby, Big League Ball."

AUGUST 7, 2020. GAME 14. IN THE LINE OF FIRE

The Miracle Marlins are healthy and continue to win, giving hope to some of the perennial bottom-dwellers in baseball. The players in that organization absolutely hate the term "bottom dwellers," and are using it as a rallying cry. The Marlins are 7-1 while trying to catch up with the rest of the schedule. In the meantime, the Cardinals continue to be hit hard by the virus. This weekend's series with the Cubs has been postponed, and the next series with Pittsburgh is in doubt. In total, nine St. Louis players and seven staff members have been infected. One player tested positive yesterday, two more today. What lies ahead for them is unknown and is quite disturbing for the proud and storied franchise, but, for now, the team remains shut down, while other teams, like the Cubs, have their schedules disrupted through no fault of their own. This is baseball in 2020.

In the meantime, things went mostly well in terms of tests around MLB this past week. The league had to test 13,043 samples and came up with only thirteen positive tests. That is only 0.1 percent. A good sign.

When it was time to go to the ballpark today, I gathered up everything I needed and got in the elevator from my twenty-second floor suite at the Westin Bonaventure Hotel, my home away from home. Because there are fewer guests, my elevator rides are usually express rides to the lobby. The elevator wouldn't move after the doors closed. The elevators at this hotel are on the outside of the building and are glassed in. They are pretty cool, actually, and there have been a lot of movies shot in and around this hotel due mostly to its unique architecture.

This elevator in which I was now stuck was used in the 1993 Clint Eastwood movie *In the Line of Fire*, where Eastwood played an aging secret service agent named Frank Horrigan. Horrigan, against all odds of course, thwarts an attempt on the president's life by tracking down a would-be assassin played by the talented John Malkovich. In one of the closing scenes (spoiler alert!), Malkovich's creepy character ends up falling from an elevator to his doom. This is the same elevator! I know, because there is a plaque outside the elevator door in the lobby commemorating it. I have seen the movie a few times and every time I look out the elevator window, I recognize the spot where Malkovich's character went splat. Fortunately, security got there relatively quickly and got the door open.

The Dodgers made the night much better by putting together another good game. They opened up a three-game series against San Francisco with a 7–2 win. It was especially great to see a live game in front of me. During this pandemic, it is not lost on me how fortunate my colleagues and I are to be able to watch Major League Baseball games in person.

Mookie returned from a three-game layoff due to a swollen finger on his left hand, showing no rust. He hit a double and a home run in his first two at-bats. According to Bill Chuck, who during a full season works as a statistical and research guy for us, Betts has had both a double and a home run in 34 games since 2015. Only the Rockies' stellar third baseman, Nolan Arenado, has more with 37.

Three other home runs were hit as Muncy, Smith, and Rios all left the yard in helping the Dodger cause and earning a win for Dylan Floro in relief of starter Julio Urías.

Again, according to Chuck, who tweeted after the game the following:

> ...the @Dodgers hit four HRs and won, making them 2-0 on the year when hitting 4+ homers. Last season, when hitting 4+ HR, the Dodgers were 19-3. From 2015–2020, when hitting 4+ homers, the Dodgers are 57-3.

This is a good nugget I would normally include in my next game, but since I have been pandemically benched, I don't have one for a while. I will use it in tomorrow's pre-game segment and give Bill credit. The Dodgers look to be on a roll but continue to chase Colorado in the National League West division standings. The Rockies finished tonight with a record of 10-3 after beating Seattle, and the Dodgers are now 10-4. It seems like it is just a matter of time before the Dodgers push past them. In just five days, we will be one third of the way through this 60-game sprint.

When the game ended and I was heading to my car, I spotted a rather large coyote, standing about twenty-five yards from where I was parked. After a game in any other season, there would be so much traffic—foot, auto, and otherwise—that you would not have the opportunity to see the coyotes, but this is a different season. The coyote didn't seem to be bothered by much, and stood there and stared back at me under the artificial light. I found it weird that I was standing, basically, a long par five from downtown Los Angeles, but there was a coyote just hanging out close to the stadium having a staring contest with me. There are some hills in Chavez Ravine surrounding this great park, and the coyotes hang around in the upper elevations. Rick Monday can hear the coyotes howling every night from his camper parked in Lot E, he tells me. He hears the owls also, but he tells me the sprinklers coming on and hitting the side of his camper at 4:30 a.m. is the only sound that bothers him while temporarily housed outside the stadium.

AUGUST 8, 2020. GAME 15. NOTHING TO SEE HERE

This afternoon we learned that Monday's game between the Cardinals and Pirates would be postponed due to the Cards' ongoing COVID-19 situation. There are legitimate fears in St. Louis and around MLB that it could be impossible for the Cardinals to play 60 games now.

Tonight, we looked forward to seeing what was supposed to be the Opening Day matchup between Kershaw and Cueto. Kershaw was not as good as he had been six days ago, allowing three home runs on top of four hits over four and a third unspectacular innings. Young San Francisco outfielder Austin Slater hit not one, but two home runs, to join an elite club of only six other players who have hit two home runs off of Kershaw in a single game.

On August 6, 2010, Adam Dunn of the Nationals was the first to accomplish the rare feat. Carlos González of the Rockies was next, two seasons later on May 2, 2012. It happened twice in 2013. Washington's Jayson Werth did it on July 21, and Jay Bruce of the Reds followed on September 8. The Mets' José Reyes slugged two on June 19, 2017, and Bo Bichette of the Blue Jays had a night on August 20, 2019.

Mike Yastrzemski, the grandson of Hall of Famer Carl Yastrzemski, hit the other homer against Kershaw. Young Yaz was in the Orioles' system, and I had the chance to see him play a number of times in spring training games against the Red Sox. The O's have to be kicking themselves for giving up on him. He has been one of the Giants' best players over the last season-plus, and he seems to be getting better.

Cueto, meanwhile, was very good tonight. He went five and two-thirds innings giving up just two hits, but one was a three-run home run off the bat of Justin Turner in the sixth inning. Cueto was twirling a no-hitter through five, pitching like he was relaxing in a rocking chair. Dodger second baseman Kiké Hernández led off the sixth with what looked like another routine fly ball out. Hunter Pence came in on the ball from left but lost sight of it in the twilight sky. Pence didn't indicate that he couldn't see the ball, so he wasn't getting much help from his teammates. I would guesstimate the pop-up landed about sixty feet behind the bewildered Pence, who would literally retire from playing just a few weeks later. Kiké was running hard out of the box and ended up with what would be scored a triple. Cueto's no-hit bid was over. Combined with Turner's blast, the Dodgers would creep within a run, but nine of the last ten LA hitters would go down and the game finished in favor of the Giants 5–4. The Dodgers and Giants have played six times so far this season, and they are even at 3-3 apiece. Tomorrow's rubber game is one the Dodgers need.

AUGUST 9, 2020. GAME 16. MOOKIE GOES BOOM

MLB has announced that the entire series in St. Louis is postponed. The Brewers, Tigers, Cubs, and now the Pirates have lost full series against the Cards. This is causing chaos with the AL/NL Central schedules and, more than likely, will end up with all of those teams experiencing some level of pitching stress in an effort to make up as many games as possible in a short stretch. The Cardinals had one more player test positive today, to bring the team's total positive COVID-19 cases to seventeen. They've only played 5 games and now have at least 11 to make up. *If* they can get back to play after this latest PPD, the Cardinals will have only forty-six days to play 55 games! They may well set a record for doubleheaders in a single season.

The Dodgers and Giants met for game three on a perfect, 82-degree day in Los Angeles and played under a cloudless sky, which made for some adventurous moments in the outfield. Pop-ups and fly balls are not easy to see against a clear sky.

Buehler started against right-hander Kevin Gausman, who had spent most of his career with Baltimore. Buehler didn't have his best command but managed to pick his way through four and two-thirds innings without allowing a hit. After walking Pablo Sandoval and plunking Austin Slater with a 95 mph heater, there were two men on without the benefit of a hit. A curveball gone wild moved both base runners up. Buehler then left a curveball just a little bit too high to Yastrzemski who poked the ball into center for a single that scored two. That was the only hit allowed by Buehler on the afternoon. He ended up walking four and hitting a man, but without his best stuff, still pitched well enough. If the right-handed Kentuckian can pitch like he did *with* his best stuff, then he is a no-hitter waiting to happen. It should happen for this guy and probably will.

Gausman, on the other side, was pitching exceptionally well. He was dotting the strike zone with fastballs that registered 98, even 99 mph. I've seen him pitch a number of times but didn't know he had this kind of velocity in him. He was nursing a 2–0 lead with one out in the seventh, when Bellinger singled to center and, with the right-handed-hitting Justin Turner coming to the plate, almost inexplicably, Giants manager Gabe Kapler emerged from the first base dugout. He was going to take Gausman out after 80 pitches. Last night he took an obviously injured Cueto out of the game two batters too late. Today, it was two batters too early for Gausman, who looked pretty upset in the dugout. He should have been.

Turner singled off of side-arming right-handed reliever Tyler Rogers, and two batters later, A.J. Pollock blasted a two-strike three-run homer over the left field fence to give the Dodgers a lead they wouldn't relinquish. It was Pollock's fourth homer of the young season. The next inning, Mookie Betts would stick a fork in the Giants with a three-run shot of his own. It was a 6–2 win, a two-games-to-one series win in raising their record to 11-5 with a talented Padres team coming to town tomorrow night.

AUGUST 10, 2020. GAME #17. HERE COME THE FRIARS

The Cardinals can't seem to catch a break. They were scheduled to get back to action on Thursday with a doubleheader against the Tigers in Detroit, but that has now been postponed as St. Louis tries to figure things out and get a squad that hasn't been exposed to the coronavirus. They will have so many games to make up now, that you wonder if whatever record they have when the regular season ends on September 27 should be considered viable at all. I feel bad for those I know in their organization who have not been able to work for a couple of weeks now. With any luck, they will be able to play a game this week.

Tonight, the Dodgers open an important four-game set with the suddenly improved and more-than-confident Padres. Taking two of three in the first series from this team was not easy, and this series should be a challenge.

The bats took a nap tonight as the Dodgers could only manage four hits off the San Diego bullpen. Six pitchers combined with Cal Quantrill, son of former journeyman pitcher Paul Quantrill, who threw for the Dodgers during the 2002 and 2003 seasons, to shut LA down. Cal's dad picked up a lot of luggage during his fourteen-year career, wearing the uniforms of the Red Sox, Phillies, Blue

Jays, Dodgers, Yankees, Padres, and Marlins. The younger Quantrill tossed three relief innings and earned his second win of the season.

Padres catcher Austin Hedges, an all-glove, light-bat backstop, blasted a home run over the center field wall in the fifth to tie the game. When Hedges hits a home run against you, you are usually destined to lose. He hit .176 in 2019 and has 47 career home runs over six big league seasons. Dodgers starter Dustin May provided the power, though, as he grooved a 99 mph fastball and Hedges got the barrel around on it. May would walk two in the sixth, and one came in on a single by Eric Hosmer. May pitched pretty well otherwise, taking a positive step forward. The Dodgers would lose this one 2–1, and May was tagged with the loss. Not the way they wanted to start this series with the upstart Friars.

AUGUST 11, 2020. GAME 18. THE JOE KELLY PODCAST

The Cardinals are still not playing, and the team they are supposed to be playing, the Pirates, are also idle. The Pirates could use the break, though, following one of the worst starts in franchise history at 3-13.

Stories are emerging that MLB is having conversations about a possible postseason bubble, with New York, Chicago, and Southern California identified as possible locations. If this comes to fruition, Southern California far and away makes the most sense. There are three ballparks, Dodger Stadium, Angels Stadium, and Petco Park, that could be used and are all in driving distance. Plus…the weather…duh. You want to play October baseball in New York and Chicago when you can stage games in perfect October weather in Cali? Easy answer.

All was going well early in tonight's game when Justin Turner raked his 1000th career hit with a double off the left field wall. He got a nice ovation from a few team executives who were sitting in a suite down the third base line. The cardboard cutouts didn't react other than to bob slightly back and forth in the light breeze, but I am sure the people they represent were happy for J.T. Chris Taylor knocked him in to give the Dodgers their only lead.

The game went sideways on starter Ross Stripling in the third inning, largely due to a throwing error he made on a sacrifice bunt by Austin Hedges. Another bunt by Jurickson Profar went in Turner's direction; he barehanded and threw errantly to Bellinger at first, who had to come off the bag to catch it. Two errors, a hit, and a fielder's choice loaded the bases after the tying run came in, and Manny Machado was due up.

Stripling thought he could spin one up there since Machado can be a double play waiting to happen on many nights and had already hit into one in his first at-bat. Machado, however, was expecting something soft and hammered it over the center field wall for a grand slam: the tenth of his career. That let the air out of the balloon for the Dodgers, who seemed to not have as much energy after that. The Dodgers lost 6–2 and were now 11-7. So was San Diego, creating a logjam at the top of the NL West standings with the Rockies, who are now 12-5.

Tonight's game was one of those you get during a season, where you just hope you can shower it off with some strong soap and move on. They cannot afford many more of these.

AUGUST 12, 2020. GAME 19

No new positive COVID-19 tests for the Cardinals and they are expected to play at some point this weekend in Detroit. Maybe.

Early in the day, MLB announced the discipline in regard to the recent bench-clearing incident between the Athletics and the Astros. A's outfielder Ramón Laureano was suspended six games, which he is appealing, and Astros bench coach Alex Cintrón got a whopping 20-game punishment. Cintrón allegedly yelled something vile about

Laureano's mother and that was said to have ignited things. Laureano had been hit by pitches a couple of times and was not happy about it to begin with, but the most interesting news was to come as the afternoon carried on.

About three hours prior to tonight's game with the Padres, MLB finally announced the results of the appeal hearing for Joe Kelly. He had a good enough case to have his suspension dropped from a surprising eight games to five. Still a lot for not hitting anyone and walking off the field. Granted, he did make what he calls a "boo-boo face" at Carlos Correa on his way to the dugout. Ross Stripling's latest *Big Swing Podcast* made national news today. Stripling and Kelly recorded it before the decision to cut the suspension by three games was handed down, but it was a doozy anyway. Kelly has never been shy about speaking his mind and he sure did, calling out the Astros players involved in the sign-stealing scandal.

"The people who took the fall for what happened is nonsense," Kelly said. "Yes, everyone is involved. But the way that was run over there was not from the coaching staff. They're not the head boss in charge of that thing. It's the players. So now the players get the immunity, and all they do is go snitch like a little b***h, and they don't have to get fined, they don't have to lose games."

Kelly was not shy with the microphone in front of him, as he never really is, when he added, "When you take someone's livelihood to save your own ass, that's what I don't like. Cheating? They cheated. Everyone knows they're cheaters. They know they're cheaters. It's over. That's 'been there, done that.' But now they mess it up by ruining other people's lives, so they screwed it up twice.... When you taint someone's name to save your own name, this is one of the worst things that you could probably do.... That really friggin' bugs me."

Alex Cora, former Astros manager A.J. Hinch, former Astros General Manager Jeff Luhnow, and Carlos Beltrán all got caught up in the undertow of the ocean of deceit pulled off by the Houston players.

"Maybe they could have called Cora and said, 'Hey, I'm sorry.' Or called Luhnow and said, 'Hey, I'm sorry.' Or called Hinch, and Beltran.... If they had said, 'Hey, I'm super-scared, I didn't know what to do, I didn't want to lose money, I had to rat.' Grow a pair and say that," Kelly added.

LA's new representative of baseball justice went on to say that he didn't consider the Astros players to be "respectable men" and that he didn't want to talk to any of them. Stripling didn't have to give Joe the third degree by any stretch of the imagination, and eventually the podcast got to the topic of the suspension. Kelly went on to describe how he didn't hit anyone, wasn't tossed from the game, or even warned by that night's plate umpire Alfonso Márquez. "It blows my mind, still," he remarked. "It's so upsetting. I socially distanced. I walked away. I didn't get close, and I followed all the guidelines of the CDC, and people on the other side didn't," Kelly barked. "Carlos Correa spit at our team. I don't know if it was at me. He spit out of his mouth.... This guy walks over to our dugout and then spits, while I follow all the rules, and I get eight games." Kelly was far from done. "They have a manager on their side, verbatim, yelling at me, 'Get your little skinny *** on the mound.' So my cuss words get eight games, and his cuss words get zero? That makes complete sense, right? Welcome to planet Earth. A debacle."

Dusty Baker, according to the audio of the incident, actually said, "Get your a** on the mound, m*********r." I was surprised Joe left that last word out when on his rant. Things are always interesting when Joe Kelly is around. He is currently on the IL for right shoulder inflammation and will serve his suspension when he comes off the injured list.

As for the game, it was exciting at times, but not as dramatic as the Stripling/Kelly podcast. Right-hander Tony Gonsolin was called back from USC to make a spot start, and he did a good job over four and two-thirds innings of work. The "Cat Man" had his splitter falling off the table. He struck out a career-best eight hitters and kept the top home run-hitting team in the ballpark. The bullpen took over in the fifth, and the Padres fired blanks the rest of the night.

The Dodgers' offense had been performing in the pop-gun category in recent days and it was apparently wearing on the skipper. During his pre-game Zoom conference, he did not seem his usually pleasant self, an observation made by *Orange County Register* beat writer Bill Plunkett.

"Dave, you seem a little salty today," Plunkett said.

"I like good questions, Bill," Roberts replied with a stern look at no one in particular.

During the fifth inning the offense got going, but not in the usual Dodger way, which would be to get a base runner or two and then hit a home run. For the first time this year, we witnessed some Small Ball. A.J. Pollock walked to lead off the inning, then Chris Taylor bunted to the left side for a base hit. Edwin Rios hit a shot off of Padres pitcher Zach Davies's glove that deflected into right field for a hit, and an RBI as Pollock scored and Taylor advanced to third. That would be the only run the Dodgers would need. With runners on the corners and no one out, Austin Barnes, who had just come into the game replacing Will Smith who had a sore neck, pulled off a safety squeeze with a solid bunt to score Taylor, who was sprinting home from third. An RBI double by Bellinger and a three-run home run by Turner in the eighth brought the Dodger offense back to life and put a bow on the team's twelfth win of the season. A split of the four-game series can be salvaged tomorrow night.

AUGUST 13, 2020. GAME 20. MOOKIE, MOOKIE, MOOKIE, I HAVE SEEN IT BEFORE

Today was another testing day, so around eleven in the morning, I headed over to the ballpark for my fifth test of the season. While driving up Figueroa Street toward Sunset Boulevard, someone in a junked-up car decided to do a U-turn right into traffic, right in front of me. I drive a bright white rental car that is very difficult to *not* see. I slammed on the brakes. My front end drifted to the right, while the rear of the car skidded left. When it stopped, and my horn stopped blaring, I was almost parallel to the other car and in perfect position to get T-boned by anyone behind me. Fortunately, the car following me was a ways back and able to stop in plenty of time.

On the baseball front, all parties involved say they are now confident that the Cardinals and Tigers will play a double header in Comerica Park on Saturday. We will see. Tony Gonsolin told the *Los Angeles Times* after last night's game that he felt he had a false positive on a COVID-19 test and that was the main reason that he reported late to Summer Camp.

There was some interesting news involving LeBron James and David Price. James helped to create the movement known as More Than a Vote, and Price became a part of it. The Dodgers and More Than a Vote, along with the Los Angeles County Registrar-Recorder/County Clerk and California Secretary of State's office, all got together and came up with a way that spacious Dodger Stadium could be used in early November. The home of the Dodgers will, for the first time ever, serve as a vote center for the Presidential General Election.

The Dodgers bludgeoned the Padres 11–2 tonight to salvage a split in the four-game series, and Mookie Betts was showing off some of his best tricks. For reasons known only inside the club, Betts had mostly been hitting second in the batting order. He made his name as a leadoff hitter, prefers to hit leadoff, and excels there. Like the team player that he is, he told his manager he would do whatever the team wanted. The team finally did what was best for the team and put him in the leadoff spot.

Betts is a career .303 hitter with an OPS of .941 when leading off. He hit .326 for Boston last year in 102 games batting leadoff. Tonight, Chris Paddack plunked him to start the bottom of the first and he came around to score on a game-tying homer by Corey Seager who returned to the lineup following a minor back issue. A. J. Pollock would blast one halfway up the left field Pavilion to go ahead 3–2.

Mookie would go on to hit home runs in the second, fourth, and fifth innings, and added a base hit in the seventh. The three home runs tied a Major League record for the most three-homer games in a career with six. Johnny Mize and Sammy Sosa also did it, but the twenty-seven-year-old Betts did it in only 813 games. Mize took 1,884 games at age thirty-seven and Sosa took 2,354 at age thirty-three to accomplish the rare feat, showing just how special Betts's accomplishment is. It is only a matter of time now before he stands alone atop this leaderboard.

I have now been a witness to five of the six games in which Mookie has hit three home runs. The only one I missed was last year when I was with the Dodgers, but the two in 2016 and two more in 2018 were as special to watch as tonight's was. Only difference with tonight's was I was not broadcasting the game like I did the other four times he did it. Next time, perhaps. Either way, it was awesome to watch.

After he tomahawked a first-pitch fastball from Luis Perdomo over some cardboard-cutout fans in left field, I looked at our radio post-game host, David Vassegh, who was in the booth to my right, and I held my index finger up and said, "He's got one more in him tonight. He will do it tonight."

Shortly after, my wife called me, and I told her Mookie had two homers and was going to get another one. She texted me after he hit his third and said, "I believe you had that."

Following the game, the humble right fielder told Alanna Rizzo from SportsNet LA when asked about tying the Major League record, "It's pretty cool. I don't think it means a whole lot, so I guess I'll just enjoy it."

Betts would go 4-4 with four runs scored and five RBIs to lead the way. Austin Barnes would hit his first homer of the season to add to a much-anticipated offensive onslaught and move the Dodgers into a first-place tie with idle Colorado with a 13-7 record. Mike Trout and the Angels are next up in Anaheim in a display of some of baseball's best talent.

AUGUST 14, 2020. GAME 21. FREEWAY SERIES

This afternoon, I received my COVID-19 test results via text and email. Negative again. I am five for five and looking to keep batting 1.000. The results arrived much later than they usually do, and I was starting to think something was wrong. I didn't want to call attention to not having a result at this point, since I am on the schedule to work the television broadcast tomorrow, so I didn't inquire with the team. Once I finally got my notification, I could relax.

There continue to be twists and turns. Today, Cleveland's Mike Clevinger and Zach Plesac were essentially put on trial by their teammates for breaking protocols, and it did not go well for them. After attempting to explain themselves, the Indians players let them know they felt let down and didn't want them back right now. Reportedly, one veteran player said that he would opt out if they came back. The players have lost trust in two of their starting pitchers, and have decided to compete without them. The Indians optioned them to their alternate site. This is unprecedented stuff. The Tribe would go on to trounce the Tigers 10–5.

Elsewhere, another positive test, though not with the Cardinals, who rented forty-one vehicles so players and staff could separate and drive themselves to Chicago for their series with the White Sox. That is what it takes these days to play. The positive test was with a still-unnamed player on the Reds, who had just completed the first of a three-game series with the Pirates at Great American Ballpark.

The Reds had won the game 8–1, but the news after the game was a gut punch. The rest of the weekend series is postponed and now the Pirates, through no fault of their own, have two more COVID-19-related postponements to make up; this, after missing a series with the Cardinals earlier this month.

The Freeway Series begins tonight in Anaheim, and the Dodgers have a chance to move into first place in the NL West if all goes well. It did. The Rockies lost 3–2 to the Rangers to allow the Dodgers to move to the top of the table without doing anything, but that wasn't the focus of the evening. It was on getting a win against the Angels, something they didn't do all of last season.

Clayton Kershaw dazzled in seven full innings of work, allowing only one hit—a home run by the Angels' key off-season acquisition, Anthony Rendon. Shades of Game 5 of 2019's NLDS when Rendon clicked Kershaw for a big one while pitching in relief.

"One of these days, I will find a way to get Rendon out," Kershaw said, following that game.

Tonight, Kershaw threw more sliders (38) than fastballs (36) while mixing in 17 effective curveballs. The slider was unhittable, his fastball velocity was up to 94 mph, and overall he was in command of the game. Mike Trout continued to struggle against Kershaw, going 0-4. Trout runs over the rest of baseball, but Kershaw has been able to hold him in check. Tonight's performance was vintage Kershaw, the sixth time in his career that he has gone seven or more innings allowing only one hit or less.

The other great news for the Dodgers was the reemergence of the reigning NL MVP, Cody Bellinger. Bellinger had been mired in a terrible slump, but clubbed home runs in the sixth and eighth innings, both off of left-handers, to literally get back in the swing of things. Justin Turner went 2-4 with an RBI and hit in his ninth straight game. The Dodgers are now 14-7 and a full game in front of the Rockies, in the division lead by themselves for the first time this season. It is time to step on the gas, with two more against the subpar Angels and four straight against the well-under-par Mariners coming up next week before going head-to-head with Colorado at home.

AUGUST 15, 2020. GAME 22. THE IDES OF AUGUST

Time to get back to work, as I am assigned the telecast for the second game of the Freeway Series. Given that I am staying in LA by myself and not going anywhere, I've got plenty of time to work on game prep. It was 2:20 in the afternoon when I pulled into Dodger Stadium. I just sat in my car with the radio on for several minutes because I knew I was super early and had most of my game prep done. The game wasn't for another four and a half hours. I just wanted and needed to get out of the hotel, as I was experiencing "bubble fever."

As anticipated, I arrived before anyone else and settled into my work space, the same workspace the legendary Vin Scully used, which can be intimidating if you think about it. It is a privileged space, hallowed ground in the broadcasting world, really, and tonight it is where I work. I have done a number of Dodger games on TV over the last two seasons, but most of my work has been on the radio side. This year is different, in all ways, apparently, but so far it looks like I will do more TV than radio. Either way, I consider myself fortunate to be in the position I am in.

After Orel Hershiser and I did our live hit back to the SportsNet LA's studios for the pre-game show, we recorded our open. I pulled a bonehead move, causing us to do a second take. When it came time to set up Orel on a transition to talk about Cody Bellinger's uptick in offense, I mistakenly referred to him by his dad's name, Clay. That might have been the first time I have had to do a second take with Orel, who just laughed it off. I shook my head like I had a bunch of rocks in them and went on to the second take. Doing a second take is something I don't like to do, especially if it is my fault. The entire crew in the truck has to re-rack everything and do it all over again. Now, there have been many times when something from the truck doesn't go quite right and the producer wants to do it over—sometimes over and over. I did a college hockey game over the winter where we had to record the open six or seven times. It has not been my experience with the Dodgers crew that they have screwed up much, and I can't remember a time that a taped open was blown because of them.

Once the open was in the can, we had about fifteen minutes before the start of the game. It is still weird doing all of this in a silent stadium with an empty field. We are also at the mercy of the Angels TV director. We didn't have any cameras showing the bullpens like we did in every other road park that we have televised from so far. Also, there were some very quick cuts on batters' swings with contact that made the ball especially difficult to see coming off the bat and to tell exactly what direction it was going. I haven't called a home game yet this season on TV but have on radio, and it is 1,000 percent better when the game is right in front of you. During some of my off time, I have been paying attention to how other TV broadcasters have been handling their games, especially on the road. It seems like most have adjusted well, but I can tell when they are not sure of how well a ball is hit and which direction it is headed. We all have had to make the adjustment.

When Mike Trout hit his first-inning home run, it sounded OK off the bat, but not a sure thing. I saw the ball make contact with the bat, but did not see it again until it hit the green artificial turf on the incline behind the center field wall. A.J. Pollock was in center and I just watched him drift back toward the warning track. Once he began to turn and face the wall, I figured it was gone, making it 2-0 Angels.

The Dodgers tied it up in the top of the second and went ahead in the third on Max Muncy's two-run single. The Angels would add one in the third and take the lead, 5–4, in the fifth. Betts would tie it in the seventh with a solo blast to left, his eighth of the season. From his familiar power swing and the way the ball jumped off the bat, I knew it was gone. "Mookie hammers it," I said, because he did. It was a no-doubter, even though I couldn't find the ball on the screen. The Angels probably couldn't find it on the other side of the fence, either.

In the tenth, the Dodgers' "placed runner," Chris Taylor, took off for third and made it. This is highly risky play. If you are going to try to steal third with no one out, you better be sure you have it. My guess is he had a solid assist from third-base coach Dino Ebel, who is adept at picking up pitchers' moves to the plate. With Taylor at third and no one out, it gave Muncy the chance to be the first player to have a "leadoff sacrifice fly" in MLB history. I didn't give that any play on the telecast because, honestly...really? This is a one-off rule for this year and it doesn't really matter, but it got the winning run in, and that mattered more than anything.

Kenley Jansen came in to close things out and caught Trout window-shopping, striking him out looking on three pitches to end the game. The Dodgers won 15–7 and extended their lead in the NL West. Just four days ago, the Dodgers were in third place; now, after winning four straight, they are two games up on Colorado and four up on San Diego.

After spending a few innings knocking off the rust, the telecast went fairly well, and I'm looking forward to the next one. It is much easier to do it every day rather than parachute in every once in a while, but this is 2020.

AUGUST 16, 2020. GAME 23. RUIZ DEBUTS WITH A DINGER

No more Reds players tested positive, but there is still some contact tracing going on. They could be playing again soon, which means we are close to having all thirty teams in action. We used to just take that for granted.

The Dodgers and Angels finish up the Freeway Series this afternoon in perfect weather conditions, though a little on the warm side with a game-time temperature of 93 degrees. Right-hander Julio Teherán started for the Angels, and the Dodgers were all over him in the third and fourth innings, putting up seven runs with the help of four homers.

The most notable home run came from twenty-two-year-old catcher Keibert Ruiz in his first Major League at-bat. He got a pitch up and pulled a frozen rope down the right field line, with the ball hitting a section of tarped-off seats and bouncing up onto the mezzanine level. The Dodgers had people, including Julio Urías, looking for the ball to make sure Ruiz had the valuable souvenir. Eventually a stadium security worker came up with it. Keibert became the seventh Dodger to hit a homer in his first at-bat. The others to do it were Garey Ingram in 1994, José Offerman in 1990, Dan Bankhead in 1947 for Brooklyn, Ernie Koy in 1938, Gordon Slade in 1930, and the first to do it was Clise Dudley in the year before in 1929. Ruiz also was the fourteenth different Dodger to hit a home run this season, with the team extending their Major League lead in long balls to 43. Corey Seager, Max Muncy, and Matt Beaty went yard as well, in the 8–3 win that completed the sweep of the Halos, allowing them to keep their two-game lead over Colorado with a 16-7 record.

AUGUST 17, 2020. GAME #24. "HITTERISH" KIND OF NIGHT

The coronavirus-related baseball news today wasn't much, fortunately. The Reds reported no positive tests again today, which will inch them closer to resuming their schedule. One other interesting note today concerns the Rockies and Rangers. Apparently, both teams have been petitioning MLB to clear the way for them to allow fans back into their ballparks at partial capacity. Since COVID-19 cases have either leveled off or gone down in those areas, the teams wanted to see if they can allow some people in. MLB said no, and put out a statement from Rob Manfred to reinforce it. "Given the state of the virus throughout the country and that most of the clubs do not have authorization from their local jurisdictions allowing for it, we are not able to consider hosting fans at this time."

The Dodgers were back home tonight, and I was glad to be able to go watch a game in person, plus I needed to get out of the hotel. Yesterday, I didn't need to go to Dodger Stadium, so I stayed in and watched the game to prepare for my post-game radio segment. I got back from working the Dodgers/Angels game on TV Saturday night around eleven at night, and I didn't leave the hotel until four this afternoon. That is forty-one hours straight. With the exception of a twenty-minute period to go into the FedEx in the hotel lobby, I never left my suite. I have a prepared food service ship me food once a week and I have a microwave, so there was no reason to go anywhere. If this were a normal season, I would get out, walk around, and get food from the many cool places to eat in the area and enjoy the things that Southern California has to offer. Not this year. I have to be more cautious than ever so I can continue to go to the ballpark to work.

When watching tonight's game against Seattle, one would wonder if it was actually being played at Dodger Stadium or the pre-humidor Coors Field. The baseball was flying! Game-time temperature was 94 degrees and the wind was still. Before the game, I mentioned to Jorge Jarrin, one of our Spanish-language radio announcers, that "the ball should be flying tonight." It didn't take long for that prediction to come true. The Mariners slipped in two runs in the top of the first inning including a couple of very deep fly outs. Mookie Betts, serving as the DH, launched a no-doubter to left in the bottom of the first to get the Dodgers on the board. It was the twenty-first time in his career he hit a leadoff home run and his first as a Dodger.

Five runs on four hits, including a home run by Corey Seager in the second inning, got the Dodgers a semi-comfortable 6–2 lead.

Then the top of the third happened. The Mariners put up a five-spot of their own with three home runs, one each by Evan White (the first of two on the evening), Kyle Lewis, and Corey Seager's older brother Kyle. All of a sudden, the Mariners were in front and starter Ross Stripling was left to wonder how this game got sideways on him so fast.

It was the first time brothers had homered for opposing teams in a game since June 7, 2001, when Felipe Crespo of San Francisco and his brother César of San Diego did it. While they were not with opposing teams, I remember a game that I broadcast that almost made a different kind of brother history. On April 26, 2009, at Petco Park in San Diego, two brothers on the Padres, Adrián and Edgar González, each hit home runs in a game against Pittsburgh. The Pirates had the brothers LaRoche, Adam and Andy, and when Adam hit one, I started to focus on Andy, who had two more at-bats left. If Andy, who came up with the Dodgers originally, had hit one, then two sets of brothers would have homered in the same game and made Major League history. It was one of those moments as a broadcaster that sticks out sometimes, and you put it away in some compartment in your brain to roll out when you might need it. I don't remember the date, but I also remember the LaRoche brothers did homer in the same game against Minnesota at PNC Park in 2009.

As the game went on, any ball hit to the outfield seemed like it had a chance to get out. Outfielders continued to drift back and make catches either near or on the warning track. After Seattle added one more run in the fourth with two outs on three straight hits, the Dodger offense didn't pick up again until the bottom of the seventh against right-handed reliever, and former Dodger, Matt Magill. Justin Turner had a base hit following one by Corey Seager to extend his current hitting streak to 11 games, and Bellinger walked to load the bases. A.J. Pollock drove in a run with a single and after Max Muncy walked, Matt Beaty hammered a two-out, two-run bomb to put the game away—apparently.

The Mariners threatened in the top of the ninth when Kenley Jansen gave up a base hit and a walk to put the tying run on with nobody out. A curveball, fastball, and backdoor slider caught Kyle Seager watching the paint dry. A beautiful sequence of pitches retired a very dangerous hitter. Austin Nola would pop out foul to Turner, then the burly designated hitter, Daniel Vogelbach, flied to right to end the game.

The Dodgers are 17-7, have won six in a row, and have quickly built a three-game lead in the division. A good night at the office for the Boys in Blue. even though it was an offensive circus on both sides.

AUGUST 18, 2020. GAME 25. GONSO VS. GONZO DUEL

The Cincinnati Reds were hoping to get back to play today and traveled to Kansas City to face the Royals. That game was postponed, likely out of an abundance of caution due to the last of the contact tracing that is going on. They are expected to play a double header tomorrow.

Players around baseball, I am noticing, including some on the Dodgers, are slowly relaxing the guidelines here and there. There is more high-fiving and handshaking going on, opposing players talking and visiting on the field before games and less social distancing. I hope players don't let their guard down.

In a Zoom presser this morning, catcher Keibert Ruiz confirmed what many in the media had suspected. He had arrived late to Summer Camp because he had been battling the coronavirus. He talked about having all the typical symptoms: headache, fever, loss of smell and taste. "Thank God I didn't go into the hospital. I just stayed in the hotel. It was a tough time. I feel good now," the youngster from Valencia, Venezuela, said.

Here is some perspective for you. The 25th game of the season is this afternoon, with 35 to play. It is a 4:00 p.m. start, so both teams can get a head start on their chartered flights to Seattle so they can complete the four-game home-and-home series. Game number 25 means that we are now 42 percent of the way through this 60-game season. Doing the math, this would be the equivalent of the 68th game in a regular season. If you convert the calendar and the season would have started on time in late March, this would be like playing a game on June 11.

The Dodgers have won six consecutive games, and have outscored their opponents during the streak 49–23 while hitting 17 home runs. Mookie Betts is the first player this year to achieve a 2.0 WAR in his bid to become just the second player ever to win the MVP in both leagues. Frank Robinson won the NL MVP in 1961 with Cincinnati and again after his first season with the Orioles in 1966. Robinson played a season with the Dodgers in 1972.

As crazy as last night's game was in terms of the offensive outbursts for both teams, today's game could not have been more different. Tony Gonsolin and Marco Gonzales locked up in an old-fashioned pitchers' duel for a while, and runs were difficult to come by. Gonsolin went six innings allowing only two hits and no runs. It was his third straight scoreless start, as he joined Rich Hill as the only two Dodgers pitchers ever to begin a season with three straight scoreless starts. It will be hard to keep Tony out of the rotation, and I would not be surprised if the Dodgers continued with a six-man rotation. He does have options and can't pitch for a few days after the start, so I also would not be surprised if he was sent back to the alternate site to wait for his next start.

Gonzales went seven innings, allowing five hits and a run with a career-high nine strikeouts, and certainly pitched well enough to win the ballgame. While the Dodgers searched for some offense, they finally pushed a run across in the sixth inning when Austin Barnes came around to score on a Justin Turner base hit. Turner extended his hitting streak to a season-high 12 games in the process. Seattle tied it in the seventh after reliever Jake McGee walked Kyle Lewis to lead off the inning, Kyle Seager doubled, and there were Mariners on second and third. A ground ball to Turner with the infield back and playing for the out in a 1-0 game allowed Lewis to come in and tie it.

A subtle mistake by the Mariners may have cost them the game. In the bottom of the eighth with one out, Barnes walked. With the count two balls and two strikes on Corey Seager, the M's dugout apparently told first baseman Evan White not to hold Barnes on first. This slight defensive maneuver allowed Barnes to get a bigger lead and a better jump, and he stole second. I wonder if they lost track of the count and thought it was full. It wasn't. On the next pitch, Seager lined one sharply into right center field and Barnes scored what would become the winning run. Bad teams find a way to lose, and good teams find a way to win. The Dodgers have won seven straight in what seems like the blink of an eye, and have gone from being behind the Padres by a half game in third place to building a four-game lead in the NL West in a week. They now have the best record in baseball at 18-7, along with the best winning percentage at .720. This team is on a roll, but doing it without that one game where they put everything together. That is coming, but, in baseball, you never know when.

AUGUST 19, 2020. GAME 26. SHOE POLICE

I drove over to Dodger Stadium around half past eleven in the morning and proceeded to Lot B to pick up my test. I was the only person there to be tested. I noticed that my last name was misspelled again, this time with an *e* at the end. I don't like it when people do that, but it shouldn't affect me getting the results. Rinse, lather, repeat, and I was on my way.

While flipping through social media in the afternoon looking for some baseball stories, I came across a beauty from someone not surprising. Reds starting pitcher Trevor Bauer, who is not shy and sometimes misunderstood, is often in the middle of something and was working on another escapade. He had posted pictures of the cleats he was planning on wearing in tonight's game, and they are one-of-a-kind classics. On the left cleat is a picture of Joe Kelly displaying the "boo-boo face" he broke out during the brouhaha with Correa and the Astros. On the right spike, in red lettering, it said "Free Joe Kelly." While a lot of people saw the post as humorous, Major League Baseball did not. They sent word to Bauer that if he tried to wear them on the field he would be disciplined. An eight-game suspension, perhaps? Bauer capitulated. The Shoe Police won. They always do.

The Shoe Police, as the players call them, showed up in a bad way during the 2016 season when then Dodger Yasiel Puig honored Vin Scully during his final year by wearing custom cleats featuring a portrait of Vin in a game against Arizona. Puig was unhappy when he received a letter from MLB saying that if he wore those cleats again he would be fined.

Back when Bauer was with the Indians and I was with the Pirates, I was in the TV booth at PNC prepping for that night's game when something caught my eye. I looked up and realized it was a drone hovering above the seats in the 300 level and almost at eye level with me. As I looked at it, I realized it had a camera on it. I stood up and looked down into the seats and there was a partially uniformed Bauer with the controller in his hands. He didn't acknowledge me; he just steered the drone away from the booth and out over the field. He was taking aerial photos of the ballpark and apparently had been doing that in all the road stadiums. I found out later that he built his own drones. You may remember that he cut his finger on one during the postseason a few years later. Now there are signs around PNC Park prohibiting drones.

The Dodgers are in Seattle for the back half of their four-game series, and many around the game are scratching their heads about the extra travel for these types of series. I thought the idea was to cut down on travel during the pandemic, but this seems like an unnecessary trip for one team. Even Dave Roberts told us on a Zoom call this afternoon that he thinks this should have been a four-game series in one city or the other. I am sure there are many who agree with the skipper, including me. When the Cardinals are playing as the home team against the Cubs at Wrigley Field and the Blue Jays have batted last in visiting stadiums, what difference does it make? Do you what you have to do to get 60 games in as safely as possible. Plus, with owners losing a ton this year, one fewer road trip for half the teams might be a meaningful savings for some teams. Ever have to rent ten busses and a 757 before for a less-than-forty-eight-hour trip? It's not inexpensive.

At T-Mobile Park, Julio Urías didn't have it. He lasted only an inning and a third, and this game began to look like it might be one of those nights. Even though he struck out the last man he faced in the second, his pitch count was at 52, and it seemed like he'd had a full count on everyone. His fastball consistently missed up and out of the strike zone, and all signs pointed to an early departure.

Dennis Santana came in leading 2–1 and left trailing 5–2 after giving up a four-spot in the third. The Dodgers couldn't recover in spite of home runs by Cody Bellinger, Joc Pederson, and Max Muncy. All three had been struggling at the plate coming into the game. Bellinger's average was .175, Pederson's .159, and Muncy was hitting only .170 at the game's start. Muncy was given a quick hook by home plate umpire Mark Ripperger when he expressed his displeasure with a strike call just before the one he struck out on. He never even looked at Ripperger and was muttering to himself. Ripperger tossed him like a nervous hunter with his finger on a hair-trigger, and then Muncy turned around and jawed with him. Prior to the Muncy incident, Dave Roberts and hitting coach Robert Van Scoyoc were both tossed when a pitch at Muncy's ankles was called a strike, so the ump was already riled up and probably went too far to make his point by chucking Muncy out of the game.

Mariners catcher Austin Nola, in an effort to "frame" the pitch in question, caught the pitch and yanked his glove north and into the strike zone. Some teams want their catchers to get on a knee and set a low target then catch the ball on the way up. The theory is that this technique should basically "steal a strike" for your pitcher. No disrespect intended towards Nola, but it looked like a little-league catcher trying to fool an umpire. Framing has to be a subtle move of the glove, and sometimes the head, to help "frame" a borderline pitch into a perceived strike zone, therefore "stealing a strike" for your pitcher. When a catcher yanks his glove from out of the zone back into it, he isn't fooling anyone. Umpires hate the term "framing," and say it has no bearing on whether they call a pitch a strike or not. Catchers and sabermetricians will tell a different story, but when you see a catcher whose glove actions resemble the motion of a windshield wiper or, in this case, an elevator, there is nothing Major League about that.

The Mariners got a good pitching performance from starter Taijuan Walker, who toiled for seven innings, allowing three runs. From the fourth through the seventh he retired 12 straight to help his cause. The final score was 6–4. The Dodgers dropped to 18-8, ended their seven-game win streak, and remain four games in front of the Rockies and now the Padres.

AUGUST 20, 2020. GAME 27. PLEASE MOVE OVER A LITTLE, MR. DRYSDALE

The Mets were all set to play the Marlins in Miami tonight when it was discovered that one player and one staff member had tested positive. The final game of the series was postponed, and the Mets moved their charter flight up and flew back to New York. The two people that tested positive, and anyone who had been really close to them according to the contact tracing process, were left in Miami and could not fly with the team. The Yankees and the Mets are supposed to square off in a subway series starting tomorrow, but that game was already postponed, and the entire weekend series is in doubt.

Meanwhile, no players or staff with the Pittsburgh Pirates have tested positive, but the president of the team, Travis Williams, released a statement that he turned up with a positive test and is staying away from the ballpark. I received my test results today and they were negative again. I am still batting 1.000, thankfully. Six for six.

Clayton Kershaw turned in another vintage performance tonight, baffling Seattle hitters for seven innings and getting the Dodgers back in the win column. The only blemish was Kyle Seager's fourth-inning solo home run off a misplaced fastball. It happens. Kershaw has allowed only 6 runs to this point in the season, while 5 of the 6 have come on solo home runs.

Kershaw reached another milestone in his storied career, passing the great Don Drysdale and his 2,486 career *K*s, moving into second place on the all-time Dodgers strikeout list and now has 2,493. Following Kershaw's 11-strikeout performance, he trails only Don Sutton. Sutton had 2,696. It was the 38th time in Kershaw's career that he whiffed 11 or more in a game, which is the 15th most in MLB history. When asked after the game about the milestone, he said, "It's obviously very cool. Just to be a Dodger long enough to accomplish something like that is pretty special. Some of the names on that list, it's pretty cool to be a part of it. Someday, I will look back on it and think it is pretty cool, but today, it was a good start all the way around." When you think about it, in this short season, Kershaw will have way fewer starts than he normally would heading into the postseason, so, in theory, he should be able to sustain his current performance level through the playoffs. Only time will tell.

Cody Bellinger provided more proof that his bat is on the way back, as he went two for three with a single, a home run, and two RBIs. Bellinger's average is still under .200, but it looks like he is almost back.

One key moment that stands out was when Matt Beaty was at the plate in the third inning with two on and nobody out. Beaty swung at a two-strike pitch that darted down and out of the strike zone. Beaty began walking toward the third base dugout when home plate umpire Adrian Johnson made the sign indicating Beaty had actually fouled it off. He didn't. TV replays showed he missed the ball completely— and by a lot! What a break it turned out to be, because on the next pitch Beaty smashed a ground rule double to right field that scored Kiké Hernández and moved Austin Barnes to third. What should have been an out turned into more than enough to win the game, as Barnes and Beatty would both score on an A.J. Pollock base hit. Pollock would also come around on Bellinger's first hit of the night. A four-run lead for Kershaw means the game is over, and it was.

The Dodgers won 6–1 to take three of four and raise their record to a Major League-best 19-8. The Padres beat Texas, while the Rockies lost again to Houston. San Diego passed Colorado by a game and now trails the division-leading Dodgers by four games.

AUGUST 21, 2020. GAME 28. DINO'S BIG ASSIST

MLB sent out their weekly testing report today with COVID-19 tests reported through August 20. During the last week, there were 12,485 total tests done on "covered individuals," which include players, staff, and various other team personnel. Of those tests, seven came back positive, which is 0.5 percent of all tested, a low number. The report indicated that three were players and four were staff members, with five of the positives being Major League personnel and two from alternate sites.

The Mets missed their game with the Marlins last night and now will miss their weekend series with the Yankees, which was postponed this morning. The Yankees are off until Tuesday when they play Atlanta. The Mets' immediate future is unclear.

The NBA has been reporting no positives from their "bubble" in Orlando at Disney World, which is helping the bubble plan for the MLB postseason gain traction. One report has San Diego and Texas as possible sites. San Diego makes sense, because of the weather and the sheer number of hotel rooms in walking distance to Petco Park. One hotel, the Omni, is directly connected to the park via a fourth-floor walkway. The new Globe Life Field in Arlington has a roof, so weather wouldn't be an issue, and the Dallas/Fort Worth Metroplex has tons of hotel space.

On Sunday, I will pinch hit for Alanna Rizzo as the SportsNet LA pre-game anchor and in-game reporter on TV, so I decided to hang with her and her crew tonight in order to get the routine down. Last season, I came off the bench for her a number of times, but it wasn't in the plans for me this year. When she asked if I was available to cover for her, I said "absolutely" and am happy to do it. I actually miss the anchoring part after doing a bunch of it in the past.

While in suite 211, which is set up for Alanna this year, Nomar Garciaparra was there. He was going to be working the pre-game show from the newly constructed set beyond the center field wall and was enjoying the air-conditioned booth on this humid, 92 degree afternoon. Nomar and I talked baseball for a while. I always enjoy talking ball with him, because he is so passionate about it and more knowledgeable than most. We talked a lot about scouting and why it is so important for baseball to have scouts at the games instead of making evaluations from home. He stressed all the details that scouts (broadcasters also) miss by not being able to be at the games with the access they are accustomed to. We talked pitching detail, base running detail, catching detail, and about details behind the plate that cost the Mariners the game against the Dodgers during the last series. He is a walking, talking fountain of baseball information, and we are fortunate to have him on our broadcast team.

During a private broadcasters' call before the series with the Angels, I asked a question of Dave Roberts. "Dave, if I can ask you about tomorrow's starter, he has been off to a slower start than, I am sure, he or anyone had hoped. When do you think Walker will be back to what people expect of him?"

Without hesitation, he responded, "Two more starts."

He was right on target, as the second start since that conversation turned into Walker Buehler's best performance of the season. The right-hander turned in an 11-strikeout gem against Colorado, working six innings while throwing 92 pitches, 68 percent of them fastballs. He landed some good curveballs that looked like they dropped right off the table. It was the eighth time in Buehler's young career that he had struck out 10 or more hitters in a game. I fully expect to see more of this from Buehler this season.

Overall, it was a pretty good game for the Dodgers, and they did it with Mookie Betts enjoying a scheduled day off. Bellinger went two for three again with a double and drove in the first run of the game. In the fourth inning, with A.J. Pollock at second following a leadoff double, Matt Beaty hit a ball to right field that took one bounce in front of right fielder Charlie Blackmon. Blackmon either assumed Pollock had no chance to score on the play or had a brain cramp. He threw the ball into second base rather than straight to first baseman Daniel Murphy, who was positioned on the infield grass as the cut-off man. Dino Ebel saw where the throw was headed and waved Pollock home. He beat the extra throw from shortstop Trevor Story, and gave the Dodgers a lead they would not relinquish. In this situation, the throw from right field goes to the cut-off man, who will either cut it off and get the base runner who would be trying to advance and protect against the runner coming home, or, if the runner is attempting to score, let the ball go on the catcher's call and try and get the out at the plate. With nobody out, Beaty was thinking that he was going to have to round first and maybe get in a run-down or attempt to get to second base if the throw went all the way through, but he just parked at first, as Blackmon's mental error allowed Pollock to score.

Cory Seager's two-out double then scored Beaty and Chris Taylor, who had singled earlier, and it was pretty much game over. The bullpen then choked this game into submission as Adam Kolarek, Caleb Ferguson, and Kenley Jansen each pitched an inning, combining to retire nine straight Rockies and put them to bed for the evening while sealing a 5–1 win.

The Dodgers are the first team to 20 wins. This is the fourth time in franchise history that the Dodgers have begun a season 20-8. Over the last 10 games, they are 9-1 and have outscored their opponents 66–32, which is great. They are also 15-5 over their last 20 games.

For some perspective on how the offense and the pitching have done so far is the team's remarkable run differential, the number that shows how many runs they have scored versus how many they have allowed. For hockey fans, it is the equivalent of the plus/minus stat, and in baseball, it is an important team metric. After tonight's win their differential is +70, by far the best in baseball. The next best team run differential belongs to the Minnesota Twins at +34. Oakland is next at +33. The Atlanta Braves have the second-best run differential in the National League at +22. While the Braves' mark is considered good, it still falls a full 48 runs short of the Dodgers.

AUGUST 22, 2020. GAME 29. WEIRD WALK-OFF

Not much going on today on the COVID-19 front for baseball. It has been a quiet day in that regard, which is welcome.

The Dodgers got off to an interesting start in the bottom of the first inning, while Mookie Betts continued to peel back layers of his uncanny baseball talent that folks around here haven't seen yet. After a walk, Betts used his best base-running instincts to go from first to third on a Cory Seager base hit to left. Usually, a runner stops at second with the play right in front of him, but knowing that Raimel Tapia was left-handed and moving to his left to field the ball, and that he would have to throw across his body to get the ball to third, Mookie flew around second, surprising many observers at the stadium and, I am sure, some TV viewers as well. Not surprising to me was the fact that he made it to third base easily. I have seen this act before. When Seager saw that the throw went to third, he headed to second base, drawing a throw from Nolan Arenado, and ended up in a run-down. Betts, seeing this, drifted off of third base about 20 feet. When he saw Trevor Story, who now had the ball, commit to getting Seager out, Mookie put his head down and sprinted for home, beating the throw for the first run of the game. That is making things happen with your feet, something Betts does exceptionally well. Dodger fans are catching on that Betts is an especially exciting, generational-type player.

Chris Taylor hit his second home run of the season in the second inning. In the seventh, with Colorado up 3–2, Justin Turner got hit by a pitch, A.J. Pollock doubled, and Cody Bellinger walked. Taylor hit into a double play that scored Turner to tie the game. In the inning, the Dodgers were walked three times, had a double, and a man plunked and only came away with one run. Normally, that would be a head shaker, but it is nitpicky stuff when you are talking about the team with the best record in baseball. This team can get away with stuff like that and still win, as they were about to.

In the bottom of the ninth, the game was tied at three with Bellinger leading off. Rockies manager Bud Black, one of the all-time decent guys in the game, put Daniel Bard on the hill. While Bard is a great story, Bellinger was about to write one of his own. Bard had a promising career with the Red Sox go sideways due to control issues, and was most recently employed by the Diamondbacks as their mental skills coach and mentor to younger players. He had not pitched in a Major League game in seven years before remarkably making the Rockies roster out of Summer Camp. His appearance would be brief. On his second pitch to Bellinger, he tossed an 89 mph slider that spun like a cement mixer. Bellinger hit it hard enough to right field, but as he looked up to where he thought he hit it, he couldn't find it. He wasn't helped out much by veteran umpire Bill Miller, who went out into short right field from his position at first base to get a good look at the flight of the ball. Miller didn't make much of a gesture indicating a home run. Right fielder Sam Hilliard, who was at the wall, leaped as high as he could but was too far from the ball to make the game-saving catch. Meanwhile, approaching first, Bellinger was looking toward left center field, where he thought he hit it. Once he heard the piped-in crowd noise and the blaring music, he rounded the bag, shrugged his shoulders, and put his palms up in the air, knowing he had won the game, but still wondering where the ball had gone. The dugout exploded with emotion, but Dave Roberts yelled to his players, "Social distancing! Social distancing!" Then the weirdest, most awkward home plate celebration took place, with players jumping up and down, air high-fiving, and limiting what usually goes on when a player hits a game-winning home run in the bottom of the ninth. Weird times.

With the win, the Dodgers moved to 21-8 and continue to dominate the Rockies. They have now won 22 of the last 26 games against Colorado, and have outscored them 181–114 during that stretch. They will go for the sweep tomorrow afternoon as we reach the halfway mark of this crazy season.

AUGUST 23, 2020. GAME 30. LUCKY NUMBER 7 AND KOBE DAY

Sunday afternoon was 91 degrees and humid, with a significant breeze moving the flags out toward the newly constructed "Front Door" beyond the center field wall, perfect conditions for the baseball to carry. And boy, did it ever.

The Dodgers were playing their 17th game in seventeen days and had gone 12-4 over the previous sixteen. I got to work on the new SportsNet LA pre-game set in the empty fan section beyond center field. Ned Colletti, the former Dodger general manager, was working as the analyst with me while I anchored a few segments for the Leadoff and Access SportsNet Dodgers pre-game shows. Ned is great to work with. He was one of the first people to call me when I got this gig in December of 2018. Not only does he work with the Dodgers on television, but, uniquely, he works as a scout for the San Jose Sharks of the NHL doing player evaluations. When he is not focusing on baseball and hockey, he is teaching at Pepperdine University in Malibu.

Today would have been Kobe Bryant's forty-second birthday. He had a great relationship with the Dodgers and appeared at the stadium every so often. Players were always enamored in his presence. I remember before Game 4 of the World Series in 2018, Kobe was on the field getting the crowd going. He got on the microphone to say Vin Scully's iconic words, "It's time for Dodger Baseball." January 26 will be remembered in Los Angeles as one of the city's darkest days. It was the day of the helicopter crash that killed the Lakers legend and his beautiful daughter, Gigi, along with a number of her teammates and family members. Such a sad day. It was one of those events that you remember right where you were when you received the news.

Prior to the game, every Dodger player and staff member stood on the third base line wearing a Bryant game jersey. Half wore his number 8 jersey, while the other half wore his number 24 jersey; he wore both numbers during his time with the Lakers. On the first base line, Matt Kemp, now with the Rockies but a longtime Dodger, was the only Colorado player with a Bryant tank top on. The bright gold color of the Lakers' home uniform stood out in dramatic contrast with the grey road uniforms.

As part of the ceremony to honor Kobe and Gigi, there was a stirring and emotional three-minute-and-twenty-one-second video played on the large video boards, carried live on the telecast and over the Dodgers Radio Network. It was narrated by Vin Scully, who can still capture you and draw you into anything. Goosebumps. I don't imagine there were too many dry eyes among the fans watching at home.

While anchoring the pre-game on TV, I said, "If the Dodgers win their next three games, they would be 24-8, which would be an appropriate record considering what is going to be happening today."

Here is a tweet the Dodgers put out after the game.

> *-Corey HR on the 8th pitch*
> *-Mookie HR on the 42nd pitch (Kobe's birthday today)*
> *-Kiké HR on the 62nd pitch (Kobe's 62 points vs. Mavs)*
> *-Cody's 8th homer and his 24th hit*
> *-11–3 win vs. Rockies (win by 8)*
> *Kobe was here.*

Wild.

In total, there were ten home runs hit in the game today. The Rockies hit three and the Dodgers launched seven. Betts had two and would become the only Dodger ever to hit two bombs and steal two bases in a game. This game was close, as the teams traded home runs until the fourth inning. With two on and two out, Kiké Hernández fired a gut shot at the Rockies, blasting a three-run homer that would effectively open the flood gates. When coming across home plate, Hernández shot an invisible basketball, a three-pointer, as he said after the game, to honor Kobe.

Seager, Bellinger, Muncy, and Will Smith, just activated from the IL, all went deep to complete the sweep of the Rockies by an 11–3 score. The Dodgers have now won eleven of the last twelve games, and are on a roll heading into the second half. I find it strange that the start of the second half of the season, the stretch run, and the trading deadline are all in the same week. The COVID Curveball strikes again.

AUGUST 25, 2020. GAME 31. TAKE IT BACK FROM THE OCEAN

Following a well-earned day off, the Giants are the opponent tonight as the Dodgers begin a six-game road trip to San Francisco and Texas. Things started off swimmingly at Oracle Park, as Max Muncy cracked a 3-run shot in the top of the first to give Julio Urías a 3–0 lead before he took the mound. It wouldn't last long. Giants first baseman Brandon Belt blasted a three-run homer of his own in the bottom of the first to tie it at 3. Urías, coming into the game, had a first-inning ERA of 7.20, not very good. But, for the innings he would pitch after the first, his ERA was a paltry 1.50. He would end up surrendering four runs before leaving the game after four innings plus.

This was a mess of a game. The Dodgers bullpen blew the lead three times, and when Kenley Jansen came in to close out a one-run lead, Belt took him out of the ballpark to tie it up and force extra innings. At the end of four hours and twenty-two minutes, including two excruciating extra innings, San Francisco's Donovan Solano hit a walk-off two-run homer to give the Giants an 8–6 win. It was the first time in three extra-innings games that the Dodgers lost. It also happened to be the suddenly confident Giants' seventh straight win. The Giants won in spite of a one-sided statistic that was squarely against them. Giants hitters went an astoundingly awful 3-22 with runners in scoring position and still won. That should tell you all you need to know about what a mess this was for the Dodgers.

On the post-game radio show on AM 570 LA Sports, I was asked for my thoughts, and I said, "This is the perfect example of how a team snatches defeat out of the jaws of victory." It is not an original quote and I'm not sure who said it first, but it seemed apropos for the situation.

For what had proven to be a rare poor performance, the Dodgers played down to their competitors' level, let them back in the game several times, and suffered the consequences. As gloom and doom as this game sounded, this stuff happens whether you play a 162-game season or a 60-game season. The short season simply magnifies it. With a record of 22-9, no one in Major League Baseball was crying for the Dodgers. This night there was a game, and for the time they played, there was a distraction from the serious events going on outside of the baseball world.

AUGUST 26, 2020. GAME 32? BLACK LIVES MATTER

Today is a day that will be remembered forever, not for the games that were played, but for the games that were not. The police shooting of a twenty-nine-year-old African American man named Jacob Blake in Kenosha, Wisconsin, poured salt into an already wide-open wound. This country has seen its share of racial injustice and systemic racism. The sports world responded in an effort to create a heightened awareness of the multiple problems people of color have been dealing with for years. High-profile players decided to make a stand and collectively say, "Enough is enough." NBA players decided against playing their playoff games. The Milwaukee Bucks began the protests, followed by the Milwaukee Brewers in MLB. The rest of the NBA followed the Bucks' lead, then the entire WNBA did the same.

The Zoom conference with Dave Roberts, originally scheduled for 3:00 p.m., was pushed off. Around 5:00 p.m., in the radio booth with Rick Monday and Duane McDonald, we awaited word on what the Dodgers would do. We kept an eye on our feed from Oracle Park in San Francisco to see if anything was out of the ordinary and whether there were any indicators that there may not be a game.

Other games on the east coast had already begun and were too late to join the NBA in any kind of unified strike, but once the Brewers decided not to play against the Reds, teams in the west followed suit, except the Rockies and Diamondbacks, though Matt Kemp opted out of the game with the support of his teammates.

Mookie Betts, one of the most prominent African American baseball players in the world, decided he would not play. Dave Roberts, who was born in Japan to a Japanese mother but whose father is black, was going to sit out the game too. He had the support of ownership, as did first-base coach George Lombard, whose father is black and mother was white. Lombard's mother, a civil activist in the 1960s, died when he was only ten years old, but she inspired George to never be quiet about social issues. Lombard is one of the best people in the game and has earned respect everywhere he has been, in and out of the game.

Unlike some teams, the Dodgers supported one another and decided they were either all in or all out. If Mookie was not going to play, none of them would play. Betts' teammates had his back and he felt it, saying during a Zoom press conference, "I was already tight with everybody in the clubhouse, but now that I know that everybody has my back even more than I already thought, it means a lot. I'll always remember this team just having my back."

"It's not a political issue…this is a human being issue," said Dave Roberts.

Kershaw, who has been outspoken and extremely supportive of his black teammates, stood with Betts, Roberts, and Kenley Jansen at the press conference and said, "We made a collective group decision to not play, to let our voices be heard for standing up for what we believe is right."

Giants manager Gabe Kapler, whose team virtually linked arms with the Dodgers, said, "I think I've been pretty consistent. Some things I think are just bigger than sports, and I don't think it should require athletes needing to boycott playoff games to remind us Black lives matter and that police brutality is unacceptable and that systemic racism needs to be eliminated."

Pro athletes have a big-time platform, and today it was mobilized. 2020 has been quite a year, one that will be remembered for the coronavirus most of all, but also for people standing up for what is right and countless protests and marches around the nation.

At 10:45 p.m., I heard a commotion through my window. I looked down on Figueroa Street and saw a protest march moving up the road. I have seen numerous marches in LA since I got here, and many seem to be on Figueroa.

This was a day that everyone who makes a living in the sports world, and hopefully many others, should have burned into their memories.

AUGUST 27, 2020. GAMES 32 AND 33. THURSDAY DOUBLE-DIP

It was late last night when it was confirmed that there would be a doubleheader today. The Giants and Dodgers wouldn't face each other again during this stunted season, so there was really no choice but to play a twin bill.

Before the first game was getting underway, there were rumblings of teams, mostly on the East Coast, who had played yesterday electing not to play today. There were a number of doubleheaders involving the teams that sat out last night and those would go on, but the participants in the single games were wanting to join the protest that they did not have the chance to take part in yesterday.

Seven games ended up being postponed. The NBA still did not have any playoff games, the WNBA boycotted games, while Major League Soccer also sat out in protest. This was, by far, the most profound and widespread statement by professional athletes in history. No question about it. Their voices were loud and clear.

I was back in the TV booth for the games and working with Orel. I had a thought in the back of my mind that I might not finish this doubleheader. Joe Davis was working for Fox, assigned to do the game between the Phillies and Nationals. Once I saw that his game was postponed, I figured there was a chance the Dodgers would pull me from the second game and have Joe come back. Sure enough, during the second inning of the first game, I was notified that I would not do the second game.

This situation was just another example of the times we are currently in, and the trickle-down effect COVID, and civil unrest, can have on the game and in the booth.

When the Dodgers' lineup card was issued this morning, there was no Mookie Betts. Joc Pederson was set to hit leadoff. Then, an hour before game time, a new lineup was issued with Betts at the top of the order. Mookie had told Roberts last night that he would not play in either game today, but after discussions with the Players Alliance, a coalition of more than a hundred black baseball players, he decided that his voice would be louder now if he played than if he didn't. The members of the Alliance donated their salaries from Thursday as well as Friday, "to combat racial inequality and aid Black families and communities deeply affected in the wake of recent events." As Willie Calhoun, one of two Black players in the Rangers' clubhouse, noted, "Mookie is the LeBron of baseball. He has a huge voice."

Betts walked against right-hander Logan Webb to start the game and eventually came around to score the first run on a groundout by Cody Bellinger. The Dodgers put up a crooked number in the fourth, plating four runs with the big hit coming from catcher Austin Barnes, who smacked a two-run double into the left-field corner. After that, the Giants went dormant. In the sixth inning, Betts hit a sharp ground ball through the left side of the infield for his 1,000th career hit.

Kershaw kept San Francisco at bay as he has for the majority of his career, turning in another vintage performance. He easily could have come away with a complete game in the seven-inning contest, but after A.J. Pollock punished an offering from lefty Andrew Suarez for his sixth home run in the top of the seventh to make it 7–0, there was no reason for Kershaw to come back out. It was Kershaw's 173rd career win and his 24th over the Giants. The Dodgers were 23-9 and still had another game to play.

Game 2 wouldn't go any better for San Francisco, and it wouldn't start on time due to Gabe Kapler getting a taste of his own medicine. At the beginning of the season, as I noted, Kapler was withholding his starting pitchers. This did not sit well with other teams, and it was theorized that Kapler may have had it suggested to him that he knock it off. After placing Walker Buehler on the IL with a blister issue, the Dodgers decided to go with the bullpen for game two. It was pretty much a game-time decision, and they only told Caleb Ferguson that he would start the game a short time before announcing their intention, but in plenty of time within the rules of the game. Kapler didn't like it, and after Ferguson had gone out to start warming up, he let the Dodgers know that the Giants were delaying the game by a half hour so they could have time to prepare for the new starting pitcher. Ferguson had to stop what he was doing and push back his warmup to accommodate the delay.

Ferguson pitched one inning and retired the side in order. So much for the extra half hour of prep. What was worse for Kapler's team would be the fact that the Dodger pen men had a combined perfecto going until the fifth inning, when Brandon Belt led off the inning with a hit. Belt would reach in the seventh on a bunt base hit and would end up recording the only two Giants hits.

Joc Pederson clubbed a second-inning home run and scored two innings later on a Will Smith double. That is all the offense the Dodgers needed in working their way to another shutout and 2–0 win. San Francisco went a total of 3-29 with runners in scoring position during the series. The Dodgers took advantage in building their record to a Major League-best 24-9, and now have a five-game lead over San Diego.

According to ESPN Stats and Info, the last time the Dodgers shut out their opponent in both games of a doubleheader was September 19, 1971, versus the Braves. The last time the Giants were blanked in both ends of a double-dip was July 25, 1943, by the Cubs, when they were the New York Giants.

AUGUST 28, 2020. GAME 34. JACKIE ROBINSON DAY

The Dodgers are playing their first game inside the new Globe Life Field in Arlington, Texas. I have done a number of games in Arlington in the past, and if any team's park needed a roof and air condition-ing, it was that one. I'm just sorry I cannot be on the trip to see the new yard.

Due to the Kapler delay and the time it takes to get out of San Francisco in general, the Dodgers did not arrive at their hotel in the Dallas Metroplex until around three in the morning, Central time. That should never be an excuse, but they did not play well in game one against the struggling Rangers. I have been on many, many late nights and all-night charter flights and it is not that day that affects how you feel, but the next day.

The Dodgers played like the next day came a day early. They were sluggish and couldn't muster any offense, eventually scoring two runs in the top of the seventh inning on an RBI double by Cory Seager and a run-scoring hit by Justin Turner. Turner stole second, and some-thing didn't look right with his gait as he approached the bag. He was lifted from the game due to what was described as a "cramp." I have seen enough hamstring issues and experienced enough of my own to know what it was. Later it would be diagnosed as a low-grade ham-string strain and Turner would miss the rest of the weekend series.

The Rangers got to reliever Jake McGee in the bottom of the seventh, after Dustin May had held them to two earned runs through six. It was May's longest and most effective outing of the season and of his career, really, as he has solidified himself as a middle-of-the-rotation starting pitcher. He has now pitched in 11 straight starts to begin his career allowing two earned runs or fewer. Only one other Dodger had a better start to his pitching career. From July 1992 to April 1993, Pedro Astacio went 14 straight.

The Dodgers' first impressions of Globe Life Park were that it was big, really big, and played like a pitchers' park. Like a number of the parks built in the past fifteen years, eventually, I predict, the Rangers will move these new walls in.

The Rangers took game one 6–2 and the Dodgers are now 24-10, the last team in MLB to lose double-digit games.

AUGUST 29, 2020. GAME 35. SPECIAL EFFECTS EXPERIMENT

It was 10:06 in the morning and I had been up for a couple of hours reading and looking at that day's baseball news when a text popped up on my phone. It was from Mike Levy asking if I was available to fill in for Alanna Rizzo, who was not feeling well. SportsNet LA would need me to conduct pre-game interviews and do some segments from the stadium, as well as some in-game features and post-game interviews. I didn't have any time to waste, because the pre-game interviews started in less than two hours and I wasn't close to ready. I am here to patch up holes, so I got ready quickly.

One of the different things we tried during the pre-game show was to have a different look in the monitor that Alanna usually stands in front of in the suite that is set up for this position. Usually, it is a Dodgers logo or something, but today the crew in the truck thought they would take a live shot of Globe Life Field in the background with the grounds crew doing some work. Our camera operator in the suite cropped out the frame of the flatscreen monitor behind me, and it looked remarkably like I was standing in Arlington and not in suite 211 at Dodger Stadium. They experimented with a couple of different camera angles that were available, and for the next shot made it seem like I had moved to a different location.

I was actually asked by a doctor that I had to see about a bum Achilles tendon a couple of days later how it was to travel with the team. The shot looked that good! We were not trying to fool anyone, and I never once intimated that I was anywhere other than where I was, but it looked remarkably real, like I had been teleported from one park to the other. The next time I do it, viewers won't even be able to see the walking boot I am now in to correct my left Achilles issues.

The Dodgers hadn't lost a series yet this season, so if they were going to prevent that, they had to win this one tonight in Arlington, and they would be counting on Ross Stripling to put them in a position to do so. Ross only lasted four innings plus two hitters before he had to be lifted from the game. He had given up back-to-back home runs to Ronald Guzmán and Leody Taveras, the eighth and ninth hitters in the third inning, along with a triple to Todd Frazier. Stripling left the game with a lead (3–2) but couldn't stick around long enough to qualify for the win. Little did anyone know at the time that this would be his last start as a Dodger, as he would be traded to the Blue Jays for two players to be named later three days from now.

Stripling's problem had been the fastball, but his curveball was better. Following the game, I asked him if he wanted to shake to some more soft stuff based on his fastball getting crushed. "The curveball was great tonight. I was really happy with the breaking stuff, especially the curveball. I feel like I was aggressive at the top of the zone and executed some fastballs at the top of the zone well," Stripling told me. "It's just the few that I tried to get down and away to get into the count, they bled back over the middle of the plate, and both those lefties at the bottom of their lineup hammered them." Stripling is nothing if not honest and his assessment of his performance and what caused his early exit was spot on. He is one of the really good dudes in baseball and will be missed. I hope he does well with Toronto as he joins his former teammate Hyun-Jin Ryu.

Max Muncy had a pretty good night at the office, driving in four runs with a double, a home run, and a sacrifice fly that might have been a home run in any other park. His batting average and overall swing are not where he wants them, but he is still a very productive offensive player. I asked Max about his long sacrifice fly during the walk-off interview I conducted immediately following the game. "I thought I got a pretty good piece of it, but after a couple of days here we have definitely noticed how big this park is. It's almost a little bit of a joke how big it is," said Muncy matter of factly. "I was just happy to get the run in and get the job done." The home run was his ninth of the season.

Bellinger added his ninth with a bomb to right field in the third inning. The Dodger hitters managed to navigate around veteran innings-eater Lance Lynn. Lynn had been unbeaten and was 4-0 for a team that is seven games under .500. Lynn gave up four runs, three of them earned, and took his first negative decision of the season. The Dodgers at 25-10 remained the team with the best record in baseball and have a chance to come back and win the series tomorrow.

AUGUST 30, 2020. GAME 36. THE BASEBALL BRUNCH

Today was a quick turnaround day and the end of the six-game road trip. A 1:35 Central time game meant brunch and baseball back in California with an 11:35 a.m. start. The Dodgers need two home runs to tie the 2019 Atlanta Braves for the most home runs hit in a month in National League history. With tomorrow off, if they were going to do it, it has to be done today. Most important, is the opportunity to win the series heading into an off day at home.

The Season

As the Dodgers and Rangers were preparing to play, the Oakland Athletics were in Houston for the final game of their three-game series with the Astros. As the team was preparing to head over to the ballpark, with their luggage being loaded onto an equipment truck, they were discovering that someone in their traveling party had tested positive for COVID-19. This was the first case detected since the season began that involved a team in the west. The A's ended up having to stay in Houston to quarantine, their game postponed until later in September.

Tony Gonsolin was called back from the alternate site (euphemism for the minor leagues in 2020) to make today's start. The team was pretty happy with his two prior performances, and he is getting close to making his mark. I spoke with Tony yesterday and we focused on his splitter, which has been a standout weapon for him this season. He told me it was a much better pitch for him this year than last, and his fastball velocity had been up.

Gonsolin didn't have to worry much about offense behind him, as Cory Seager popped his ninth home run of the season over the center field wall for a quick point and a 1–0 lead before Tony even took the mound. Will Smith cranked one out to left field in the second inning to make it 2–0, and Cody Bellinger would help the Dodgers set the new National League record with his 10th of the season and team's 57th of the month. I do understand that there is a DH being used in the NL this season, and there are more chances for regular hitters to get shots at home runs, but still, for any team to hit 57 in less than 30 games is truly outstanding.

Gonsolin's pitch count got up to 62 early and he left after only three innings, but he was still pretty effective. Victor González got the win after one and a third solid frames in relief. The Dodgers figured out how to conquer Globe Life Field's deep fences and won 7–2 to take the series. They still have not lost one this season, and are the only team in baseball to do so. Tomorrow is this season's trading deadline, which should be interesting. Arizona will be in to start a three-game series on Tuesday night.

SEPTEMBER 1, 2020. GAME 37. IT'S THE LAST MONTH ALREADY?

The coronavirus strikes again. Today, the good news for the A's is that no one in their group had a positive test and they should be playing again soon. Out of caution, however, their three-game series that was to begin tonight against the Seattle Mariners has been postponed, assuring that the front-running A's will have to squeeze in a number of double headers to complete sixty games. They hold a three-game lead in the AL West over Houston, but that could change with Houston still playing. The Astros recently had to shut down their alternate site due to a positive test, but it didn't impact the big-league club.

The way it looks now is that the Athletics will be challenged with at least four double headers over the final two to three weeks of the regular season. No one said it would be easy, but with the way that the playoffs are formatted this year, there's not much benefit to winning your division; it's just a nice thing to be able to say about your club. Making the postseason this year is the equivalent of a college football team being "bowl eligible," in my opinion.

Earlier in the afternoon, all the Dodger broadcasters were on a private Zoom call with Dave Roberts to discuss the matters of the day and the series with Arizona. Dave told us the moves of the day that wouldn't be announced until later, including Justin Turner going to the IL with a left hamstring problem. We also learned that Walker Buehler's blister has healed enough, and he would be coming off the IL to pitch tomorrow, the second game of the series. I enjoy these private calls because he trusts us with information ahead of when it is put out to the public and it gives us insight as to what is going on with the club in a season where we are not allowed near the clubhouse.

Another thing Roberts talked about was Julio Urías working on a different grip and shape to his slider, which makes it "tighter," "more slurvy," and we should notice a difference in the game tonight. He couldn't have been more correct, as Julio looked very good and turned in his best performance of the season. As noted, Urías has had a lot of trouble getting through the first inning unscathed. That changed with a quick 1-2-3 top of the first that included a strikeout. That set the tone for the rest of his outing, which encompassed six innings allowing four hits and one earned run. That came on a solo home run in the third off the bat of catcher Carson Kelly. Most pitchers won't even blink at giving up one solo home run. Home runs happen. These are called the Big Leagues for a reason. You only hope there is no one on base or the game is not on the line, but an early inning solo shot is more than survivable for any pitcher. This outing was a big step forward for Urías.

The Dodgers were without Turner and also Cody Bellinger, who reported some soreness in his side before the game. He sat out for precautionary reasons, but his team didn't really need anything from him that Arizona didn't provide themselves. The Diamondbacks gifted the Dodgers with seven walks, including one with the bases loaded in the first inning to Chris Taylor, along with two errors. Walks and errors resulted in four of the six Dodger runs and were more than enough for the margin of victory in a 6–3 decision. Taylor had a night with two doubles and four RBIs. Urías raised his record to 3-0, and Kenley Jansen faced one man in the bottom of the ninth after lefty Scott Alexander gave up a two-out walk to Kole Calhoun, and then a home run to Nick Ahmed to push the game into a save situation. It was the tenth save for Kenley. The Dodgers were now 27-10, and their divisional lead was back to five games over the idle Padres.

SEPTEMBER 2, 2020. GAME 38. SOMETIMES YOU JUST HAVE TO BUNT

Fantasy football is more important in baseball than anyone not involved in the game would ever think. Aside from the NCAA Basketball Tournament pools that occur during every spring training, fantasy football is the biggest contest taking place in Major League clubhouses each season. Just prior to the draft is the daily watching of the Little League World Series games on ESPN. Except in 2020, of course, the LLWS is on every TV in every clubhouse. In an effort to recover some sense of clubhouse normalcy, the focus beyond the game itself has shifted to the next thing on the regular calendar, and that is which player is the biggest expert on something else other than baseball. Fantasy football comes with a cash prize, but more important to these young, elite, competitive types, and something money can't buy, is bragging rights.

Today was the day the Dodgers had the important task of deciding the draft order for their league. Led by commissioner Walker Buehler, who was scheduled to pitch tonight, the boys gathered out in left center field under the afternoon sun with a flag and measuring tape. The flag was placed at home plate and the game of "closest to the pin" was on. It was a golf contest, as players brought clubs and golf balls out to the pavilion and teed off. There is a new area that is cut out of the stands as part of the off-season renovations that made for a perfect tee box and players tried their luck from there, approximately four hundred feet from home plate. Clayton Kershaw produced the measuring tape and kept track of who was closest to determine the draft order.

Tonight's game didn't start out like any kind of fantasy for the home club, due to one of the best pitching performances against them all season. Arizona right-hander Zac Gallen is a guy that looks like he will give the Dodgers some problems now and in the seasons ahead. His changeup was terrific and kept hitters off balance. In fact, from the end of the second inning through the end of the seventh,

Gallen retired 16 straight hitters from one of the best lineups in baseball. That is a big-time performance and Gallen, despite his youth, is showing ace-like stuff. If you saw a pitcher who retired 16 straight, pitched seven-plus innings, allowing no runs and only one hit while whiffing seven, you would think he and his team would win that game, right? In the case of this particular game, you would be wrong.

Sometimes numbers lie, and tonight that was the case for the struggling Diamondbacks, who have lost 12 of their last 13 games. The Dodgers got a good start from Buehler, who pitched five shutout innings. Newly ordained Dodger killer Christian Walker hit a sixth-inning solo homer off of Caleb Ferguson in a rare bullpen mishap to make it 1–0. That lead lasted until there was one out in the bottom of the ninth when Mookie happened again.

Betts provided another of what should be a number of "Mookie Moments" in Los Angeles when he crushed a Kevin Ginkel fastball over the center field wall to deadlock the game at a run apiece and force the new extra-innings rule to make its coming out party at Dodger Stadium. The Dodgers have done just fine in the extra frames so far, but they have yet to play bonus baseball at home.

Max Muncy made the last out of the bottom of the ninth, so he was the "placed runner" at second to begin the last of the tenth. I hear some people refer to the placed runner as a "ghost runner." There is nothing "ghostly" about that runner. He is very much alive, with red blood pumping through his veins. He is extraordinarily tangible and can easily be identified by the naked eye. His run counts, and will often decide the game. While growing up playing tons of wiffle ball and tennis ball with friends, we seldom had enough players on each team to account for all the base runners. It was great for the number of at-bats you would get, but you didn't get to run the bases a relative number of times. The runners that you could not actually see that got credit for base occupancy and, by this New Hampshire kid's ground rules, were allowed to advance as many bases as the runners in front of and behind were able. That kind of Casper is what a "ghost runner" is. Let's establish the term as "placed runner," in the event the rule is here to stay. I am starting to look at this new rule as the equivalent of when the NHL brought in the shootout to decide ties after a short overtime. Fans in hockey tend to stay longer in close games, and maybe MLB hopes for the same reaction when fans are allowed back in the ballparks.

Anyway, off the soapbox and back at the game, while now in extra innings at home and trailing by a run after the D'Backs' placed runner Daulton Varsho was walked in during a subpar Kenley Jansen performance, the Dodgers employed a different strategy offensively. I actually saw a Dodger non-pitcher shorten up and show bunt. It is the smart play in this case, as you are playing to extend the game more than just attempting to win it as the home team. Chris Taylor laid down a bunt that went to the third base side, but just a little too close to the mound to be a perfect bunt. It worked well, as it turned out. Arizona pitcher Junior Guerra moved off the mound and had the idea to get Muncy, the lead runner who represented the tying run, at third. Normally, this would be a sound decision. As Guerra fielded the ball, his legs were out of whack and he attempted to make a short throw off the wrong foot to Eduardo Escobar. The throw, too, was out of whack and went right past Escobar, allowing Muncy to score the tying run and Taylor to move up to second on the throwing error. Huge play, as the game would now be extended and the chance of winning increased tenfold.

Joc Pederson made an out but showed what a good out is all about. With nobody out and the winning run in scoring position, Pederson hit a grounder toward the middle that was to the left of Taylor, just enough so that once he recognized what direction the ball was headed off the bat, he bolted for third and made it easily, while Pederson was thrown out at first by shortstop Nick Ahmed. To some, this might have just appeared as though Pederson had made the first out of the inning by simply grounding out, which he sort of did, but it was much more than that. This is how you play the game, and he showed the definition of a purposeful out in what was a key at-bat in deciding the outcome of the game.

With one out and the winning run at third, the Arizona infield played in to cut down the run, while the outfield played shallow to shorten the throw to the plate on any possible sacrifice fly. Will Smith got a pitch up in the zone that he could easily handle from Guerra and barreled it over the head of left fielder David Peralta, scoring Taylor and earning the Dodgers a 3–2 walk-off win.

In spite of the challenges the Diamondbacks are going through this year, this was one of the harder-fought wins the Dodgers have recorded during this strange season. Things are certainly going their way as they moved to 28-10. To be 18 games over .500 in a 60-game season is pretty remarkable when you sit down and do the math. It was really good to see some old-school baseball with a bunt being one of the biggest plays of the game. Granted, Arizona screwed it up while trying to defend it, but it comes down to the age-old fact that good teams find ways to win, while the bad teams find ways to lose. Tonight's game was certainly evidence that both are still true.

SEPTEMBER 3, 2020. GAME 39. 2500 KERSHAWS AND COUNTING

One of the cool things about this season is that on most nights I sit in the front row of suite 215 to observe the game. Directly to my left, sitting in the front row of suite 214 is Baseball Hall of Fame broadcaster Jaime Jarrin of the Dodgers Spanish-language radio broadcast crew. Over the course of this series, I have appreciated what the umpire-in-chief Alfonso Marquez has been doing before each game. Just before the lineups are exchanged, when it is just the four umpires standing at home plate, Marquez and his crewmates, Cory Blaser, Tom Woodring, and Malachi Moore, turn and look up at Jarrin, take their caps off, and salute him. In an empty stadium with only cardboard cutouts in attendance, the special gesture to Jarrin does not go unnoticed.

Hats off to Marquez for another reason. The three umpires on his crew are all relatively new, mostly minor league call-ups working a busy schedule due to the fact that it is "all hands on deck," with many older umps having opted out due to possible health concerns. I found it to be a great teaching moment of respect for one of the legends of the game of baseball. More often than not, the Spanish-language broadcasters do not get the attention and accolades that their English-speaking brethren receive. Not a lot of teams employ Spanish-language broadcasters, so there are far fewer of them in the game. Jarrin has been broadcasting Dodger games since the team arrived in LA for the 1959 season and were playing at the LA Coliseum. He predates Dodger Stadium! It makes me happy and appreciative to see the umpires, particularly Marquez, recognize the velvety-voiced Ecuadorian broadcaster. Hopefully, we will see more of this.

Clayton Kershaw was on the bump tonight and didn't take long to establish his presence. He has been dynamite, with a record of 4-1 and a minuscule ERA of 1.82. His mound opponent couldn't have had numbers that were more on the other side of the rainbow. Arizona right-hander Luke Weaver's fastball had been hit like a bad boxer's face. It was getting punished. He was only 1-5 with an obese ERA of 8.23. On paper, it looked like a mismatch, but they still have to play the games.

Weaver pitched well, allowing only two runs over five and a third innings and retiring 14 Dodgers in a row at one point. Normally that effort would be good enough to win, or at least keep your team in the game. While the Diamondbacks appeared to be in the game, only trailing 2–0, it may as well have been 20–0 while Kershaw was conducting the Dodger orchestra. He can be an artist out there some nights, and like any great performer, leaves you wanting to see more of what he can do.

Kershaw turned in a clean first inning, striking out Kole Calhoun and Christian Walker for career strikeouts numbers 2,498 and 2,499. In the top of the second, after issuing a rare walk to start the inning to David Peralta, Kershaw broke off his signature pitch and whiffed Nick Ahmed, who flailed at "Uncle Charlie" for the milestone. Strikeout number 2500. The southpaw would punch out Andy Young to end the second, then pitch a perfect third, striking out Carson Kelly and Tim Locastro. Locastro, a former Dodger, was the sixth strikeout victim of the game, which would be fitting. It was career strikeout number 2,503, and with it, Kershaw passed the "Big Six," Christy Mathewson, who pitched for seventeen years for the New York Giants, for 38th on the all-time list. Back when Mathewson pitched in the early 1900s, more than 200 pitches per game and 20 to 30 complete games a season was the norm. Times and the game may have evolved, but it is still rare air in which Kershaw exists.

"I don't ever want to discredit any of the stuff that is happening because it is cool. It really is," Kershaw said in his post-game Zoom presser that is so 2020. "It is just hard to think about, honestly, or wrap my head around being associated with names like that and getting to see your name on different types of leaderboards. It's hard to grasp, really."

Kershaw has always maintained that he would just take care of business now and then count 'em up at the end of his career, when he might take a step back to reflect on what he has accomplished. Certainly, he will be the last person to wear the number 22 on a Dodger uniform, and it shouldn't take him more than five or six years to be elected to the hall of the greats once he hangs up the spikes, but he is only thirty-two and there is still significant high octane left in his tank. Tonight he became the third-youngest pitcher in the history of the game, behind only the great Nolan "The Ryan Express" Ryan and Walter "Big Train" Johnson, to register his 2,500th strikeout.

Kershaw tossed 99 effective pitches over his six innings of work and finished with 8 strikeouts for a new career total of 2,505. Kershaw now needs 9 more punches to pass A.J. Burnett (2,513) for 37th all time. "It's obviously a huge honor, and I am thankful that I have been able to be here long enough to do it, and hopefully, I can keep going," the lefty added.

If you were going to show a young pitcher how to pitch, you might want to start by showing him the absolute clinic Kershaw put on tonight. The strikeout milestone aside, think of another, under-the-radar remarkable number for a moment. Kershaw faced 22 Arizona hitters, and only gave up a measly infield single to his usual nemesis Christian Walker. Of the 22 hitters, he had an 0-2 count on 11 of them! That is unreal. In this day and age, consistently pitching ahead like that is something you just don't see a lot. This feat was more impressive to me than anything else he did in the game.

The Dodgers plated enough runs for a win in the bottom of the first when Cory Seager and Max Muncy reached on back-to-back singles. Seager would score on a throwing error by Walker, and Muncy came home on a Chris Taylor hit. The insurance policy was signed in the seventh, when A.J. Pollock came off the bench to hit for Pederson and smashed the first pitch he saw from Keury Mella, sailing it over the center field wall. This was the perfect example of a pinch hitter coming to the plate ready to hit. It was the first pinch-hit homer of the season for the Dodgers and the third of Pollock's career.

Kiké Hernández would single and score on a base hit by Betts. Taylor would double in the eighth and score on Hernández's second base hit of the game. Kershaw, with six shutout innings, would lower his already almost-invisible ERA to 1.50 and moved his career ERA to 2.43, substantially lower than any left-handed pitcher in the history of this great game whoever registered as many as 2,500 strikeouts. Baseball Reference's new stat tool in 2020, Stathead.com, backs this up.

Rk	Player	ERA	SO	From	To	IP
1	Clayton Kershaw	2.43	2505	2008	2020	2310.2
2	Warren Spahn	3.09	2583	1942	1965	5243.2
3	Steve Carlton	3.22	4136	1965	1988	5217.2
4	Randy Johnson	3.29	4875	1988	2009	4135.1
5	Jerry Koosman	3.36	2556	1967	1985	3839.1
6	Cole Hamels	3.42	2558	2006	2019	2694.2
7	Mickey Lolich	3.44	2832	1963	1979	3638.1
8	Tom Glavine	3.54	2607	1987	2008	4413.1
9	Frank Tanana	3.66	2773	1973	1993	4188.1
10	CC Sabathia	3.74	3093	2001	2019	3577.1
11	Chuck Finley	3.85	2610	1986	2002	3197.1

Provided by Stathead.com. Generated 9/4/2020

The Dodger machine just kept on grinding, and another win was produced to go along with a three-game sweep of Arizona. After the first 39 games, the Dodgers are an MLB-best 29-10 and have built their lead over the second-place Padres to six games. It also, following the Padres being shut out 2–0 by the Angels, shaved two games off the Magic Number. Yup, we are starting to talk about the Magic Number, which is now at 16 and counting.

SEPTEMBER 5, 2020. GAME 40. DRONE DEAF

Another COVID-19 test today. This will be the eighth time I have been tested, with the next test already scheduled for just five days from now. I have self-administered enough of these tests now that the folks who hand them out don't even ask if I have questions anymore. On my way into the stadium I looked over at the public testing site that was off to my left and it seemed especially busy today. Cars were lined up, snaking around a massive trail of orange cones with drivers waiting patiently for their turn.

Major League Baseball released their updated COVID-19 test results, and this was the best week ever. Knock on wood. There were 12,780 test samples, with only one positive test from a player (Oakland) and no staff members for a 0.008 percent positive rate. They reported that there were no new positive test results for a fifth consecutive day, and for the tenth time in the past twelve days. So far, there have been 103,668 tests conducted, with a total of eighty-five positive cases. There have been 0.08 percent positives, with fifty-five of them players and thirty of them staff members. MLB and its teams have done a good job keeping the positives under 1 percent, and they continue the daily battery of tests across the league.

Dustin May continues to make positive strides. He did not get the decision, but he did quite well for five and two-thirds, and for the 12th time to begin his career allowed two earned runs or fewer. He mixed in his off-speed stuff a little more and is enjoying great results. He has put a solid down payment on the potential number-three starter heading toward the postseason.

During the bottom of the second, the few allowed to work at the stadium witnessed something different and a little unnerving. Dodgers security came onto the field and notified home plate umpire Gabe Morales that something wasn't right and he needed to get the players off the field. Somebody, hidden nearby, was hovering a drone high above the infield. This is serious stuff, as no one has any idea what the controller of the drone has in mind The players quickly left the field. Kiké Hernández, who was in the middle of a live TV interview with Alanna Rizzo, jokingly yelled, "I don't feel safe, I don't feel safe!" tossed the headset down, and ran off. He came back and told a story of a strange game delay he experienced during his first week in AA ball, when he was told by his manager that he had to dance to entertain the crowd while the game was paused. He has plenty of stories and is one of the big personalities on this team.

Mookie Betts had another good night at the plate, going three for five with a home run and two runs scored. In the eighth inning, he drove in his 500th career RBI with a two-run smash, his team-leading 13th of the season. The 10–6 win over Colorado improved the Dodgers' record to a Major League-best 30-10 and won their 24th game over the Rockies in the last 28 contests at Dodger stadium. I am expecting the Colorado Department of Revenue to call the Dodgers and demand property taxes be paid since they absolutely own the Rockies.

SEPTEMBER 5, 2020. GAME 41. CAT-QUICK SPLIT

The Rockies have to be tired of getting spanked by their big brothers in blue and played like it tonight. Right-hander Germán Márquez faced righty Tony Gonsolin. Márquez, the Rockies' best pitcher, held the best offense in the game down with a stellar performance, throwing seven innings, allowing 2 earned runs on 5 hits, and striking out 5. Gonsolin, on the other hand, had his splitter and slider working well and took a great step forward to solidify his newly found spot in the starting rotation. He went six innings and tied his career high with 8 strikeouts, half of them on sliders.

The game was a 2–2 battle until the top of the ninth when the Dodger bullpen had another case of the blues. Right-hander Blake Treinen, who has been one of the more reliable back-end-of-the-pen guys in baseball this season, had a bad night at the office. He allowed three runs on three hits, and the game went upside down in the blink of an eye.

Last night, the Dodgers were able to overcome a late-inning go-ahead grand slam by newly acquired Colorado center fielder Kevin Pillar, a southern Californian, formerly of the Red Sox, Giants, and Blue Jays. But it was not in the cards tonight, as the Dodgers went quietly into this good night. Colorado won game two 5–2. The Dodgers still had baseball's best record, with a now-Magic Number of 14 to clinch the division, and were still six games up on San Diego.

SEPTEMBER 6, 2020. GAME 42. SPA DAY

Tonight's rubber game with the Rockies ended up bouncing like a bad check. It was highly disappointing, based on the fact the offense delivered plenty enough for another win, but the guys throwing the rock were not in sync. The bullpen is now officially struggling, allowing 10 runs over the course of the three-game set. The Dodgers had the Rockies on the line and were reeling them in, but the bullpen allowed them to spit the hook.

The Dodgers were short-handed tonight, with Joc Pederson leaving the team to tend to a family matter (we would later find out his wife was getting ready to give birth to their second child), and Dave Roberts having decided to give Mookie the night off—entirely off— and did not use him to pinch hit even with the game on the line in the ninth inning. When Mookie gets the day off (this was just the second time) Roberts jokingly characterizes it as a "spa day." This was a game backed up by an off day and, oftentimes, when managers are trying to keep their stars fresh, they will give them the off day against the travel day in order to give them a couple of days down from baseball activity. This is part of managing the people in uniform, and Roberts has done a good job with it.

The Dodgers hit four of the game's six home runs and still found a way to lose, dropping the game 7–6. This is rare altitude for this Colorado team, who had lost 24 of the last 29 games at Chavez Ravine. This is baseball, and stuff happens that you don't expect sometimes. Hey, they are professionals over in that other dugout who work at the game, too. They are going to win sometimes. That is how it goes in this sport.

The Dodgers ended up going the first 13 series of the season without losing one, which is one of the better marks of all time. The 1977 Dodgers went 14 series without losing one, and the record is 17 straight by the 1990 Cincinnati Reds. No matter how you slice it, the Dodgers have had a remarkably good start to the season. That being said, they are starting to show signs of vulnerability—bullpen problems, too many runners left on base, and starters not going deep enough into games. Again, this is baseball, and stuff happens, so every now and then you just have to chalk up a loss to that axiom that is so well known inside the game.

It is evident the Dodgers could use tomorrow's day off. It will be a travel day, and when they arrive in the Phoenix area ahead of a three-game series with the Diamondbacks, they will hold one of their major annual bonding exercises: the fantasy football draft. Many players wore the NFL jerseys of their favorite teams and players on the flight.

SEPTEMBER 7, 2020. OFF DAY/TRAVEL DAY

The *Wall Street Journal* published an article yesterday by Louise Radnofsky and Jared Diamond titled "MLB's Coronavirus Tutorial for America." The article highlights the diversity in patients that MLB has tested, how they implemented health and safety protocols, and how they have played through outbreaks and fixed them.

"The sport has helped demonstrate how the novel coronavirus spreads and incubates; its potential damage to the cardiovascular health of young and healthy people; and how stringent testing and isolation protocols must be to limit outbreaks. It has even offered a vivid glimpse of the social costs when co-workers disagree over health protocols."

The MLB response to COVID-19 has been both praised and criticized, but intentionally or not, collectively they have come up with some real-life solutions to playing during the worst pandemic in a hundred years. Plain and simple, it is working. I can tell you that the Dodgers players feel safe and so do the employees. I feel safer going to Dodger Stadium than I do anywhere else in the Los Angeles area.

Some of MLB's policies and procedures have been deemed worth emulating by the NFL, who will be using the "Tiered" personnel system instituted by MLB, even using the same nomenclature.

The last positive test was on the Oakland A's two weeks ago. The positive person was immediately contained, quarantined, and contact traced. He was tested and the results were negative a short time later. The A's were able to get back to play after missing a handful of games that were quickly rescheduled, and it was back to business. After the messes with the Marlins and Cardinals, MLB and the teams got things under control, even though it took a while. Things were contained and both teams were able to continue. There were many lessons learned by everyone involved in pro sports by the examples, both good and not so good at times, that Major League Baseball has set. There is now a playbook for this situation.

At this point of the season, we continue to hear rumblings of a postseason bubble as MLB does not want to take any chances on losing valuable television revenues if games have to be cancelled. The plan we are hearing currently is: after the Wild Card round, the NL teams will reconvene in Arlington and Houston, Texas, while the AL teams would move to the stadiums in Southern California. Also, at this point, I am not so sure the MLB Players Association is on board. With less than three weeks to go in the regular season, teams need to hear a solid plan this week so they can prepare. Frankly, from what I have witnessed this season, I am not 100 percent sure a bubble is needed, and teams who have earned home-field advantage should be able to take advantage of it and be able to continue to live at their local places of residence and be with their families as they have been all season.

SEPTEMBER 8, 2020. GAME 43. TWISTED BLISTER

Tonight's game seemed like an exhaustive process just to get through. Four hours and twenty-six minutes of baseball bliss from Chase Field. The game saw a grand total of 15 pitchers who threw a combined 398 pitches. The Dodgers took 12 walks in the game, left 15 runners on, and were a not-so-good 5-17 with runners in scoring position while playing a team that has lost 16 of their last 18 games, and has waved the white flag by trading away high-profile players like outfielder Starling Marte and closer Archie Bradley at the August 31 deadline. That said, the players in the home uniform are still trying to win because that is what they are paid to do, so they gave the Dodgers a game.

One main concern is the right index finger of Walker Buehler. Despite throwing several pitches in the triple-digit range, Buehler has been dealing with the blister issue again. A pitcher with a blister on his index or middle finger is like an opera singer trying to hit every note while suffering from a mild case of laryngitis. The pipes will sound good for a while, but continued use will slowly damage the instrument and make it more difficult to utilize.

One shot on SportsNet LA as Buehler came out of the game showed his right index finger looking rather chewed up. Orel Hershiser speculated that there could be "some glue" on there. There have been many pitchers over the years that have tried to patch up blisters and pitch through them by applying airplane glue. That reminded me about a conversation I had, for some reason, with former Pittsburgh Pirates pitcher James McDonald about a decade ago, who had recently been traded from the Dodgers to the Pirates for reliever Octavio Dotel. McDonald was having blister problems and showed them to me in the clubhouse one afternoon. He admitted that, at the time, it was the Dodgers' way to have pitchers repair blisters with airplane glue and that the Pirates were not allowing him to do that. McDonald said that he experienced further problems as a result of the glue not holding up during the time he was on the mound, along with having to peel it off after his outings, and it took much longer to heal properly.

While Buehler started the game retiring the first nine hitters almost effortlessly, a home run allowed to rookie Daulton Varsho and some shoddy defense behind him ensured that "Butane" never made it out of the third inning. He would have to be lifted after two and two-thirds innings while allowing five runs, two of them earned. Roberts said after the game that he expected Buehler to make his next start.

One of the Dodgers' top prospects, infielder Gavin Lux, had a bit of a coming-out party with three hits, two of which were home runs. Lux's tenth-inning three-run shot gave the Dodgers enough of a cushion after Kenley Jansen had to labor excessively to finish the game. Jansen would surrender three runs in the bottom of the tenth, two on a home run by the newest Dodger killer, Christian Walker, and managed to get the final out with the tying run on base and the winning run at the plate. All this after entering the inning with a four-run lead.

The Dodgers limped their way to a 10–9 decision in extras, and are 4-1 with the new placed runner extra-inning rule. While you could pick your way through the game and find all the warts, in the end, they scored one more than the other guys and that, ultimately, is the name of the game. This is the type of game that is typically described by players as "a pig." Not the most attractive of contests would be the guesstimated translation. The Dodgers, as of late this evening, improved to 31-12 and remain four-and-a-half games in front of the red-hot Padres. Both teams have won seven of their last ten. The Giants, incidentally, have also won seven of their last ten, and continue to battle to sneak into the postseason field. There are two more games with the flailing Diamondbacks, and the Dodgers need to grab that low-hanging fruit.

SEPTEMBER 9, 2020. GAME 44. MAGIC NUMBER IS 13

All is not quiet on the Western Front. Deadly wildfires are raging in California, Oregon, and Washington. The fire that began in the Angeles National Forest in Palmdale continues to roar and spread. The forest is in the San Gabriel Mountains that serve as the picturesque backdrop for Dodger Stadium and is about fifteen miles from the ballpark. The smoke continues to mix with the air day and night, and blue sky is hard to find.

From the twenty-second floor of the Westin Bonaventure, my view looks west from downtown toward Hollywood and Griffith Park. On any other day, I can see the Hollywood sign and the Griffith Park observatory clear as a bell, along with all of the surrounding mountains that stretch from the west to the north past Pasadena. Today is the first day that I had trouble discerning the outline of the mountains due to the smoke that has enveloped the skies.

Today was also another COVID-19 test day at the stadium, so around eleven in the morning I made my way over there to be tested for the ninth time. While nine tests might sound like a lot to you, that is nothing for the players and staff that are in Tiers 1 and 2. Those people are tested pretty much every other day. Baseball has been doing its part, and the Dodgers, in particular, are a model in how to keep COVID-19 out of the workplace.

While out, I decided to take the short drive from Dodger Stadium to Silver Lake to see a just-completed mural of Joe Kelly making his "boo boo face" at Carlos Correa. The local artist, Jonas Never, said he wanted to complete the painting before the Astros got to town, which they will on Saturday. Never painted this baseball masterpiece on the back wall of a building that houses Floyd's 99 Barbershop at the corner of Sunset Boulevard and Parkman Avenue. It is not visible from the Sunset side, so you have to turn the corner at Parkman to see it. When I found out about it, I had to go see for myself because that was the neighborhood I lived in for most of the 2019 season. I got my hair cut at Floyd's 99 and walked that area all the time. After taking some photos, I texted one to Kelly with the message, "Joe, look what I found today. Hope you are doing well." He responded in about sixty seconds with "That thing is amazing. I am going to try and stop by that tomorrow. It's so cool. Feeling good finally should be back soon." He showed up the next day with his family and took photos with Jonas that made for some great images.

Back in Phoenix, the team is playing game two of the series with the Diamondbacks. Kershaw has been pitching so well that it is worth bringing up his name in the 2020 Cy Young conversation. His numbers are worthy, and he is looking for a few more solid starts before the postseason. Arizona has lost 18 of their last 20 games and are one of the worst teams in baseball. Games are never won on paper, though.

Mookie Betts started things off on the right note. On right-hander Taylor Clarke's second pitch of the game, Betts blasted his

22nd career leadoff home run for some instant offense. It was his team-leading 14th of the season. The Dodgers would add another run with two outs in the second when Kiké Hernández, a native of Puerto Rico, sent one over the left field wall.

There was some added significance to Hernández's homer since it happened on his first at-bat wearing Roberto Clemente's number 21 to honor The Great One on Roberto Clemente Day. MLB, in conjunction with Clemente's sons, Luis, Roberto Jr., and Enrique, gave players born in Clemente's home country permission to wear his long-retired number. Edwin Rios was the only other player on the Dodgers eligible to wear it, which he did. Rios is from Caguas, while Hernández is from San Juan. The entire Pittsburgh Pirates team wore 21 in their game tonight in Pittsburgh. I was happy to see that. Finally. When I was broadcasting games there, I used to mention it on the air on Clemente Day, in probably five of the seven years that I was there. I always thought that would be a great idea to have the Pirates, just the Pirates, wear his number on that one day.

On Clemente Day each year, I got tabbed by the club to emcee the activities that we held at local schools with the Clemente family, including Roberto's late wife, Vera, and his sons, along with the entire team. The only player who was excused from attending was whoever that night's starting pitcher was. It is an appropriate and overdue honor to see the additional attention that Clemente is getting now. He was so influential and so important in helping to open many doors and inspire so many Latino players in our great game. As Hernández came across home plate after smacking his second-inning home run, he patted the red number 21 on the front of his gray road jersey and looked up to the sky above Chase Field.

A bunt, an infield hit, a walk, and a sacrifice fly in the home half of the second inning tamped down what started out as a solid beginning for Kershaw. Speedster outfielder Tim Locastro cleaned up the base runners with a triple, giving the D'Backs a 3–2 lead. The veteran lefty did not record a decision after going five innings and was victimized some by his own team committing three errors behind him over two batters in the bottom of the fifth. The game finished nine innings tied at four and headed to extra innings for the second night in a row. Chris Taylor and A.J. Pollock came up with RBI singles in the tenth and Blake Treinen closed it, retiring all three hitters he faced to wrap up a 6–4 win and secure the series. The Dodgers are now 5-1 in extra innings.

The new extra-innings rule is still a hot-button discussion among baseball people, and the reviews are split. Kershaw made his side known right after the game. "It's not real baseball," he said. "It's fine for this year, but I hope we never do it again." His manager, however, seems to be leaning the other way. "I think it really shortens the game," Roberts said. "It adds strategy for the fan, the managers, the players. I think it's playing out pretty well…I like it permanently, but I don't like it for the postseason."

SEPTEMBER 10, 2020. GAME 45. MAGIC NUMBER 12… BUT HEARING FOOTSTEPS

When I looked out my window this morning, it looked like there was a fog over Los Angeles. The smoke is thicker today and the *Los Angeles Times* reported that LA was experiencing the worst smog in thirty years. The Hollywood Hills were not visible and neither were any other mountains that ring part of the city. As the day went on, I noticed a lot of helicopter traffic, more than usual. I wondered if this was an effort to get the air and smoke moving and clear it up. That is just a theory. By early evening the hills and mountains were visible again.

I woke up to news of another negative test. Nine for nine and still batting 1.000. Major League Baseball continues to release their testing information weekly, and this week is very good news, maybe the best they have reported yet. There were 11,669 monitored samples tested this past week, and there were zero positives among players. There was, however, one positive among staff members. Of this week's tests, 0.009 percent were positive. MLB continues to show they can smother the virus and keep playing. There now have been zero positives among players for twelve straight days, and twenty of the last twenty-one.

As a result of the success, there is growing chatter from the players that they do not favor a postseason "bubble" and would like to continue along the path they have taken this season. This is interesting because there is basically a bit more than two weeks remaining in the regular season, and still nothing definitive about where postseason games will be played.

In an article in *The Athletic* by esteemed baseball writer Ken Rosenthal, he said the Dodgers were the team pushing back the hardest. Why does MLB want a postseason bubble? According to Rosenthal, there is $787 million postseason TV money on the line, and the league does not want to risk any kind of outbreak that could cause the postponement or cancellation of any games. The players have an interest, as they will split fifty million of those dollars. Everyone involved stands to gain, including the owners who have not had any ticket, concession, or parking revenues this season and have sustained tremendous losses. So, if everyone has something to gain, you have probably asked yourself, "Why would the players push back?"

The players are not in favor of what MLB is proposing regarding quarantines for themselves and their family members. MLB is asking players who play for teams that are still in playoff contention, which due to the expanded playoff is most of them, to quarantine at local hotels away from their families for seven days at the end of the regular season and before the playoffs begin. That quarantine would have to begin in ten days when the season ends on the twenty-seventh. That is one item of contention. The players pushing back contend that they have been living with the same people all season long and an end-of-the-season quarantine shouldn't matter. Some veterans want to keep things just as they are in terms of home field advantage and team travel. There is a lot to this story and a lot more detail of the bubble proposal from MLB being discussed with the Players Association.

There are more requirements of the bubble to consider as well, such as broadcasting. Do teams send their radio teams to broadcast inside the bubble or would they be relegated to calling games off screens? There are more questions than answers, but the more time that goes by, the more I think that MLB will have to keep things as simple as possible and have radio broadcasters do the games just like they have been for regular season road games: either in a studio or at the home ballpark watching the feed. If, for some reason, MLB and MLBPA cannot agree on a bubble format and the games are played at home ballparks, then postseason games will be played status quo and we just have to keep our collective fingers crossed that there is no outbreak. It would be more of a gamble financially than the bubble concept, but, again, like most everything that has gone on this season, we will have to wait and see what happens.

Things didn't go so well on the field, as the Dodgers attempted to sweep Arizona in their final matchup of the season. Dustin May got drilled on the instep of his left foot by a rocket off the bat of leadoff hitter Josh Rojas. It looked painful. May was also drilled in Arizona last year but off the head that time. It turned out, miraculously, that he was just fine after getting skulled, but he was limping around the mound tonight. He finished the inning without allowing a run and when he went out to start the second, his foot was throbbing, so Roberts lifted him.

Starting pitching is getting a little thin in Dodger world all of a sudden. Earlier in the day, Walker Buehler was put back on the IL due to the nagging blister on his right hand. Tony Gonsolin was told he would skip his next start and be available out of the bullpen. That turned out to be a blessing. Gonsolin was tagged with the 5–2 loss, but he covered five innings.

While the Blue would win the series two games to one, this was not a good series. Not even close. They played three games against one of the worst teams in baseball and there were some hidden warts. Defensively, they committed seven errors in three games while allowing 18 runs (6 RPG), more than triple their season runs per game average of a little over two. Offensively, while still scoring runs, they did not score as much as they should have, stranding a whopping 37 men on base. There was an inning tonight, the sixth, when the Dodgers had three walks, a base hit, and came up empty! Will Smith was caught rounding first too far after a hit had just set up a first-and-second no-out situation, and Hernández was thrown out at home when he got off of third base too late at the back end of a double steal. That happened with one out and their best hitter, Mookie Betts, at the plate.

The record is still great at 32-13, but the Padres, still chasing, beat San Francisco again to cut the division lead to 3.5 games. The Dodgers are off tomorrow; a weird and highly unusual scheduling quirk to have a Friday night off for something other than a rainout, but the smoking-hot Padres are playing the Giants again. If San Diego wins again, they will cut the lead to three games with a head-to-head series coming up in San Diego on Monday. The Dodgers have two with the Astros to deal with back at Dodger Stadium on Saturday and Sunday. This is a big weekend.

SEPTEMBER 11, 2020. OFF DAY

I can't remember having a scheduled Friday off. It just doesn't happen, but due to a scheduling quirk to accommodate the final two games of the Dodgers and Astros four-game home-and-home series, we're all home on a Friday night. So, while there was no baseball for the LA team, there was definitely baseball news in Southern California, and it was not good.

The Padres were hosting the Giants at Petco Park. The teams were warmed up and lined up on the chalk lines for the National Anthem. Right before the Padres were to take the field, they were called back when it was revealed that a member of the Giants had recorded a positive test. The game, along with tomorrow's game, has been postponed. The Dodgers are scheduled to play the Padres in San Diego on Monday.

MLB had gone twelve days without a positive player test. While running out the calendar and still a bunch of games to makeup, this could have an impact on the postseason seeding. The Padres had been carrying a ton of momentum into the game tonight, steamrolling their opponents and climbing to within three and a half games of the Dodgers.

ESPN's Jeff Passan reported that the bubble plan is all set and laid out the locations. There has been no word from MLB because they are still discussing with the MLBPA and putting together a plan to allow families. There will be two bubbles, with the ALDS occurring at Dodger Stadium and Petco Park. The NLDS will take place in Texas at Globe Life Field and Minute Maid Park. The ALCS will be at Petco, while the NLCS will be at Globe Life. The World Series will be played at Globe Life as well. If the Dodgers win the best-of-three Wild Card round, there is a chance they could play the NLDS, NLCS, and World Series at the same park.

SEPTEMBER 12, 2020. GAME 46. HOUSTON GOT LUCKY IN MORE WAYS THAN ONE

The skies over the greater Los Angeles area have been filled with smoke for days, but today seemed a little worse. The Bobcat Fire in the Angeles National Forest continues to rage. This thick smog is the kind I last saw in 2008 in Beijing, China, during the Summer

Olympics. That was the last of four Olympic Games I would work for One Sport, an international consortium of television networks that provided English-language commentary to one hundred and ten different countries. I was there to call play-by-play of men's and women's basketball along with baseball and softball. The skies over Beijing for much of the time I was there were grayish-brown and hung over the region like a heavy, wet blanket. I read an article that the Chinese government would be shooting some sort of rockets into the sky to seed the clouds and force them to rain. The theory was that the rain would clear up the smog and create "blue sky days." The morning of the Olympic Marathon, the runners passed by my temporary residence at the Hubei Hotel in the Haidian District. It was raining.

Following the clearing of the athletes and security personnel a few hours after the morning race, I went out for a walk under what was, for the first time since arriving, blue skies. I could finally see the picturesque green tree-covered mountains in the distance that had only been a rumor. Looking at the ground, there was brown stuff everywhere, puddles of brown water on the street and sidewalks. Parked cars had strong evidence on the windshields and windows that some sort of brown liquid had fallen on them. Basically, there was brown stuff on everything. This was the thick smog that had been beaten down from above by the supposed government-induced precipitation. We were all encouraged to blow our noses a few times a day. What we found when we did that was a dark residue that showed we were expelling at least some of the unhealthy air we were breathing in.

The LA air doesn't seem quite at that level yet, but it seems like it is getting close. Accompanying the bad air are the bad feelings from Dodger fans over the clouds of disenchantment the mere presence of the Houston Astros has brought. The Astros are quite fortunate. The coronavirus has created a void of fans and a void of high-volume, full-capacity, and well-deserved jeering at road games. The same players that admitted they cheated, the same players who were allowed to keep their entire generous postseason and World Series shares, while players with other teams (the Dodgers, for instance), under equitable game situations in Houston in 2017 and who knows what other seasons, might have been able to earn their fair shares of the money. It is no secret why many players, especially those who crossed paths with the Astros in 2017, are not happy with the players who participated in one of the most egregious cheating scandals in baseball history. Their actions are and will remain a stain on the game and a number of Dodger fans showed up today to remind them.

Fans clad in Dodger blue appeared, carrying creative signs and trash cans that they were banging with sticks while one of the Astros' team busses pulled up to Sunset Gate A guided by an LAPD motorcycle escort team. Team buses coming from the team hotel on game day never have a police escort. The Dodger supporters were loud and impossible for the Houston players to ignore. Joe Kelly, stopped at a red light at the entrance to the stadium, saluted the die-hards with a few quick blasts of his horn, much to their delight.

Dave Roberts was asked during his pre-game presser about his thoughts on the fans who showed up. "I loved it. They have every right to be upset. It just shows the passion that Dodger fans have."

Roberts cancelled batting practice due to the air quality. There was limited activity outside as infield coach Dino Ebel pounded ground balls to second and third. Fielding at second were Gavin Lux and Mookie Betts, who has taken infield grounders almost daily throughout his career. Edwin Rios was getting in some work at the hot corner, as was Clayton Kershaw. I realize he is doing it to stay active, but the veteran probably should have been captured and held in solitary confinement back in the clubhouse. With Buehler on the IL, Dustin May possibly headed there, and no starter available for tomorrow, the Dodgers need to be more careful with their ace. Instead, Kershaw moved to second where he was turning double plays. Fortunately, he escaped unscathed and got some throwing in to stay loose. Kershaw is so valuable to the Dodgers' fragile pitching situation right now. They can't afford any freak accidents or injuries.

Before the game began, a plane began to circle Dodger Stadium pulling a sign in big, black capital letters that read "HOUSTON CHEATED...BANG BANG." The Astros were largely trying to ignore it. The plane circled Chavez Ravine several times at a relatively low altitude and seemingly inside the legal three-mile radius pilots are allowed to fly near the stadium on game days. Pictures and videos of the sign went viral on social media and became national news. The game was still an hour away. Can you imagine how rocking Dodger Stadium would have been with fifty-thousand-plus fans in the seats? As it was, there was extra security near the Astros dugout and more police presence at the stadium gates.

The Astros came into this game on a terrible run, having lost eight of their last nine games and struggling at the plate and on the mound. A bad combination. Julio Urías was having one of his better outings on the bump, getting through six innings allowing only one earned run on three hits. Back-to-back home runs by Chris Taylor and Kiké Hernández in the second inning gave the Dodgers the lead. A triple by Corey Seager along with a sacrifice fly by A.J. Pollock added another in the third. In the fifth, Seager drove in Betts from second with a sharp opposite-field single. The Dodgers' pitching, hitting, and defense were all clicking far better than during the series in Arizona, and it looked like, as I said on the radio broadcast in the bottom of the eighth, "the Dodgers have put a solid down payment on their thirty-third win of the season." Yogi Berra was famous for saying a lot of things, and "It ain't over 'till it's over" is one of his most well-known quips.

The Dodgers led 5–2 heading into the top of the ninth. Kenley Jansen has been in this position hundreds of times. He had a rough go of it on Tuesday in Arizona and hadn't pitched since. Things were about to go in the wrong direction. Jansen was named the NL Reliever of the Month for August, but won't repeat in September. He faced six Houston batters and every one of them reached base. Max Muncy was charged with an error when George Springer smoked a short-hop missile to Muncy's glove side that skipped into the outfield. When it was over, Jansen allowed five runs without recording an out. He had a few of the hitters in 0-2 counts and failed to put them away. The Astros had scored a total of five runs over their previous 26 innings and matched that in a third of an inning. It was a major come-from-behind win for the checkered franchise.

A somber Jansen appeared on Zoom after the game. "I can't execute pitches to put them away and it is just frustrating. I went back and watched the video. I am ahead in the count on everyone and just didn't execute like I used to. It's unacceptable and this feels terrible," he offered on what was easily the most disappointing loss for his team in 2020.

The Dodgers lost 7–5, with the demoralizing top of the ninth as a wart on this season that has to be removed within the next twenty-four hours and a bullpen game looming. The lead in the division shrunk to just three games and the Magic Number is stuck at 12.

It was determined tonight by the powers that be that the Giants' Alex Dickerson came up with a false positive test result and the Giants and Padres would be cleared to resume play after missing two games. They will have a doubleheader at Petco tomorrow and make up the other lost game during the next series.

SEPTEMBER 13, 2020. GAME 47. DODGER FANS FLYING CIRCUS

One of the great things about baseball is that every day is a new day, and players are wired to have short memories.

Smoke is still present in the sky, but not nearly as bad as yesterday. The sun forced some blue sky through the hazy gray cover that has been omnipresent for the last several days, making the sky better for visibility, especially if one just happened to be piloting a small plane pulling a sign behind it.

On the way to the ballpark at 1:30 p.m., I turned right off of Sunset Boulevard and onto Vin Scully Avenue. As I got over the apex of the hill, I could see Dodger fans milling around Gate A. Some brought lawn chairs, perhaps figuring they would be there for a while, to greet the multiple busses that would carry the Astros. There were more trash cans and signs, with the largest reading "FRAUDS."

The afternoon was going on as normal for a 5:08 p.m. scheduled start time for ESPN's Sunday Night Baseball. It would be the second night in a row I was assigned to do radio play-by-play, and only the first time all season I will have worked back-to-back games. Being a bench player for the first time in my career hasn't been easy, but I have had to be understanding of the situation we are in as it has affected everything I am associated with.

The Dodgers had completed their pre-game work on the field and the Astros had taken over for batting practice. Rick and I started to record the first of our two pre-game radio segments, and I planned on teeing him up on some topics related to the game when I noticed something out of the corner of my eye. Appearing high over the rim of Dodger Stadium was a plane pulling a message for the Astros. *Just like yesterday*, I thought, but it wasn't. A second plane appeared with another message. Then a third plane appeared towing another banner. I lost my train of thought and went straight to a "live to tape" description of the flying circus.

My favorite of the three signs said in big bold letters, "HEY ASTR*S, TRY STEALING THIS SIGN!" Another said, "ASTROS CHEATED. NEVER FORGET. GO DODGERS." The trolling didn't stop just because there were no fans in the stadium.

My career has been spent in stadiums and arenas and I have soaked in the atmosphere of every event. The Dodgers have done such an incredible job of creating a realistic game atmosphere that if one closes their eyes and just listens, they would never know there were not actual people in attendance. Stadium organist, Dieter Ruehle, who also tickles the ivories at Staples Center during LA Kings hockey games, is the best stadium organist I have ever heard. His creativity and up-to-date new-school approach really works, as he has great tunes that he plays for each player on the Dodgers and has some good trolling ditties for opponents. When Mookie Betts hit his 15th home run tonight in the fifth inning, Ruehle cranked out the theme from *Hawaii Five-O*, not only because Mookie wears number 50, but because it made the score 5–0. That is good stuff. He finds songs that have a title or lyrics that may relate to a player or what is happening on the field. I love it when the Rockies are in town because he has some funny ones for those guys. When Charlie Blackmon, with his trademark long, bushy, and unwieldy beard comes up to hit, Ruehle plays the Warren Zevon classic, "Werewolves of London." When Trevor Story comes up, he plays a couple of things, like *The NeverEnding Story* theme, which is a layup, but also the theme from *The Brady Bunch*, where the first lyrics are, "Here's the story…" Funny stuff.

For this series, Ruehle, along with chief house sound man DJ Severe, came loaded for bear. Ruehle played such tunes as, "Banging on a Trash Can" by Doug, "Bang on the Drum" by Todd Lundgren, "The Sign" by Ace of Base, and "Lyin' Eyes" by the Eagles. Severe had a good list of troll songs that he added: "Bang Bang" by Jessie J, "Truth Hurts" by Lizzo, "The Payback" by James Brown, and "Cry Me a River" by Justin Timberlake. The musical attacks went on and on for two days. It was creative, fun to hear, and wonderful for everyone but the Astros.

Brusdar Graterol made his first Major League start and led a parade of different and successful pitchers out of the bullpen en route to getting the Dodgers back in the win column. The hitters would hand former LA standout Zack Greinke his worst loss of the season.

Greinke is now 1-5 at Dodger Stadium since 2016 and has allowed 16 home runs during that time span.

Chris Taylor's three-run blast halfway up the left-field pavilion in the bottom of the eighth to greet new Houston reliever Cy Sneed put the cherry on top of a decisive 8–1 win while clinching the season series three games to one. The Astros will return to Dodger Stadium for a two-game series in early August of 2021 and, by that time, fans may be allowed back. I don't suspect anyone is going to forget about 2017 anytime soon, and Houston should face an angry wrath. Good luck finding tickets for that series.

The Dodgers are now 33-14, and with the Padres gaining a half-game following a doubleheader sweep of the Giants, just two-and-a-half games separate the teams with the start of a three-game series in San Diego looming tomorrow.

SEPTEMBER 14, 2020. GAME #48. A RIVALRY IS BORN

As of today, there is still no announcement from MLB on a postseason bubble, but they are working on it. The Dodgers have begun their final road trip and don't know if they will be required to sequester at a hotel for the final week of the season. Word is, the bubble is coming. An announcement is expected by tomorrow.

The first of three between the Dodgers and Padres was expected to be a pitchers' duel, as Clayton Kershaw was on the mound against burgeoning staff ace Dinelson Lamet. The game lived up to its billing as the pitchers traded strikeouts, each landing wicked slider after wicked slider. Kershaw's curve was good, but not up to his lofty standards. His fastball, however, was excellent and registered the most velocity it has all season at 94 mph.

The Dodgers drew first blood in the third inning when Austin Barnes drew a walk, Mookie Betts doubled, and Barnes scored on a groundout by Corey Seager. The 1–0 lead would stand until the bottom of the sixth when the seeds of a new rivalry were sowed.

Center fielder Trent Grisham led off the home half of the sixth inning. The left-handed hitter out of North Richland Hills, Texas, was a first-round pick by the Milwaukee Brewers in 2015 and is in just his second season. Any young player from Texas knows all about Kershaw. North Richland Hills is a straight thirty-minute drive due west of University Park, which is Kershaw's hometown. Dallas Metroplex locals were about to face each other, with one a decorated veteran and the other part of a new breed of players that don't show the level of respect toward the players that have come before them that was given in years prior.

Kershaw's first pitch to Grisham was a 91 mph four-seam fastball for ball one. Kershaw came back with a pair of sliders and worked the count to two balls and one strike. The lefty sent another four-seamer toward the plate that was up and in, a dangerous spot. Grisham swung out of his shoes and barreled a ball that came off the bat at 104.9 mph. Grisham paused for what seemed like a minute. He then tossed the bat and started his long trip around the bases. He was going to enjoy it, at the expense of Kershaw. As Grisham came around third, the personnel in the Dodgers' dugout were at full throat, giving it to him verbally. Not a soul on the Dodgers' side was happy. Grisham yelled back, and the Padres' dugout erupted like the ball had just dropped in Times Square on New Year's Eve. The game was tied 1–1.

In the old days, either the next hitter or their best hitter would have the tower buzzed, or would wear a pitch in the back pocket or the ribs. That doesn't happen in baseball today, though a lot of the "get off my lawn" crowd would like to see it. Baseball players have long memories.

Following the game, Kershaw, presumably keeping his feelings to himself, said of the incident, "I'm not going to worry about their team. Let him do what he wants."

Opening night at Dodger Stadium from behind the fan cutouts, July 23.

Shot of fan cutouts from the field on the first base side, July 23.

Matt Beaty during batting practice wearing his "Legend Of Chico" T-shirt.

The author broadcasting from the socially-distanced radio booth. Rick Monday is obscured by a video monitor, but is two rows behind me.

Orel Hershiser and Joe Davis in the SportsNet LA TV booth. Notice the hand sanitizer on the wall to the right.

Team photo day with the players spread out. September 12.

First Base Coach George Lombard (now a bench coach with the Tigers), Bench Coach Bob Geren, Manager Dave Roberts, and Third Base Coach Dino Ebel posing in the dugout before a game versus the Angels.

Kobe Bryant Day at Dodger Stadium, August 23.

Inside the Dodger Clubhouse prior to a game with the Angels, September 25.

Dave Roberts on a Zoom call in his office at Dodger Stadium prior to the NL Wild Card Game, September 30.

Corey Seager in the Dodger Clubhouse with Walke Buehler going in another direction.
Notice the hand sanitizer and sanitary wipes on the left. September 30.

Cody Bellinger eavesdropping on two masked members of the Houston Astros. September 13.

Mookie Betts attempting to break up a double play versus the Padres in Game 2 of the NLDS at Globe Life Field. October 7.

Clayton Kershaw unleashing a pitch during Game 2 of the NL Wild Card series versus Milwaukee. The cutouts are on the edge of their seats in the left field pavilion. October 1.

stin Turner loosening up in the clubhouse at Globe
Life Field with a handful of bats. October 23.

Walker Buehler prepares to take the
field. NLCS Game 2, October 17.

A light moment in the Globe Life Field indoor batting cage prior to Game 3 of the World Series. Cody Bellinger
(with bat), Mookie Betts, Chris Taylor, Justin Turner, Hitting Coach Robert Van Scoyoc, and Coach José Vizcaino.

World Series MVP Corey Seager putting the ball in play during Game 6 versus Tampa Bay. October 27.

Game 6 starting pitcher Tony Gonsolin taking in some TV in his socially-distanced locker set up in the Rangers clubhouse at Globe Life Field. October 27.

The moment and the reaction with a celebration to follow. Julio Urías being hugged by catcher Austin Barnes. Edwin Rios, Max Muncy, and Brusdar Graterol are closing in. October 27.

** Photos by Jon SooHoo/Dodgers **

Grisham countered with, "It's a big situation off a big pitcher, a Hall of Fame pitcher in a big game. Stakes were high. It got the guys going."

It did get them going, with the help of some shoddy Dodger defense in the seventh. The Friars sent nine men to the plate and scored five. Wil Myers added a solo shot in the eighth to put the punctuation on this 7–2 loss. One bad half-inning did in the Dodgers for the second time in the last three games, and now the division lead is reduced to a narrow one-and-a-half games. The Dodgers can feel the Padres' breath on the back of their collective neck.

SEPTEMBER 15, 2020. GAME 49. BUBBLE BALL

Major League Baseball announced the postseason format. The Dodgers are in a position that, no matter what, they will play at home during the Wild Card round. Now that the Padres have the Dodgers firmly in their crosshairs, the NL West Division crown is very much in play. The unprecedented bubble plan will have the players, with certain exceptions, like if they live alone, staying in a hotel for the last week of the season if their team is playing home games. The Dodgers will wrap up the regular season at home against Oakland and the Angels.

The AL and NL Wild Card rounds will be played at the home stadium of the higher-seeded teams. Then the bubble comes into effect. The highest seed from the NL will then relocate and play in the ALDS at Globe Life Field. The other matchup will be at Minute Maid Park. Dodger Stadium will host one round of the ALDS, while Petco will host the other. The ALCS will then be played at Petco, while the NLCS will happen in Arlington, along with the World Series. Weather won't be an issue for the postseason, but smoke and poor air quality from wildfires is a concern. The smoke should be dissipated by the time the postseason rolls around. Chase Field in

Phoenix is a backup location if the air quality becomes a problem in Southern California. There are whispers from Rob Manfred that baseball is even looking into ways to open the bubble up to a percentage of fans. That would be something. It is certain that teams, not just in MLB, but in every sport, need to have fans back as soon as it is possible, even if it has to be gradual at first.

One aspect that I have not heard anyone mention is the financial bonus for players and members of the traveling party. They won't be getting a check unless they win and get a playoff share. I am not talking about playoff shares, though. I am talking about state income tax. When you earn at the level of professional athletes, or if you don't and have to travel with them for your job, there are a few states you really like to work in. Texas is one of them. Unlike most people who work in the United States, athletes and traveling parties are targeted by local governments in an effort to collect more income taxes. You may not know this, but when you work for a Major League Baseball team, state and local taxes are withheld from your paycheck from every state that you set foot in to work, unless there is no state income tax. I have had years when I have had to sign up to fourteen tax returns. Once, I had to write a one dollar check to the State of Colorado, and I have received checks for a dollar, five dollars, and up to a few hundred dollars from other states. It is a joke, frankly, that because we travel with a Major League team that the IRS and local governments come after us to collect. In a lot of cases, it costs more to file the state tax return than the actual amount they are coming after. If you make players' money, then the numbers are significant, whether you are paying or getting a refund.

If you were a salesperson, or you did a job of some sort that required you to travel out of your home state frequently, I am sure that your company doesn't withhold state taxes from every state you had to visit to do your job. Because major sports teams are high profile and play on TV, people who work for them are targeted by the states. The NFL, NBA, and NHL also have people who get hit with these taxes. The city of Pittsburgh gets you for an extra 1 percent "entertainer's tax." Believe it or not, and it is strange to even write this, but it is expensive to work in this field. Many professional athletes take up residence in Texas, Florida, and Nevada to put themselves in a better financial situation because those states have no income tax. The NL teams playing in Texas will catch a break, because for the time they are there they will be exempt from state taxes, and will not have to pay California taxes for the period they are not in California. On the other side of the coin, the teams from the AL coming in for the playoffs will be making tax payments payable to the California Franchise Board. The Franchise Board is basically California's version of their local IRS, and they may be the most vicious of the state collection organizations. I know; I have written many checks to them over the years.

Earlier today it was announced that the Mariners and Giants game is postponed in Seattle due to terrible air quality. The M's played a doubleheader with the A's yesterday under awful, smoky conditions. Both teams will get on planes to San Francisco and continue the series there. The air quality index (AQI) gives people a tangible measurement of the quality of the air they breathe and whether it is healthy. One source for that is Airnow.gov. According to that site today, the AQI in Seattle registers at 241 which is considered very unhealthy. The AQI in San Francisco, a city that has also been affected by nearby wildfires, registered at 68, which is considered moderate. In 2020, if it is not one thing, it is another, and MLB keeps diligently working around the issues.

The quality of the baseball was very good tonight in San Diego in a huge swing game. A win for the Padres, and they close the gap in the division to just a half a game with eleven to play. A win for the Dodgers would get them back to two-and-a-half games up and cut the Magic Number to 9. There was a lot on the line for Tony Gonsolin, and he showed up big time.

Gonsolin frustrated San Diego hitters with a good splitter and fastball. The "Cat Man" scratched his way through seven innings, giving up just one earned run on four hits and threw 90 pitches. He retired the side in order in four innings, faced four men in two innings, and five men in one inning. He was super-efficient in going deeper in a game than ever before. After the game, Gonsolin told Alanna Rizzo that he was happy to be able to use all of his pitches to get the job done in a big game. "I thought early on the splitter and the slider were pretty good. Later on, the slider kind of tapered off but the curveball kind of came around. It was nice to be able to use everything today."

Padres starter Zach Davies has been exceptional this year and had won his last five starts. The last Padre pitcher to win six straight starts was Andy Benes in 1991. Davies would not catch him tonight, as he surrendered eight Dodger hits over six innings. Justin Turner came off the IL and went 3-4, Mookie Betts had two hits, and Edwin Rios hammered a fifth-inning home run that travelled 413 feet.

Dave Roberts is giving Kenley Jansen some rope. Blake Treinen had to come in earlier than planned when Caleb Ferguson felt something painful in his pitching elbow after striking out Jurickson Profar to start the bottom of the eighth. Ferguson called for a trainer, then exited. It's worrying, as he's been really good this season and the Dodgers need him. Treinen got the next two outs on four pitches. Since he'd finished the inning, despite the new three-batter minimum, Roberts was free to keep him in the game or move on to Jansen. Roberts elected to show confidence in his closer, who would have to go through the teeth of the Padres lineup to notch the save. He got Tatís Jr. to ground out to Seager for out number one. He left a 3-2 pitch up to Machado, who drilled a line drive to left for a single. Newly acquired first baseman Mitch Moreland popped up to shallow center, but with the Dodgers playing "no-doubles" defense, A.J. Pollock was too deep, and the ball dropped in for a hit. Austin Nola drew a walk to load the bases. The tying run was at second, the winning run on first.

Will Smith alertly called for a mound meeting with the entire infield, to discuss their defensive strategy. They didn't even have to move, as Jansen would get the hot-hitting Wil Myers to swing and miss at a nasty slider for strike three, then whiffed NL Rookie of the Year candidate Jake Cronenworth on a high cutter to put a capper on the game. Dodger Nation exhaled. Jansen earned his eleventh save after walking a tightrope without a net. Unfortunately, that has been the norm lately, and his outings have been nerve-racking. This may be the late-season turning point that he and the team needed.

The series is even after the Dodgers' 3–1 victory and puts an end to San Diego's eight-game winning streak. Their record expands to 34-15, which is still the best in baseball with the White Sox (32-16), Padres (32-18), and Tampa Bay (31-17) the next closest. When checking out the standings after the game tonight, I noticed something I had not really paid attention to before today. As of the completion of games tonight, the only team the Dodgers have played with a record over .500 is the Padres. Oakland is 30-19, but they have not played the Athletics yet and will meet them for their only scheduled series a week from tonight at Dodger Stadium. These games with the Padres could end up being incredibly significant in preparing the Dodgers for the postseason.

SEPTEMBER 16, 2020. GAME 50. MAKING TRACKS

I love mid-week matinee games. Baseball under the sun on a weekday is the best. Don't ask the players for their opinion, though. Publicly they may say all the right things, but players generally prefer night games for a number of reasons. Some say the ball is harder to see in daylight. Others don't like shadows. And others will tell you they don't like getting up so early.

Today is a day game under the beautiful and warm Southern California sun. The Padres have an off day tomorrow, but the Dodgers have to fly to Colorado. Could they have a night game and still charter to Denver? Sure, but they are in San Diego, which presents a unique challenge to the schedule makers and directors of team travel. San Diego International Airport has a curfew of 10:00 p.m. Some teams have paid hefty fines to depart after curfew and, in the past, other teams would fly out of the nearby military installation, where the former commander was a baseball fan. The more recent commander is not as big a fan and put a stop to the practice a few years back.

It was another bullpen day for the Dodgers, as they decided Dustin May would come out of the pen and try and eat up a bulk of the innings rather than start. We found out before the game that Caleb Ferguson has a torn ulnar collateral ligament (UCL) and is done for the season. Tommy John surgery is scheduled next week and there will be a long recovery ahead. This will be the second TJ for Ferguson, who had it done in high school. His loss will be felt as he really took a step forward from last year. Brusdar Graterol served as the opener, which worked out well, just like it did against Houston on Sunday.

Pollock clubbed a two-out solo home run in his first at-bat to give the Dodgers a 1–0 lead in the second. The home run was his 100th, but he wouldn't get to relish it long. He'd leave the game later with hamstring tightness. Will Smith continued to crush and came up with a huge two-out two-run double in the top of the fifth that pretty much put the game away. Mookie went 2-5 and stole three bases. The MVP conversations continue to swirl in his direction. Zach McKinstry, a thirty-third-round draft pick out of Central Michigan University in 2016, made his Major League debut as a pinch hitter for Justin Turner in the ninth. While he struck out swinging, he got on the other side of it. He could be a good player for the Dodgers in the very near future.

May was very effective through five-and-a-third innings. He did not get the win, even though the official scorer could have given it to him for being the "effective" reliever rather than Adam Kolarek, who only pitched two-thirds of an inning, allowing a hit and two walks. Either way, it finished 7–5, with the Dodgers taking the series and ownership of the tiebreaker for the division title at the same time. They pulled off the rare feat of knocking three games off of the Magic Number in one night, dropping it to six. The Dodgers are now 35-15 after 50 games. The last three teams to go 35-15 in the first 50 games were the 2016 Cubs, the 2007 Red Sox, and the 2006 Tigers. All three of those teams were in the World Series, with the Cubs and Red Sox emerging victorious.

SEPTEMBER 17, 2020. GAME 51. ROCKY MOUNTAIN HIGH RUN TOTALS

Today's COVID-19 related news is that one of the Rangers' announcers, TV analyst C.J. Nitkowski, tested positive. With only ten games left, The Rangers are out of it. C.J. is a good guy and one of the regular hosts on MLB Network Radio on Sirius/XM. He pitched in the Big Leagues as a journeyman left-hander for the Reds, Tigers, Astros, Mets, Rangers, Braves, Yankees, and Nationals. He also pitched in Japan, Korea, and the Dominican Republic. Have left arm, will travel. He is the second Texas-based TV announcer to test positive. Earlier in the season, Astros play-by-play man Todd Kalas, son of Phillies legend Harry Kalas, had to miss time.

Today was another COVID testing day, my tenth.

While preparing my pre-game segment for tonight's radio broadcast for the road game in Colorado, I also spent considerable time preparing for the class that I teach every Thursday at my Alma Mater, Emerson College in Boston, where I am a professor in the School of

Sports Communications. I conduct the entire class on Sports Advocacy on my iPad and am able to give assignments, class announcements, grade papers, and more, completely on this wonderful piece of technology. I conduct in-person classes every so often on the occasions when I am available.

Tonight, the Dodgers open a four-game series with the Rockies, the only team to hand the Dodgers a series defeat this season. The Rockies are 22-26, and clinging to a remote shot at the playoffs as the last Wild Card team. On paper, they have a good offensive team, and it makes one wonder why they don't win more games. Their home ballpark has more square feet of playing surface than any other park. The outfield is huge. I won't be surprised if a team uses four outfielders there someday. I once asked Tony Gwynn about almost hitting .400 one season. He was the head coach at San Diego State, and we were sitting in his office inside the baseball stadium that bears his name. "If you could pick a ballpark to play all eighty-one home games in that would give you the best chance to hit .400, which would it be?" Without hesitation, Gwynn answered, "Coors Field, easy."

Runs are usually easy to come by at the corner of 20th and Blake Street in the lower downtown section of Denver, and tonight would be no exception. Locals call a high-scoring game a "Coors Field Classic." Tonight was not a full-blown classic, but it had a good result for the visitors.

The scoring began in the first, when Julio Urías, again struggling early, allowed two runs on three hits. Corey Seager continued his outstanding season when he smashed his 13th home run to lead off the fourth. Justin Turner singled and so did Cody Bellinger. Chris Taylor drew a walk to load the bases and Kiké Hernández was hit by a pitch to drive in the tying run. In the top of the seventh, the Dodgers took advantage of a poor Colorado bullpen and sent eleven men to the plate. They put up a six-spot in the inning, the most runs plated in a single inning this season, without the benefit of a home run. A round tripper came in the eighth off the bat of Edwin Rios, his fifth of the season.

With the Padres idle, the Dodgers increased their lead to four games and shrunk the Magic Number to 5. Their record is still the best at 36-15, with a chance to clinch home field for the Wild Card as early as tomorrow and a chance to clinch the division as soon as Sunday.

SEPTEMBER 18, 2020. GAME 52. MAGIC NUMBER 4. ROLLING, ROLLING, ROLLING

I wake up to a text and an email late each week with that all-important word—negative. The only one to test positive this week, that I was aware of, was C.J. Nitkowski.

News of the passing of legendary Supreme Court Justice Ruth Bader Ginsberg permeated every corner of America today, including the baseball world. Baseball people realize how important she was to the rule of law and what the untimely vacancy means.

The number of tests conducted was 12,381, with only two positives. None of the positives were from anyone on a roster or coaching staff. The two came from one team's alternate site. That's nineteen straight days without a positive test at the MLB level. A total of 127,718 total tests have been conducted with eighty-eight positives since testing began, for an overall positive rate of 0.007 percent, far less than 1 percent, which is really good considering the circumstances. MLB's plan was criticized by some at first, especially in the beginning. Give credit to them and all of the teams that followed the plan, the protocols, and the science to keep the positive rate so low.

As MLB considers allowing a percentage of fans to attend the postseason, a story out of Kansas City caught my eye. The NFL, in certain cities, allowed some fans into the stadiums. There is no way of knowing how safe this is, as it takes weeks to learn. The sports world is keeping a close eye on how the NFL and college football manage with fans in attendance. The story out of Kansas City was of a fan at the season opener between the Super Bowl Champion Chiefs and the Houston Texans who tested positive. There was immediate contact tracing and everyone who sat nearby was asked to quarantine. Major League Baseball is monitoring the situation closely as they attempt to come to their own resolution.

The Dodgers took the Rockies out behind the woodshed tonight and showed them a thing or two about scoring runs. My scorebook was a mess. When that happens, it's a good thing. They pushed across a season-high 15 runs on 17 hits, and everyone in the starting lineup had a hit. Everyone in the lineup except Austin Barnes, who went 2-2 with two runs scored, had at least one RBI. Cody Bellinger has changed his stance, backing slightly off the plate, and it is paying off. He went 3-5 with three RBIs and was a triple away from the cycle. Gavin Lux had a couple of hits, including a massive upper-deck 453-foot homer in the second, just three batters after Bellinger hit his. Mookie Betts hit his NL-leading 16th in the sixth, then hit a two-run triple in the eighth, while scoring three runs. Betts, as of tonight, has to be the odds-on MVP favorite. He has exceeded expectations and has Dodger fans giddy over what they will see in the future out of this special athlete who is just entering the prime of his career.

After the game, Mookie was asked if he pays attention to the MVP stuff. "I don't pay any attention to it," he said. "I'm just doing what I can to win a World Series. I am who I am. Those things, I think, come from playing the game. You can't think about those things and think about the game as well. I just have one goal and that is to win the World Series."

The Dodgers have won four in a row, and one of the reasons is that they have been better with runners in scoring position. During this streak, they have gone 17-34 with RISP for a .500 average! That will win you some games. The formality of clinching home field for the Wild Card has come and gone, and the focus now is to prepare for the playoffs with eight games to go. The Dodgers are 37-15 and are rolling.

Speaking of rolling, the ground was rolling tonight in Los Angeles. While sitting at my desk watching an HBO documentary about the 1990 UNLV basketball team at 11:38 p.m., the building began to shake. The wall of windows to my right sounded like it was starting to crack as the tower was swaying. I could feel the floor moving under my feet. I looked to my left and noticed the two-and-a-half-gallon plastic water dispenser was shaking, and waves of water were moving around violently inside. I have been through earthquakes a number of times before but never from this high up. Last year, we played a game right through an earthquake with Kiké Hernández at the plate. He said he didn't even notice it, but our TV cameras were shaking. From ground level, or a second floor even, earthquakes will move you, but they are generally not that bad. For a second or two, it felt like my floor was tilting toward the windows. I grabbed the key on the desk and headed for the door. By the time I got there, the rolling had stopped. I stood still, not realizing yet that it had been an earthquake, and made sure the floor wasn't moving. I slowly walked back to my desk, sat down, and processed everything that had just happened. About two minutes later, a notification popped up on my iPad from the *Los Angeles Times* confirming there was a quake that registered at 4.5, which is not too alarming to many Angelinos. Most locals don't experience them from twenty-two stories above the earth, however, which is far more unnerving, in my opinion. The epicenter was one mile away from South San Gabriel, which is only twelve miles east. What's next in 2020? Locusts? Famine? What a year.

SEPTEMBER 19, 2020. GAME 53

One of the greatest things about being in the Pacific Time Zone is that college football on Saturdays comes on in the morning. After taking in a socially distanced version of ESPN's College Game Day, I watched the game between Oklahoma State and Tulsa from Stillwater. Boone Pickens Stadium. Officials at OSU had allowed approximately 25 percent capacity, roughly fifteen thousand fans, with each receiving instructions on how to safely be there to cheer on the Cowboys. Masks and face coverings were mandatory, as both the university and Stillwater have a mask mandate. It was encouraging to see people back inside of a sporting venue.

Clayton Kershaw made his penultimate start of the regular season and was stellar once again, inching the Dodgers a little closer to their eighth straight division title. Kershaw threw the slider more than his fastball, with both connecting for strikes. His curveball was effective as well, inducing a number of strikes. After allowing a double to speedy outfielder, Raimel Tapia, Tapia swiped third. It is easier for a runner to steal third against a lefty because the pitcher's back is to the runner and once he turns his head he can't step over like he can to first base. Often, good base stealers will get a shot at a bag early in a game against Kershaw, as Tapia did. With one out, a routine groundout to short by Nolan Arenado produced the first and only run for Colorado.

After that, Kershaw applied the sleeper hold, and the Rockies never got their eyes back open. Assisted by two double plays and a base running goof by second baseman Garrett Hampson, Kershaw would only face one batter over the minimum for the seven innings he pitched. He took the mound in the bottom of the first with a 2–0 lead after a two-run triple by Chris Taylor, so Kershaw never trailed at any point. Taylor would homer in the fourth, and Pollock homered in the seventh to spark a three-run inning. The 6–1 dispatching of the Rockies was done in an efficient, businesslike manner and only took two hours and thirty-two minutes to complete. It is rare to have a game this quick at Coors Field. With the Dodger win, Kershaw picked up his 24th positive decision over Colorado, the most by any single pitcher against them in franchise history. The record that continues to grow and is simply amazing—Kershaw is now 122-1 when he receives four runs or more of support in a game.

The play of the game came in the seventh after Mookie picked up his only hit of the night. He advanced to second on a wild pitch by reliever Mychal Givens, while Austin Barnes scored from third. Betts had a decent lead at second and Givens decided to wheel and attempt a pick-off play. The throw sailed high and into center field and was backed up by Kevin Pillar. Pillar figured that Betts would only take third and tossed the ball lackadaisically to Trevor Story. Anticipating this, Betts didn't break stride and took advantage of the lazy play, beating Story's late relay throw with a headfirst slide. Betts's teammates, though elated at what they just witnessed, were collectively in awe. Mookie continues to show people how to play this game.

Kershaw has seen a lot in his storied career, but he hasn't come across the likes of Betts before. "He's leading the league in homers, doesn't strike out, has great at-bats, runs the bases well. He is the best right fielder I have ever seen," Kershaw said after the game. "He took third base on a bad pickoff and scored on a throw to shortstop. Who does that?" Nobody but Mookie.

Roberts agreed, adding, "I just don't see anyone else in that category. That's one of the better plays you will ever see. He has exceeded even the high expectations I already had for him."

38-15 is the record, the Dodgers have outscored the Rockies 30–10 after three games and, with the Padres losing to Seattle, have cut the Magic Number down to 2. With a five-game lead and seven to play, it is pretty much a lock right now. A mathematical disaster would have to take place to not win the division. Since the Dodgers own the tiebreaker, the Padres would have to win their remaining seven games, while the Dodgers would have to lose them all. There is just one more game in Colorado to wrap up the road portion of the season.

SEPTEMBER 20, 2020. GAME 54. MAGIC NUMBER 2

Today is a quick-turnaround day game after a night game. This is a pretty typical occurrence for a Sunday, but the Dodgers have played on the two previous Sundays, which is not so common.

There was some good news during Dave Roberts's 10:00 a.m. pre-game Zoom. Walker Buehler pitched a simulated game at Coors yesterday afternoon, throwing 90 pitches, 75 without protection on his finger. He had been throwing during the week with his finger covered, but it cannot be covered up during a game. Buehler will come off the IL on Thursday at Dodger Stadium to face the Oakland A's. The Dodgers need Buehler to make a deep October run.

Tony Gonsolin was on the bump this afternoon and looks like he is turning into a legitimate weapon for the Dodgers. His fastball has become one of the elite four-seamers in the game, largely because he has one of the best splitters to work off of it. Through the first three innings, "The Catman," as Gonsolin has stitched into the thumb of his glove in gold thread, had the Colorado hitters chasing their tails. He struck out the first six and got the first nine in order. He gave up two runs in the fourth, all on soft contact and well-placed hits, but struck out the final two to get out of the inning. Following his solid five innings, he collected a career-best ten strikeouts, all swinging. He ended up taking the loss in the end, but mostly because the offense didn't help him out any.

This game, at times, looked like the final game of the final road trip. Sometimes you see teams go through these types of games without their best effort. Anthony Senzatela had one of his better outings, scattering just three hits and allowing only one run to the most prolific offensive team in the league. It is these games where one wonders how much credit goes to the pitcher and how much blame goes on the hitters. This may have been a combination of both, and it ended up favoring Senzatela and the Rockies, who ended up salvaging a game in this four-game series by a final score of 6–3. There were no home runs by either team, a rarity in the thin air of Coors Field.

There would be no clinch of the division today, and with San Diego beating Seattle in eleven innings, the Magic Number remains at 2. Both teams are off tomorrow so the earliest date to clinch will be Tuesday. I am expecting the inevitable clinch celebration this week to be somewhat low-key, as MLB announced recently that booze will be forbidden as part of post-game celebrations.

SEPTEMBER 22, 2020. GAME 55. VOTE FOR A CLINCHER

With eight days before the start of the postseason, players and staff members who had been temporarily housed at the Westin Bonaventure Hotel had to check out this morning and report to a new hotel to sequester for the final week of the regular season prior to entering the bubble. I won't be traveling with the team to Arlington. As of today, the Dodgers still don't know how exactly they are going to handle the radio broadcasts. Many teams are dealing with this situation on the fly and most have no definitive plans.

At 12:30 p.m., the Dodgers held a company-wide Zoom meeting moderated by Alanna Rizzo. Stan Kasten announced that all Dodgers employees will have a paid day off so that they can vote. Special guest Alex Padilla, the secretary of state for California (who later was tabbed to fill Vice President, Kamala Harris's vacant senate seat) and a big Dodger fan, explained that on November 3, Dodger Stadium will be transformed into a polling site so that people who are worried about waiting in line during a pandemic can be outside, vote comfortably, and "take a few selfies," which will give voters more incentive to show up. Alanna had great questions, and Padilla had great answers. I wished that this was something that had been televised nationally. The best and most accurate information on voting anyone can get is directly from your state's secretary of state. They operate and oversee every function of the elections and are the most informed. The Dodgers were great in bringing in Padilla to set the record straight.

News from the NFL today indicates that the league is not fooling around. Three head coaches, Pete Carroll of Seattle, Kyle Shanahan of San Francisco, and Vic Fangio of Denver were fined one hundred thousand dollars each for not wearing masks during games. Further, each team was fined two hundred fifty thousand dollars for allowing the violations. That swift action sent a strong message. In college football, The University of Notre Dame announced that their upcoming game on Saturday against Wake Forest has been postponed due to thirteen Fighting Irish players testing positive. This is probably not the last time we will see this happen.

Things have to break just right for the Dodgers to clinch their eighth straight NL West Division Championship. Even in a shortened season, it is a big deal. It is hard to win in baseball, and to do it as consistently as the Dodgers have been doing it is a testament to the organization and the way they draft and develop players. The A's are one of the better teams, and the Dodgers will need a win along with a Padres loss to the Angels to clinch tonight. The Angels have done their part, knocking off San Diego 4–2.

Dustin May started and found himself down 1–0 after only one out when left fielder Robbie Grossman hit a slicing, opposite-field fly ball off the left-field foul pole. With no fans, you could hear the clang off the pole loud and clear. Mookie singled and scored almost immediately in the bottom of the first when Corey Seager drove him in. Seager would go three for three with a home run to lead the offense. His bat has been on fire, and hitting behind Betts should result in a few extra RBIs. Seager's homer was one of four hit today. Max Muncy smashed his 11th and A.J. Pollock recorded his 13th in the fourth, two batters after Chris Taylor led off the frame with his 8th.

May allowed one other run on a walk, two ground ball outs, and a wild pitch. The bullpen was activated in the sixth and slammed the door with Victor González, Dylan Floro, Joe Kelly, Pedro Báez, and Jake McGee turning in scoreless outings. McGee would strike out the last two he faced to wrap up the 7–2 win and the division title. The Dodgers made their way out onto the field happily but awkwardly as there were some hugs and handshakes as well as the distribution of the customary postseason hats and T-shirts. There was no champagne, no beer, no plastic sheets to protect players' lockers. I have been lucky enough to be in a number of those clubhouse celebrations, including a World Series win. They are wildly fun and get ingrained in your memory. Nevertheless, they will adjust and find another way to celebrate this year, as the Dodgers are hoping for a few more. During the post-game interview with Mookie, the team lined up near the mound for a team photo. Alanna interrupted him and said, "You need to be in that team picture. Go."

On Zoom for the post-game presser, Seager commented on the unorthodox celebration. "It's really weird…. You want to enjoy it, you want to live in the moment, and to not be able to do it kinda sucks, you know."

Muncy was especially happy that his home run came against the team that gave up on him a few years ago. The A's made a mistake designating Muncy for assignment. Asked about the celebration, Muncy said, "Not as fun. One of the best things about baseball is that you get to do the champagne all over the place. It's just one big party. It's very unfortunate that we don't get to do that but, we know what's at stake here."

SEPTEMBER 23, 2020. GAME 56. CLINCHED AND LOADED

The team that clinches usually has a hard time winning the next day, due to it being a hangover game, but that would not be a factor tonight. The Dodgers have wrapped up the division and assumed the National League's number one seed. They do not yet know who their

Wild Card opponent will be, and may not until the last day of the season. What they do know, however, is that should they make it out of the Wild Card round and have to go to the bubble, they will be in Arlington for the duration.

The heavy lifting on the regular season is done, but home field throughout the postseason can be achieved with a win over the A's. The Dodgers have a different plan for the men on the mound tonight, making Joe Kelly the opener to see if skipping Julio Urías in the first alleviates him of his first-inning troubles. Brusdar Graterol is lined up for the second and Urías will come in for the third as the "bulk innings" guy. Urías did a good job, only allowing one run on two hits while striking out five and turning in the longest relief appearance for the Dodgers in 24 years—since September of 1996 when Pedro Astacio logged six and a third innings. Unfortunately, Kelly was tagged for three runs when he allowed back-to-back doubles by Tommy La Stella and Robbie Grossman to open the game. Kelly walked the next hitter, Marcus Semien who would later score on a throwing error by center fielder Cody Bellinger. Mark Canha would drive in another A's run to make it three to nothing.

Urías was able to hold Oakland down as the Dodgers chipped their way back into the game. Max Muncy clubbed his 12th of the season with Justin Turner aboard to cut the Athletics' lead to 3–2. The teams traded runs in the seventh to make it 4–3 heading into the eighth. In the home half of the inning with one out, Edwin Rios, who replaced Justin Turner two innings earlier, hijacked a Jake Diekman pitch and hit a frozen rope over the short wall down the right field line to tie the game. Diekman, a lefty and one of the most effective in the AL, had not allowed a run this season and had not given up a home run to a lefty since late in 2018. Rios was in rare air.

Just as it seemed like the pendulum was swinging in the Dodgers' direction, Blake Treinen began to struggle in the top of the ninth. After striking out pinch hitter Matt Olson, he allowed a base hit to

Stephen Piscotty. Two batters later, Ramón Laureano went down and got the barrel on a poorly located sinker, popping it down the left-field line and over the fence. That would ice it for the A's with a 6–4 win.

This series was a good test and a dress rehearsal of sorts for the best-of-three Wild Card round looming on the horizon. The Dodgers still have MLB's best record at 39-17 and will await the deciding game of the series tomorrow with an excellent Oakland club who are 34-21.

SEPTEMBER 24, 2020. GAME 57. BUEHLER'S DAY ON

The rubber game with Oakland tonight was a good distraction from the uncertainty of whether or not I need to plan for the postseason or plan to go home, especially with Walker Buehler coming off the IL to pitch. He was good. Really good. The best game I ever saw him pitch was Game 3 of the 2018 World Series. He was on a different level that night. He got a no decision, which is still hard to believe, but the game was decided in eighteen innings on a Muncy opposite-field walk-off home run after seven hours and twenty minutes of riveting baseball. A lot happened in that game, and Buehler was a big part of it. Without his performance, I believe the white-hot Red Sox would have won and gone on to sweep the Dodgers. If not for an error in the bottom of the thirteenth by second baseman Ian Kinsler, the Red Sox would have won that game and won it a lot earlier.

Buehler's appearance tonight, to no one's surprise, wasn't long and didn't need to be, during what was his final tune-up before the post-season. He had his signature fastball on cruise control, threw more curveballs than usual, and cut back on the cutter. The cutter, due to the grip Buehler uses combined with his release, was probably the biggest culprit that led to the annoying finger blister that landed him on the IL, twice limiting his regular season work. Buehler faced one over the minimum in four innings of work with six punch-outs. He looked strong, and the Dodgers saw all they needed to see before letting the bullpen get some work in.

Betts singled and scored in the first, Seager blasted his 15th homer in the second, and the Dodgers added a three-spot in the sixth led by a Bellinger RBI double. The only blemish to the pen was when catcher Sean Murphy hit his eighth-inning solo home run off a Jake McGee fastball that was left up in the zone. The game ended with the Dodgers banking their MLB-best 40th win of the season on a 5–1 score. The Dodgers guaranteed themselves home field throughout the postseason, which is one of the few rewards available during the COVID season playoff structure.

SEPTEMBER 25, 2020. GAME 58. THE CORONAVIRUS HITS HOME

Every day, it is hard not to pay attention to the rising case numbers all over the country.

Today, I received a phone call that I was hoping not to get. I picked up right away. The voice said, "I haven't been feeling very well so I went and got tested today. I just got a call from the lab. I've got it. I'm positive." It was my twenty-six-year-old son, Matt, who lives in Las Vegas with his brother, twenty-four-year-old Kyle. Fortunately, his symptoms have been mild to this point. He called his employers and immediately went into quarantine and began his own contact tracing. Kyle scheduled a test for tomorrow and his employer won't allow him to come in until he tests negative, so he is quarantined on the opposite side of the apartment they share. He says he feels fine. My worry is not the short-term symptoms but the possible long-term effects. COVID-19 has entered the Neverett family domain and it is unnerving.

MLB's weekly testing numbers are out and a total of 13,279 samples were examined. There were two new positive cases, but none from players. Something I also learned today is that postseason broadcasting plans have changed again, though not regarding my participation. After further consultation, the Dodgers decided that they will only travel the radio crew if the team makes the World Series, handling games remotely until then. Most teams are not sending their broadcast crews. The Reds, who clinched their first postseason berth since they were dumped out of the Wild Card in Pittsburgh in 2013, will be the only team sending their crew. Our Spanish-language broadcast team told the Dodgers a while ago that they did not want to travel. That was a veteran move by Jaime Jarrin.

While so many want to fast forward and land somewhere in the middle of 2021, the Dodgers and their fans are holding onto the present, at least in the baseball sense, as this team attempts to make history. They continue to grind their way through the season, beating the teams in front of them almost every night. The countdown to the postseason is on.

The Angels have made their way up Interstate 5 to wrap up the regular season and play a game they have to win to keep their mathematical playoff hopes alive. They are hanging by an awfully frayed thread.

The ball was flying at Dodger Stadium as eight home runs were hit, five by the Dodgers. The Angels had built up a 3–1 lead in the top of the third inning when Clayton Kershaw hung a curveball that Mike Trout obliterated. Trout got the better of Kershaw in this at-bat, but Kershaw has typically dominated Trout. It was only the third career hit for Trout off of Kershaw in 18 at-bats against him. This was a cool game to watch from the point of view of anyone who appreciates the game. It featured five former MVPs and four surefire Hall of Famers. Trout and Albert Pujols for the Angels won the big awards. Pujols won it three times in the NL with the Cardinals in 2005, 2008, and 2009. Cody Bellinger is the reigning National League MVP, Mookie Betts won the American League MVP in 2018, and Clayton Kershaw picked up the NL award in 2014.

Justin Upton and Jared Walsh went yard for the Halos, while the Dodgers quintet featured Justin Turner with two, Will Smith, A.J. Pollock, and Edwin Rios. In the "something you don't see every day" department, there was a delay of game in the top of the eighth. A fire alarm was triggered. It could barely be heard above the canned crowd noise, but anyone could see the flashing white strobe lights that line the jagged outfield pavilion roof stretching from bullpen to bullpen. Upton was at the plate with one on and one out when it started at 9:43 p.m. He struck out looking and appeared to be distracted by the strobes. Angels manager Joe Maddon asked home plate umpire Chris Guccione what was going on. When the umpire realized it was an alarm, he halted play until it was shut off several minutes later.

Kershaw didn't have his best stuff and left the game after four innings, but he was going to leave early anyway with this being his last start before the playoffs. Ironically, the Dodgers' 9–5 win secured a playoff spot for the dreaded Astros. The Angels were eliminated. The Dodgers moved their record to 41-17, and have hit an MLB-best 113 home runs.

After the game, I spent some time with Rick Monday and our radio producer, Duane McDonald, out at Rick's RV. Mo's Bar & Grill, I call it. We shared a few beverages and swapped stories and laughs. Rick showed us how the coyotes had come within about three feet of his RV recently. I guess they wanted to share his food. With the hum of a nearby generator used to light up the parking lot below, we recounted the details of the three-hour-and-forty-one-minute game. Duane left to go home after a while, and I hung out with Rick for a while longer. I took a quick look at my watch, saw it was 1:15 a.m., and figured it was time to go.

The Season

SEPTEMBER 26, 2020. GAME 59. POWER OUTAGE

It is a slow Saturday, the last of the regular season. Realizing the season is almost over and I will be heading back to New England, I began packing and straightening out my suite this morning. I can feel the clock winding down on the 2020 season. I needed something to do while I waited for Kyle to let me know the results of his test. It took a while, but the test was negative, and he and Matt continued their quarantines. No matter a kid's age, a parent always worries.

Baseball may be stiff-arming COVID-19 for now, but today Major League Soccer could not. A game scheduled between Sporting KC and the Colorado Rapids in Denver was postponed because one player and three staff members tested positive. New cases are going up in many states. Delays and postponements in pro and college sports due to positive tests look like they will continue.

Having college football on TV in the background was certainly welcome as ambient noise. It is just so different to watch Florida and Ole Miss with hardly anyone in the seats in Oxford. The same goes for Army and Cincinnati in the Queen City. Nothing is the same this year, but having some of something is better than nothing.

The middle game of the season-ending three-game series was about as meaningful as a spring training game. The only thing on the line were answers to who might be the last few to make the roster for the Wild Card. The Dodgers certainly wanted to win and set the high-water mark for a 60-game season. May we never see a 60-game season again.

Tony Gonsolin started on the hill with a chance to solidify his spot as a possible Game 3-type starter. Dylan Bundy was the probable starter for the Angels, but Joe Maddon scratched him and gave the ball to Julio Teherán instead. That turned out horribly for the Halos, as Teherán was brutal. He threw half a game, an egregiously high 52 pitches, before he registered three outs. He hit Mookie with a pitch in the left hip and walked both Muncy and Bellinger following

Justin Turner's base hit. Three runs later, the Dodgers had control of the game.

Gonsolin was very good for five of his six innings. The "Catman" used up one of his nine lives in the third when he allowed four runs on four hits, including a two-run triple to Jared Walsh, which flipped the script, giving the Angels a 4–3 lead. Gonsolin used his splitter and fast ball to put up zeros over the next three innings and wrapped up his regular season on a positive note.

Will Smith led off the Dodger half of the sixth with a free pass to first. Joc Pederson, who was in left, lifted a pitch off the end of the bat to the opposite field. The baseball was carrying and didn't have enough slice to make it sail foul. Left fielder Taylor Ward was drifting after the ball but ran out of room, and Pederson flipped things right back in the Dodgers' favor with a two-run homer and a fresh 5–4 lead.

The game was moving along until the top of the seventh. Joe Kelly took over for Gonsolin and was warming up while up-and-coming Angels outfielder Jo Adell was approaching home plate to take his place in the right-hand batter's box. Then at 8:34 p.m., sudden darkness. The power went down, and for a couple of moments, it was completely dark and quiet. It was a brief vacuum in time and space. Some lights and power came back on, enough so that one's eyes could adjust. Apparently, there was an issue with the local power grid in Echo Park and it tripped the grid momentarily at Dodger Stadium. It took a bit to get all the power back on and would take even longer to warm up the stadium lights again. The broadcasters got back on the air quickly and following a twenty-five-minute delay the game resumed at 8:59 p.m. Imagine if a 98 mph fastball from Kelly was on the way to the plate when that happened.

The power came back on for the Dodgers as well. Edwin Rios hit a home run to center in the seventh, helped by a deflection off Adell's glove. In the eighth, Smith didn't need any assistance when he hit a screaming liner over the left-field wall for his eighth of the season.

Smith has been very good with the bat and looks like he is going to be a legit number-one catcher for years to come. Rios has now homered in back-to-back games, in three of his last four, and is making a strong case to be on the Wild Card roster. The Dodgers were able to hold off a late Angels comeback and win the game 7–6. They are sitting on an impressive 42-17 record after 59 games.

SEPTEMBER 27, 2020. GAME #60. LOOKS LIKE WE MADE IT

There were many who felt we may never get to this point considering the once-in-a-century pandemic we are in. This season will go down in history for a number of reasons, and one of them is the fact that it was completed.

Every game in Major League Baseball, for the fifth straight season, will start at the same time. Many fans wonder why. I can tell you because I was in the middle of it in 2014 when a situation developed on the last day that ended up giving a team a competitive advantage.

I was with the Pirates, finishing up the regular season in Cincinnati, still clinging to a slim hope of tying the Cardinals for the Central Division title and forcing a one-game playoff the following day in St. Louis. If the Buccos beat the Reds and the Cardinals lost to the Diamondbacks later that day, there would be a tie. If the Pirates lost, then St. Louis would claim the division title before a pitch was thrown in their final game. With the Pirates/Reds in the Eastern Time Zone and the Cardinals/Diamondbacks in the Pacific Time Zone, their game would start three hours after the Pirates' game did.

Johnny Cueto was on the hill for Cincinnati, looking for his 20th win of the season. Gerrit Cole got the nod for Clint Hurdle's team. It was a good matchup. In the top of the ninth with Pittsburgh trailing, Cardinals ace Adam Wainwright was warming up in Arizona. Manager Mike Matheny had a plan. The Cards were monitoring our telecast, and the second the last out was recorded in the Reds'

4–1 victory, Matheny stopped Wainwright and replaced him with the unknown Nick Greenwood, who made his only career start that day. Wainwright was a late, non-injury, non-illness scratch, and the Cardinals saved him for Game 1 of the NLDS. Matheny ran his version of the option offense. He wanted Wainwright to pitch only if the Pirates won, but by pulling him out the Diamondbacks had no time to prepare. The Cardinals beat the Diamondbacks 1–0. The Pirates then hosted the Wild Card game and lost to Madison Bumgarner and the eventual World Series Champion Giants.

That offseason, MLB came up with a new policy to prevent pitching manipulation by making every team start their final regular season games at 3:00 p.m. Eastern Time. It's been that way ever since.

A chamber of commerce afternoon with sunny blue skies and a game-time temperature of a perfect Southern California 79 degrees welcomed the Dodgers and Angels to this strange regular season finale. The Dodgers were looking to sweep the Angels into the offseason and themselves into the postseason. Everything went as planned.

Left-hander Victor González, who has pitched so well this year he has simply made it impossible for the team to send him down, got the nod to start. Just a couple of years ago, he was so frustrated with baseball he almost walked away. In fact, he did for a short time, but the people around him convinced him to contact the Dodgers. He was given another chance, made more than the most of it, and is shining at the Big League level for the first time. González would serve as the opening act for Dustin May, who blew away the Angels for four innings. The rest of the staff tossed out donuts as well, to send the Angels quietly away. Mike Trout did not play the last two games. Joe Maddon was not taking any chances with his superstar now that they'd been eliminated.

The Dodgers had all the offense they would need after their first batter came up. Pollock led off with Betts getting the day to rest and cranked his 15th home run of the season, and the first of two on the afternoon. His second came in the seventh, and not only tied Betts for the team lead but passed his own total from 2019.

As the seventh inning went along, a message popped up on the signature Dodger Stadium video screens above the right and left field pavilions that was as good a symbol of the 2020 season as anything else I have seen. "We'd like to thank our cardboard cutouts for their support all season."

At the end of the two-hour-and-fifty-four-minute baseball exercise, the Dodgers shut out the Angels 5–0.

It may have been a 60-game season, but the last day wasn't unlike a regular 162-game slate. In the bottom of the eighth, reports on social media from baseball reporters began to surface. Angels GM Billy Eppler had been fired. The game wasn't over yet, so you know this conversation between owner Arte Moreno and Eppler had taken place hours before.

The Dodgers would finish the season with the best record in baseball at 43-17. They used 56 different lineups and had zero issues with COVID-19. They finished with a dominant +136 run differential, scored the most runs, and gave up the second-fewest in the game. They boat raced just about every team they played and lost only one series (to Colorado). After all of this, it comes down to winning thirteen more games. *If* they lose a series now, then everything they accomplished during the short regular season may be forgotten.

SEPTEMBER 29, 2020. GOING HOME

The season was over for me, as I was told that I would not be working any postseason games and I was free to go home, if I wanted. So I did. At LAX today, the traffic was lighter than I had ever remembered seeing it, and there were not many people flying. Getting my bags checked was quick and easy as there was no one in line. I was asked to answer questions from the CDC regarding my health and other questions regarding how I packed my luggage. There was no line going through security either, and since I belong to CLEAR, it literally took me forty seconds to get through. LAX has a lot of signage in multiple languages informing people they must wear a mask or face covering. While sitting at a workstation reading from my iPad, some unmasked guy decided to sit in the seat next to me and talk loudly on his phone. I got up and left. United Airlines did a good job, I thought, in enforcing the mask rule and doing what they could to spread people out on the plane. The middle seat was open, and I was in seat 9A on the way from LA to Denver where I would switch planes. On the way from Denver to Boston, my entire row was open and so was the row behind me.

As we were on our final approach to Logan Airport, the lead flight attendant was making her announcements and finished with something that stuck with me. She said that due to the pandemic and lack of any government assistance to the airline industry that she and her fellow flight attendants were taking their last flight before being laid off. Thousands of United Airlines workers were laid off within the next two days.

PART 3

The Postseason

SEPTEMBER 30, 2020. WILD CARD SERIES GAME 1. THE POSTSEASON BEGINS

This was the first game at Dodger Stadium that I would not be sitting in the front row of suite 215. Lefty Brent Suter started for Milwaukee and had a terrible first inning. It was the equivalent of a golfer having a bad case of "first hole anxiety." Suter had walked only five men all season but walked four Dodgers in the first. Mookie led the inning off with a double, then Seager, Muncy, Smith, and Pollock all walked, with Smith and Pollock forcing in runs. The two runs felt like too few as they could not come up with the big hit. Another run came in the next inning when Chris Taylor and Betts recorded back-to-back doubles.

Walker Buehler started, but would not go too long due to the ugly blister on his right index finger. He has cut down on throwing cutters and has been sticking with the fastball and curveball to avoid making the blister worse.

Prior to the game, Justin Turner had agreed to wear a microphone and IFB (earpiece) so that he could communicate with the ESPN announcers while playing third. This kind of thing, especially in a playoff game, can be risky. Fortunately, nothing happened that caused Turner to make a mistake, but he did have to adjust his earpiece a number of times between pitches. This action did, however, raise more than an eyebrow of Dave Roberts, who banned his players from wearing a wire for the rest of the postseason. I can see doing this in spring training for sure, and sometimes during the regular season (without the earpiece and on tape), but during the playoffs is probably not the best idea.

Cory Seager continued his torrid pace when he ripped a 447-foot monster blast over the center field wall in the seventh for some insurance to lead the Dodgers to a 4–2 win, and a one-game-to-none lead. After 72 pitches, Buehler's game was done and Urías took over, pitching three innings to earn the win while Jansen picked up the save.

The blister remains the story with Buehler. ESPN showed close-ups of his finger during the game, and analyst Eduardo Pérez suggested that there possibly was a substance that was not allowed to be there. "It is what it is," the understated pitcher said during his post-game Zoom presser. "We are managing it."

"There have been times when the blister shows itself a little bit. It wasn't necessarily the pitch count," Dave Roberts said. "I just felt right there that we could end feeling good about things where they're at and get him ready for his next start."

OCTOBER 1, 2020. WILD CARD SERIES GAME 2. MORE VINTAGE KERSHAW

MLB released their most recent testing results. 15,024 samples collected, two positive tests, for a 0.01 percent positivity rate. Both positives came from Tier 2 staff members from the same team. Thirty-three straight days with no players testing positive.

A win tonight will eliminate the Brewers and move the Dodgers on to the NLDS in Arlington. It will also give the Dodgers four days off to reset their pitching before facing either San Diego or St. Louis. Buehler, blister permitting, would be on full rest for Game 1 followed by Kershaw for Game 2.

Milwaukee sent tough right-hander Brandon Woodruff to the mound to counter Kershaw, and an old-fashioned pitchers' duel broke out. It seemed like Woodruff was just playing catch with catcher Jacob Nottingham. He struck out nine Dodgers over four and two-thirds innings and was cruising. He looked dominant.

Kershaw also looked good, and as the game went on, he got better. It was more of the vintage Kershaw we had seen a lot of this season. The only chance the Brewers had was to keep MLB's highest-scoring team off the scoreboard.

With one out in the fifth, Cody Bellinger singled. Taylor singled to follow him, but Bellinger was then erased at third on a fielder's choice by Pollock. With two out and two on, catcher Austin Barnes came through, breaking the ice with a run-scoring single. A "Mookie Moment" followed, when Betts pulled a two-run double inside the third base bag and down the line to make it 3–0. It was his third double of the series. Woodruff was upset at home plate umpire Quinn Wolcott over a few close pitches called balls. When manager Craig Counsell came out to remove Woodruff, he let Wolcott hear about it and was immediately ejected. His dominance on the hill, frustratingly for him, went sideways in the blink of an eye. It was like he was being smacked in the back of the head and couldn't see who was doing it.

When the Dodgers got the lead, there was blood in the water and the sharks were circling, led by Kershaw. Clayton turned in one of his best playoff appearances. He punched out a postseason-career-high 13 hitters including former NL MVP Christian Yelich twice. The Dodgers swept the Brewers.

The ALDS will now move into Dodger Stadium as the Dodgers head to Texas. Three key players may have played their final games at Dodger Stadium. Joc Pederson, Kiké Hernández, and Justin Turner are all in the final years of their contracts.

Kershaw was in a great mood following his classic performance. "This was a fun night for me," he said. The Dodgers moving on to Kershaw's home state is just another symbol of the pandemic season. "If you would have told me that the first time I'd ever pitch in Texas would be in the Division Series against somebody other than the Rangers—it's like the craziest thing ever. It's going to be weird. I live ten minutes from the team hotel. I am going to be staring at family through a glass wall."

OCTOBER 6, 2020. NLDS GAME 1. GAME 1 WALKATHON

The question heading into this game was who would be pitching for the Padres. Mike Clevinger was a big question mark. He could not pitch in the Wild Card Series against St. Louis due to an impingement in his right elbow, and it had been thirteen days since he last threw a pitch in a game. San Diego's first-year manager, Jayce Tingler, knew he needed Clevinger to be just good enough to have a chance to get a leg up in the series with the Dodgers. I don't know too many competitors that wouldn't tell their manager they were able to play, and Clevinger ultimately convinced Tingler that he was good to go. Well, he wasn't. He lasted only one inning and had to be taken out after just two pitches in the second. He joined another Padres starter, Dinelson Lamet, on the disabled list. This put Tingler in an untenable spot and forced the Padres to set a new NLDS record by using nine pitchers in a game, with most not on the same page.

Walker Buehler gave what he had while continuing to fight through the untimely blister issue on his right middle finger. He lasted four innings, while Dustin May came on to cover two innings, ultimately earning the win. While the Dodgers trailed by a run early, they tied it up in the second inning then rolled after that. The Padres gift-wrapped this one for them. The Dodgers had a lot of free traffic on the base paths throughout the game, drawing ten walks along with a hit batsman. Garrett Richards was tagged for the loss. A 5–1 Dodger victory got the series off to a good start for the Boys in Blue, taking a one-game-to-none lead in the process.

OCTOBER 7, 2020. NLDS GAME 2. MAXWELL'S SILVER HAMMER

Kershaw was not his best, but good. Six innings pitched but left after giving up back-to-back home runs to Manny Machado and Eric Hosmer in the sixth. It looked like Blake Treinen, who came on for the seventh, was about to watch the 3–3 game go the way of the Padres. Fernando Tatís Jr. launched a high fly ball to center field. Bellinger was tracking it and timed his leap perfectly, robbing Tatís of a go-ahead home run. It was the defensive play that shifted the series.

In the bottom of the seventh, Mookie reached on a fielder's choice and Seager singled. Betts and Seager pulled off a double steal before Justin Turner's sacrifice fly to center scored Betts. Muncy drove in Seager with a base hit for what would be the game-winning run. The Padres still had a pulse in the top of the ninth, scoring two after Kenley Jansen, with one out, allowed a single to Jake Cronenworth, a double to the pinch-hitting Mitch Moreland, and an RBI single to Trent Grisham, allowing them to pull the score to 6–5. Dave Roberts came out to get the struggling Jansen, but the high-wire act would continue. Joe Kelly needed one out but had to face the top of the order. He walked Tatís and followed that up with a walk to Machado to load the bases. San Diego had the tying run at third and the go-ahead run at second. Kelly can be an adventure from time to time, but he was able to induce a game-ending ground ball to second baseman Kiké Hernández to wrap up the game 6–5 and take a commanding two-games-to-none lead. Kershaw got the win, Joe Kelly picked up the save, and Padres starter Zach Davies took the loss.

OCTOBER 8, 2020. NLDS GAME 3. BROOMVILLE

The Dodgers changed uniforms but not dugouts at Globe Life Field. These are the Playoffs in 2020. This is the first elimination game of the postseason. Dustin May started, facing Adrián Morejón. The game was close…for two innings. The Dodgers struck first in the top of the second when Muncy walked and Will Smith doubled. Bellinger brought Muncy home with an RBI groundout. The Padres countered in the bottom of the inning and took a 2–1 lead when Cronenworth walked with the bases loaded and Grisham followed with an infield single plating the go-ahead run.

The top of the third was one of two innings in which the Dodger bats exploded. Betts led off with a walk and scored, while Seager, Turner, Pollock, and Pederson had hits. Joc's long single scored two runs. Turner's was his 64th postseason hit for the Dodgers, passing Steve Garvey for the most postseason hits in Dodgers history. Nine men came to the plate and five scored, to give the Dodgers an insurmountable 6–2 lead. It would get worse for San Diego. The Dodgers added another run in the fourth, another in the fifth, and four more in the ninth, spearheaded by Bellinger's two-run triple. It capped off a decisive 12–2 win, to give the Dodgers a sweep of the Division Series. They'll now face the Braves in the NLCS and have the opportunity to reset their pitching, given the three off-days in front of them.

OCTOBER 12, 2020. NLCS GAME #1. FREDDIE AND FRIED GET IT DONE

The quest for the National League pennant begins against a very good team from Atlanta. All-star first baseman Freddie Freeman clubbed a first inning home run to right off of Walker Buehler to open the scoring. Braves left-hander Max Fried arrived as a front-of-the-rotation stud and has not disappointed. Fried cut up Dodger hitters over six solid innings, allowing only one earned run and striking out nine. Kiké Hernández's solo home run in the fifth knotted the game, which remained tied until the top of the ninth. Blake Treinen was summoned to keep the score where it was, but twenty-three-year-old sometimes-third-baseman, sometimes-left-fielder Austin Riley led off the inning by taking him deep to give the Braves all they would need. Ronald Acuña Jr. doubled, and Marcell Ozuna drove him with a base hit and scored on a two-run shot by Ozzie Albies that put the icing on the cake. The Braves drew first blood, beating the Dodgers 5–1.

OCTOBER 13, 2020. NLCS GAME 2. CATMAN-DON'T

Tony Gonsolin had a great start, then he didn't. The "Catman" was purrfect his first time through the Braves batting order. Then, after walking Acuña, Freeman got him for a two-run homer. Three of the four runs that came in during the fifth belonged to him. Atlanta starter Ian Anderson had a different fate. He only went four innings but gave up only one hit. Manager Brian Snitker lifted him after 88 pitches. Atlanta was up 7–0 heading to the home half of the seventh when the Dodger bats began showing signs of life. Seager lit a fire with a three-run smash, scoring Joc Pederson and Chris Taylor who had both singled, making it 7–3 and opening a new ball game. In the ninth, lefty Adam Kolarek surrendered a solo homer to Albies to make it 8–4, but the Dodgers were not done. With one out in the bottom of the ninth, Betts singled, Seager doubled, and Muncy hammered one to right to make it 8–6. The Dodgers were down to their last out when Will Smith reached on a throwing error by Albies and Bellinger knocked him in with a triple to make it a one-run game. Pollock had the chance to tie the game but came up short when he grounded out to third. The Dodgers almost completed the comeback, but find themselves in a hole, losing 8–7, trailing two games to none, and looking at a must-win tomorrow.

OCTOBER 14, 2020. NLCS GAME 3. ROAD WARRIORS

This is the first game in the series that the Dodgers are wearing their road gray uniforms and playing as the visiting team.

"Momentum in baseball is only as good as your next day's starting pitcher." The axiom might be from the origin of the game. The Dodgers had momentum in the ninth inning last night and almost tied the game after being down by seven. They were about to prove the axiom wrong.

Fourteen men came to the plate in the first and eleven scored. The Dodgers lit up starter Kyle Wright, to the point where he might need therapy to get over the experience. Wright is a very good pitcher, but he was in the wrong place at the wrong time. Prior to the game, Mookie told the media that being down 2-0 in the series was on him, and he has to be better as the leadoff man to get things going. He did with an infield single. Betts was called out by umpire Dan Iassogna, but the play was challenged, and the folks at the Replay Operations Center in New York overturned it. The leadoff man was on for the first time in the series. Seager doubled, scoring Betts, and Smith doubled, scoring Seager—2–0 out of the chute. Turner and Muncy grounded out consecutively making it seem as if Wright had righted the ship, but with two outs, the Dodgers took him out behind the woodshed. Pederson hit a three-run bomb, then Rios followed him with a solo blast. Taylor and Betts each walked, and Seager drove in Taylor with a base hit. Turner was then hit by a pitch (surprise) to load the bases before Muncy pounded the stake through the heart with a grand slam. Nine runs after two outs. Eleven–nothing after a half inning. The game was over minutes after it had started. Just when it looked like the Braves were going to get on the board in the bottom of the inning, Bellinger made another defensive gem, robbing Albies of a home run. Bellinger followed that spectacle with a homer in the top of the second. Seager hit one in the third as the Dodgers tacked on a few for fun. Atlanta scratched out a couple of runs late but it was way too little, way too late. During the first-inning offensive onslaught, I texted Rick Monday who was at Dodger Stadium calling the game remotely, "They seem to hit better on the road." Dodgers win 15–3.

OCTOBER 15, 2020. NLCS GAME 4. ATLANTA STRIKES BACK

For five innings this was a game. Clayton Kershaw gave up just one run on a fourth-inning solo shot by Marcell Ozuna. The only Dodger lead of the game would come briefly, after designated hitter Edwin Rios hit a bomb in the third inning, his second in two games. The importance of this game was obvious, and LA knew that their World Series hopes rested heavily on tying this series up. Kershaw allowed three Atlanta baserunners in the bottom of the sixth before being lifted. Brusdar Graterol came in from the bullpen and allowed three to score, plus three of his own. Ozuna would homer again in the seventh off Dylan Floro, and the beat was on. Atlanta was just 27 outs away from knocking off the top-seeded Dodgers and advancing to the Fall Classic. The Dodgers, however, still had a pulse. Braves 10–2.

OCTOBER 16, 2020. NLCS GAME 5. BRAVES ON THE VERGE

Elimination and the abyss of another failed World Series bid faced the Dodger organization as they looked into the mirror this morning. This might bother some groups, but it's not making a dent in this one. Dustin May got the start in a game that turned out to be of the "bullpen" variety. May gave up a first-inning double to Freddie Freeman, who scored on a Travis d'Arnaud sacrifice fly. May walked Dansby Swanson to start the bottom of the second, then, with one out, rookie outfielder Cristian Pache knocked him in with a single to make it 2–0. The Dodgers struggled against starter A.J. Minter, a reliever in to give the Braves whatever length he could. He ended up giving them the start of a lifetime as he struck out seven of the ten batters he faced in his three innings of work, allowing only a first-inning double to Justin Turner. Many wondered just how long they'd ride him, but once he left, the Dodgers went to work. Corey Seager hit the first of his two home runs to lead off the fourth and make it 2–1. The game was ultimately decided in the sixth, when Will Smith banged a two-out, three-run homer, making it 4–2. Chris Taylor doubled and scored when he exchanged places following a Mookie double. Then Seager hit a two-run shot to cap it off and give the Dodgers a 7–3 win; they were off life support, their pulse growing stronger.

OCTOBER 17, 2020. NLCS GAME 6. SEAGER SLUGS

The Dodgers are loose. To observe them you would think they were in the driver's seat tonight, but their backs are against the ropes again. There were no days off or "virtual" travel days in the championship series, so as the Dodgers flipped back to being the home team for the remainder of this best-of-seven series, both team's bullpens could be sorely tested. That left the heavy lifting to be done by two very good starting pitchers, Max Fried and Walker Buehler.

The Dodgers hitters learned from their last meeting with Fried in Game 1 and put him on notice right away. Seager continued his onslaught against enemy pitching, blasting a one-out home run. In the blink of an eye, Justin Turner made it 2–0 with a bookended long ball. The back-to-back homers shook Fried, as he walked Muncy and allowed consecutive base hits from Smith and Bellinger to score Muncy and make it 3–0. It was like Fried was sucker-punched in the mouth and staggering to find his way.

Buehler went to work like a surgeon, carving up the Braves hitters for six innings. The only run Atlanta scored was in the seventh off Blake Treinen, when Ronald Acuña Jr. drove in Nick Markakis following a triple by the veteran outfielder. The Dodgers were able to move past their near-death experience with this 3–1 win and even up the series at three games each, forcing an all-hands-on-deck, winner-take-all Game 7 tomorrow.

OCTOBER 18, 2020. NLCS GAME 7. ANOTHER MOOKIE MOMENT

Winner moves on, loser goes home. It's as simple as that, but it was a nail-biter. As in Game 5, the Braves took a 2–0 lead. Dustin May started, and the Dodgers were hoping for some length from him, but it didn't work out. Nerves may have gotten the better of Dustin in the first inning, as he was pitching in the biggest game of his life and was only a few minutes from his hometown of Justin, Texas. Dustin from Justin walked the first two batters before surrendering a run-scoring single to Marcell Ozuna. Tony Gonsolin replaced May after just one inning and promptly allowed a leadoff solo home run to Swanson to make it 2–0. That wouldn't hold. The Dodgers tied it with, what else, two outs in the bottom of the third. Turner walked and Muncy doubled. Smith came up with a two-run single for the equalizer.

It was punch and counter punch in this heavyweight baseball fight. Gonsolin faltered in the fourth, walking the first two hitters before Austin Riley put Atlanta ahead 3–2. Roberts went back to the pen looking for zeros. He got just what he wanted, but it wasn't easy. In the fifth, Freddie Freeman hit what he thought was an insurance home run but flew into another Mookie Moment. Betts, who has been beyond outstanding defensively this postseason, timed his leap perfectly and yanked the ball back from over the wall in a classic case of highway robbery.

The biggest blow was yet to come, but the tying one came off the bat of Kiké Hernández, who was pinch-hitting for Joc Pederson to lead off the bottom of the sixth. The Braves went to the bullpen and brought in lefty A.J. Minter to face Pederson. Atlanta had to know Roberts would counter with Hernández. The Braves wanted the greater home run threat out of the game, which they got. What they didn't get was the result they wanted, as Hernández hammered a Minter pitch way up into the left-field seats to tie Game 7 at three runs apiece.

The score was still 3–3 in the bottom of the seventh when hard-throwing right-hander Chris Martin struck out Muncy swinging at a sinker and caught Smith looking. With two outs never seeming to be an issue for the Dodgers, Cody Bellinger came to the plate with a plan. He knew chances were good that he would see a decent two-seamer, but he had to be aware of Martin's cutter. Martin started him with a cutter for a called strike. Two sinkers were outside the strike zone, and another cutter resulted in strike two. Bellinger was down to his last strike. He would hang tough and foul off the next three offerings to stay alive. On the eighth pitch, Martin settled on a sinker, and from the time it left his right hand, Bellinger thought he had something to work with. The reigning MVP uncoiled and launched one well into the Texas night to give the Dodgers their first and only lead.

Julio Urías was in a zone and Roberts could tell. He'd already retired the first three batters he faced and would mow through the next six hitters to slam the door shut on a 4–3 win, completing the series comeback and advancing the Dodgers to their third World Series in their last four seasons. Incredible performances by incredible players in an incredible Pennant-winning game. Bring on Tampa Bay.

OCTOBER 19, 2020. CALM BEFORE THE STORM

The Dodgers took some time to exhale and regroup after their emotional come-from-behind win. The gears have to be shifted, and the team seems exceptionally focused. The buses to Globe Life for the workout today are full, where normally you might see players staggering their arrivals the day after a late night, winner-take-all game. It was right back to business. Most people associated with the Dodgers probably didn't get a lot of sleep and are running on adrenaline. Dave Roberts got only about five hours last night and said he mostly tossed and turned. It is hard to come down from big moments like that because the brain and body are fired up and it can't just be switched off on command.

The semi-bubble the teams have been experiencing with their families has been a success so far and the latest testing numbers bear that out this week. There were 5,026 samples tested with zero positives. No new positives among players for forty-seven straight days and fifty-five of the last fifty-six.

Today was the day to take care of anything that needed to be taken care of and dive into preparations for the coming opponent, complete strangers due to the regional schedule this season. Either way, tomorrow's game should be an advantage for the Dodgers. They are the home team and have not had to travel. The Rays were playing in San Diego and are coming to Globe Life for the first time. This will also be the first time the Rays will be playing in front of live bodies. It may be disorienting for them. Things are lining up for the Dodgers in 2020.

On the eve of the Fall Classic, the players are focused on the task at hand, but Dodger fans can't help but wonder if this will be the last set of games they see a few of their favorites in a Dodger uniform. Justin Turner, Kiké Hernández, and Joc Pederson are counting down the final days of their current contracts and almost certainly will not all return. Maybe one or two, but not all three. The economic losses endured by franchises are sure to carry over for seasons to come, and it will have an impact on the free agent market and to which players' teams make qualifying offers once the season is over. Without fans, there is no industry, but in order to stay in business, the industry is sure to be reshaped in many facets. Every department from baseball operations to marketing, ticketing to broadcasting will be affected in some way. My educated guess is that, in the very near future, we will begin to hear talk of expanding to thirty-two teams.

I have proposed this expansion idea to a few people in the game this year. By expanding by two teams sometime within the next five years, it would be a financial windfall for owners at a time when they collectively need help. The expansion fees divided among the individual clubs could be in the billions of dollars, an injection of cash that could be a savior for some franchises. I don't know for sure, but I would guess that there are a number of teams leveraged to the hilt, and that there are banks that have continued to issue lines of credit that could technically claim more ownership than some actual owners. MLB does not want to get into a position again like when they took over the Expos, and guided them through the Montreal/San Juan experiment, and finally connected them with new owners in Washington, DC. They don't want to be forced into operating teams on the verge of bankruptcy, nor will they allow franchises to go into the tank, either. My guess is that there is a team or two out there, not the Dodgers, that are in tough financial straits.

OCTOBER 20, 2020. WORLD SERIES GAME 1. THE MALEDICTION OF MOOKIE

Shifting gears is not easy, especially when your team has just completed an extraordinary comeback to claim the National League pennant. If adrenaline were fuel, it would be the highest-octane version of it over the last thirty hours for this Dodgers club. The message, however, has to be: put the win in the rear-view mirror and fast.

Tonight brought a new team and the ultimate challenge. Win four games before your opponent does. There has been a lot of talk about pressure this postseason. Pressure on the Dodgers because they have not won the big prize since 1988, despite several opportunities. Pressure on Dave Roberts because he has had teams that could have won the last three World Series. Now a new, unfamiliar, but highly talented opponent stands in their way, applying even more pressure.

The Rays do things differently. Much of the new vernacular in baseball as it relates to pitching can be credited to their organization. The "opener" was theirs, so was the "run preventer," and the "bulk innings guy" too. The Rays gave baseball gifts that keep on giving, that other teams have employed and many have embraced. The four-man outfield and five-man infield? The Rays have done it all and then some, in an effort to compete with the big boys of the American League East, the Yankees, and Red Sox, on an annual basis. They are a team that wants to drink champagne, but on a budget that can only afford discount beer. I look at it like they are a service academy football team (like Army, Navy, or Air Force) that runs the wishbone offense to create an "equalizer" against their bigger opponents so that they can somewhat level the playing field. This season, albeit short, the Rays took care of business against their big-market brethren and fought and "sabermetricked" their way into their second-ever World Series.

I still have the image of the Phillies' Brad Lidge striking out the Rays' Eric Hinske to end the 2008 Fall Classic, the only time Tampa Bay has participated. The following spring training, before a Pirates exhibition game with the Phillies in Bradenton, Florida, I sat down with Harry Kalas, the legendary Phillies announcer and longtime voice of NFL Films. Kalas was preparing for the telecast while the small visiting TV booth was being set up, and he had no room to work. He took temporary refuge in our radio booth in the seat I usually sit in, which I was glad to give him. I was just excited to talk with him. Looking more frail than I remembered seeing him, he was still beaming about the World Series win for his beloved Phillies and told me in that deep, deliberate, and unmistakable voice that it was the most fun season that he had ever experienced. And he experienced a lot of them. A little over a month later, Kalas was found unresponsive in the visitors' TV booth at Nationals Park. The sports world and the city of Philadelphia lost one of the all-time greats that day.

Prior to tonight's World Series lid lifter, things are going as routinely as they can. At one point, the Dodgers had a brief scare when Max Muncy took a bad bounce off the face. He shook off the pain and walked himself into the Dodger clubhouse. Roughly ten or twelve minutes later, he emerged virtually unscathed and resumed his pre-game routine. Meanwhile, all eyes were on Cody Bellinger in the batting cage to see how his right shoulder was responding after his celebration mishap following his Game 7 pennant-winning home run. He smashed shoulders so hard with Kiké Hernández that his own shoulder had been dislocated. Tonight, there is no visible sign of discomfort, as he stroked pitch after pitch during his rounds of batting practice. Not every swing was at 100 percent, but hitters have a BP plan that doesn't include every swing being full blast. There was a thought that Bellinger would wear a brace of some sort during the game, but since it felt well enough after a day's rest, he decided he didn't need it.

The focus is on Clayton Kershaw, as he prepares to make his fifth career World Series start. Kershaw has had his issues during the postseason, when everything is magnified a hundredfold. In 35 postseason pitching appearances, 29 of them starts over a ten-year playoff history, Kershaw has a record of 11–12, one game under .500. He has, however, won two of his last three, and will be a major key to a Dodger win. During the NLCS, back spasms crept up and his start was pushed back to Game 4. Because of that, and the NLCS going seven games, Kershaw just happened to line up for Game 1 tonight. Once he got going, he bounced a few sliders and had to sight in the scope.

The first batter of the game, Yandy Díaz, singled to right and two batters later, Kershaw walked the Rays' hottest hitter, Randy Arozarena. Both Díaz and Arozarena are Cuban defectors with stories of harrowing escapes, so playing in a World Series game and reaching base in the first inning against a future Hall of Famer, while a thrill, probably doesn't get their hearts pumping like it does for others. Kershaw then tuned things up, found his good slider, struck out Hunter Renfroe, and got Manuel Margot to bounce out to the mound. Kershaw would retire thirteen in a row before Kevin Kiermaier clicked a misplaced slider for a solo home run to right. The tall Texas southpaw struck out the next batter, Mike Zunino, to end the fifth and record his 201st career postseason strikeout, passing John Smoltz (199) on the all-time playoff strikeout list and becoming only the second pitcher ever to have 200 or more playoff strikeouts. He will have a chance to be tops all-time, if he gets another start in the series. Justin Verlander sits atop that list with 205. Kershaw struck out a total of eight Rays over six innings and threw just 78 pitches to get closer to his 12th playoff win. A two-run blast in the fourth by Bellinger would give Kershaw a 2–0 cushion.

As good as Kershaw was, a certain superstar right fielder was making Dodger fans jump out of their seats and Red Sox fans smack their foreheads in disgust. Mookie Betts put a solid down payment on a World Series MVP award. He was absolutely spectacular and showed, again, why the Dodgers did what they had to do to acquire him. After a quiet first half of the game, Betts was walked by starter Tyler Glasnow. It was one of a career-high six walks for the flame-throwing right-hander with a slow move to the plate. Betts took advantage of Glasnow's inability to hold runners and promptly swiped second. This was the second time in his career that he provided anyone who wanted a free Doritos Locos Taco from Taco Bell. A shaken Glasnow walked Corey Seager. After a close pickoff attempt on Betts at second, the two orchestrated a double steal to put runners at second and third, and the Go-Go Dodgers were in business. The last team to steal three bases in a single inning in a World Series game were the 1912 New York Giants in Game 6 against the Red Sox.

With runners at second and third and one out, the Rays infield was playing in to cut down a run at the plate. Muncy hit a sharp grounder slightly to the right of first baseman Edwin Díaz, who made a slick grab and a quick throw to the plate in the same motion, but Betts was running on contact and had a great secondary lead and the perfect jump. Joey Wendle at third was well off the bag, guarding the hole against the lefty, Muncy. This allowed Betts to get a better lead and was the difference in beating the throw home with a headfirst slide to make it 3–1.

"Once I get on the base paths, I am just trying to touch home. However I get there is how I get there, but I'm going to be aggressive on the base paths," Betts said after the game.

The display with his legs was like gasoline on a fire, as the Dodgers added three more runs, making it 6–1. Betts was far from done, as he led off the bottom of the seventh with his second career World Series home run. Ironically, Betts's first homer in the Fall Classic had come off of Kershaw in the fifth inning of the decisive fifth game at Dodger Stadium in 2018. Back-to-back doubles by Turner and Muncy continued the boat race and got the score to 8–1.

Kershaw left the game and the Rays scratched out two runs, but it was barely a dent. Betts added another base hit in the eighth. Some more historical perspective on Mookie's game: he is the only player to walk and steal two bases in the same inning of a World Series game other than Babe Ruth, who turned the trick for the Yankees in 1921, in Game 2 against the Giants. It was also, by coincidence, in the fifth inning. Also, by coincidence, both Betts and the Bambino did it the very next season, after being traded away by the Red Sox. The Curse of the Bambino's World Series drought lasted from 1918 to 2004 in Boston. Will there now be the Malediction of Mookie in Beantown for the next eight decades? Only time will tell.

Following the game, Betts's teammates couldn't wait to heap praise on him. "We are so lucky to have him on our team. He is a superstar guy, superstar talent, but he does all the little things right," said Bellinger.

Austin Barnes added, "The pressure Mookie puts on the other team is huge. We've felt it before in the World Series. He brings a different element to the game for us."

Kershaw was a beneficiary of the play of Betts, along with a fortunate seventh-inning double play started by relief pitcher Victor González. The Rays had put two on the board and had two on, with Zunino up. The Rays catcher smoked a ball up the middle that landed right in the glove of González, who had not yet completed his follow through after releasing the pitch. Kiké Hernández was now at second base and actually broke the other way, so he would not have had a play if the ball was past the pitcher. It was hit so hard that González, realizing the ball was in his glove, had to wait for Hernández to change direction and get back to the bag to accept a throw that completed the timely twin kill.

"I hit it well, and after seeing the replay it was a little more frustrating," Zunino said. "If it gets by, who knows what happens?" What happened was that the Dodgers took a one-game-to-none World Series lead.

OCTOBER 21, 2020. WORLD SERIES GAME 2. BULLPENNING BACKFIRE

The Dodgers tried to out-Ray the Rays, using their own plan against them, but it turned out to be the wrong solution. Seven different pitchers were used to cover 27 outs. During the 1981 World Series, the Dodgers used seven pitchers *total* to win four games against the Yankees and capture the Fall Classic. In 1963, the Dodgers only used four pitchers to sweep the Yankees. Sandy Koufax pitched complete-game victories in Games 1 and 4, Ron Perranoski saved Game 2 for Johnny Podres, and Don Drysdale went the route and won Game 3. If that doesn't give you an idea of just one way the game has changed, or, as many like to say, "evolved," I don't know what will.

Winning tonight and going up 2-0 in the series could be huge. Teams that take a 2-0 lead in the World Series, which has happened on 56 occasions, win 80.4 percent of the time. Also, teams that go two games to none have won the World Series twelve consecutive times and have brought home the big prize eighteen of the last nineteen times. Winning tonight is big, but losing is not the end of the world.

Tony Gonsolin is tabbed to start the game, and internally the plan is to have him get through the top of the order and maybe, depending on his performance, let him get through the order once. He got designated hitter Austin Meadows to pop up to Corey Seager at short and then faced struggling second baseman Brandon Lowe (pronunciation rhymes with cow). Manager Kevin Cash had to be getting close to sequestering Lowe after compiling abysmal postseason batting stats. Lowe had been 5 for 56 (.089 avg.) with 19 strikeouts in 15 games. The count was three balls and one strike, and Gonsolin released a 95 mph fastball. Lowe took a healthy cut and barreled up a ball that left the bat at 106 mph and went over the right field wall: 1–0 Tampa.

Gonsolin faced only two men in the second, walking one, before being replaced by Dylan Floro, who was good. The former Rays pitcher went an inning and a third and kept the Dodgers out of trouble. Victor González came on in the fourth and got into trouble immediately. Once he reached the three-batter minimum, he was replaced by Dustin May. May was tagged for two hits and a run in the fourth and, in the fifth with two outs, allowed a single to Meadows and the microwaveable Lowe launched his second home run of the game. Joe Kelly allowed a run on two hits while striking out two in the sixth. Lefty Alex Wood hurled two scoreless frames, while Jake McGee mopped up with a scoreless ninth.

At the plate, this was a different game for the Dodgers. The home hitters struck out 15 times with far too many swings and misses at middle-middle fastballs. The 2018 American League Cy Young Award winner, Blake Snell, pitched one of his better games, locating the fastball and landing a number of backdoor breaking balls to right-handed hitters. The Dodgers made him work for it, but they came up almost empty. Snell was working on a no-hitter until he walked Kiké Hernández with two outs. That walk left the door cracked for Chris Taylor, who forced the first Dodger hit of the game over the right field wall to make the score 5–2 and get the Dodgers on the board. Snell, who was cruising, watched things begin to unravel and was lifted after four and two-thirds. While he was an out away from qualifying for a win, he left with a lead. In the past, you would see many managers give starting pitchers an opportunity to pitch for the win, especially if they only needed one out, but the Rays don't play that game. Kevin

Cash has made it clear to his staff that the only win that matters is the team win.

Will Smith and Seager hit solo home runs in the sixth and eighth innings respectively, but the Dodgers did not put up a fight in the ninth. Lefty Aaron Loup whiffed Edwin Rios looking and got Austin Barnes to fly to left. Cash brought in the burly closer, Diego Castillo, who got Taylor swinging for the one-out vulture save while securing a 6–4 Rays win for Tampa Bay's second-ever World Series game win. They won one against the Phillies in 2008.

Whatever strong feelings of victory and goodwill that were washing over Dodger Nation after the Game 1 win have come to a screeching halt. During the middle innings, I had the feeling this game had the chance to go the wrong way, but I have witnessed the Dodgers come back in the late innings time after time. They simply swung and missed too many times. The Rays were able to record a low twelve of twenty-seven outs when the ball was put in play and only ten times did the Dodgers put the ball in play in fair territory. That will not win many games.

Tomorrow is an off day. In the World Series, the off day replicates what would normally be a travel day and gives the pitchers an extra day of rest. Not by coincidence, there was an NFL game between the Eagles and Giants televised on Fox on Thursday night that would have been right in the same time slot as a World Series game. I am sure that football game was scheduled a long time ago, before the abbreviated MLB schedule was worked out.

OCTOBER 23, 2020. WORLD SERIES GAME 3. BUTANE IGNITES VS. GROUND CHUCK

It is a Friday, so MLB has issued their latest testing results. All around the country cases are up. The president has been saying that "when you have more testing, you have more cases." I am sorry, but basic math doesn't work that way. We have more cases because we have a lot of virus! This past week there were 3,597 samples and zero positives for fifty-four straight days without a positive test among players or staff. With a week or so to go in the 2020 season, a collective sigh of relief will be exhaled soon. Make no mistake, however, there will be severe lingering effects from the coronavirus as baseball is headed into a dark time, with more layoffs and furloughs expected and unknown economic mountains to be climbed. For most teams, they may not return to their financial summits for a long time to come.

The weather in the Dallas/Fort Worth Metroplex took a bit of a turn today. So far, temperatures have been in the 80s for Dodgers games with only a little bit of wind. Earlier today, there was thunder and lightning, the wind was howling, and temperatures had dropped into the upper 50s. The temp climbed to 74 by game time, but MLB made the decision to close the roof for the first time this postseason, even though they had hoped to keep it open for fan and player safety. We will see if the ball carries.

For a guy with the first name of "Walker," Buehler sure does strike a lot of guys out. I used to work with former Phillies, Braves, and longtime Pirates pitcher Bob Walk on Pirates radio and TV games, and always thought that would be a tough name to wear as a pitcher. Maybe the most productive name ever was Early Wynn, who was a switch-hitting right-handed pitcher who won 300 games over 23 seasons with the Senators, Indians, and White Sox. Buehler's first name could be anything else because the guy can flat out pitch and is building one of the better big-game resumes in the sport. As well as he pitched tonight, I still think the best game I ever saw him pitch was Game 3 of the World Series in 2018 at Dodger Stadium against the Red Sox. He gave up two hits over seven marvelous innings, carving up the best-hitting team in baseball that year. He would get a no decision as the game went eighteen innings and took a record seven hours and twenty minutes to complete, before Max Muncy walked it off with an opposite field home run off Nate Eovaldi that sent this bleary-eyed and weak-voiced broadcaster to bed.

Buehler pitched to Tampa Bay as though they were snoozing. It lined up to be a great pitching matchup as veteran right-hander Charlie Morton was on the hill for the Rays. Morton has really figured it out in recent years. When he was a young pitcher with the Braves, they were not sure what they had. Folks from the organization told me that they didn't think he was mentally tough enough, prompting a trade to Pittsburgh for outfielder Nate McLouth. With the Pirates, Morton began to grow, and his two-seam fastball, at times, was as nasty as we see now with Dustin May. He got so many ground balls off of his two-seamer that he earned the nickname, "Ground Chuck."

I remember former Pittsburgh catcher Ryan Doumit, who occasionally played first base, relaying a story about Morton. One night in St. Louis, Albert Pujols, in his prime at the time and one of the toughest outs in the game, was walked by Morton. When Pujols got to first he said to Doumit, "I am glad he walked me. I can't hit that guy." Pujols was then baseball's version of Superman, and he was telling Doumit that Morton was his Kryptonite. Once he left Pittsburgh for Philadelphia, he learned to rely on his curveball more and the two-seamer less. When he went to the Astros they told him to throw his four-seamer more, which he did, getting his velocity up to 97 mph on a regular basis. Morton became a World Series hero in 2017. I know…I know…2017 Astros…but Morton still had to throw the baseball, and he didn't hit. Did he benefit from the cheating scandal? Perhaps, but he was still good and didn't cheat.

It took only three batters for Morton to realize that this night was going to be different. He had been nearly flawless in the postseason so far and hadn't given up more than one run in a playoff game since the ALCS in 2018. Justin Turner stepped in after Mookie Betts and Corey Seager had made outs. On the fourth pitch, Morton left a 95 mph fastball up in the zone and Turner crushed it for a quick 1–0 lead. That home run, his 11th career postseason homer, tied the great Duke Snider for the most postseason round trippers by a Dodger. Turner would double in the third, reaching another milestone. His 18th career playoff double tied Braves Hall of Famer Chipper Jones for the most postseason doubles in history. Muncy would drive in Turner and Seager, who was hit in the right foot by a pitch, to make it 3–0.

The Dodgers would add two more in the fourth against Morton. Bellinger led off the inning with a single through a gaping hole in the middle of the infield, with the Rays employing their four-man outfield alignment. Joc Pederson advanced Bellinger to third with a single down the first base line. With one out and the nine hitter, Austin Barnes, at the plate, Dave Roberts pushed the right button. Barnes pulled off a perfectly executed safety squeeze, laying it down the first base side and allowing Bellinger to walk in with the Dodgers' fourth run. Bunts have been leaning toward extinction during the COVID-19 season since the DH is employed in both leagues. I hope we go back to NL rules for the 2021 season at least, before MLB and the Players Association puts them in mothballs for good, once they finalize the next collective bargaining agreement. Pederson came in to score on a Betts base hit to make it 5–0. Morton lasted four and a third innings and was charged for five earned runs while striking out six. "I never really felt comfortable out there. Combine that with who they are with the bat and it made for a rough night," Morton admitted after the game.

Barnes was again a factor offensively, with two outs in the sixth, when he got around on a hanging slider from reliever John Curtiss and blasted his first career World Series home run. It was the fifth run of the six scored that came with two outs, and each of the runs scored when the batter had a two-strike count. This has happened 36 times this postseason, the most in history. Two-out lightning has been the calling card for this Dodger team during the playoffs, scoring 50 runs so far in two-out situations, another mark that is more than any other team in history.

A man who speaks from experience, Mookie Betts, told the press after the game, "Obviously there are two outs, but you can still build an inning…not give away at-bats. That's just the recipe for that. That's how you win a World Series."

Buehler, the twenty-six-year-old burgeoning ace from Lexington, Kentucky, spun six remarkable innings, allowing one run on three hits, and struck out ten for the first time in his playoff career. In fact, in his two career World Series starts he has allowed only the one run on five hits, with 17 total punch-outs in 13 innings pitched. Buehler is beginning to identify as an October Legend. He is not there yet, but it won't take much longer with these kinds of performances. "I haven't wrapped my head around all that he's accomplished in such a short period of time," Dave Roberts reflected after the game. "Being a big-game pitcher and really succeeding on this stage…there are only a few guys around currently and in history. He's in some really elite company."

No big deal for Buehler. "I think the more you do these things, the calmer you get," said the icy-veined pitcher. "I don't want to keep harping on it, but I enjoy doing this and I feel good in these spots." One of the main things I like about watching Buehler is he has an edginess to him when he is on the mound. This is not a bad thing. He is ultra-competitive and lets the opposition know it. And he backs it up big time.

So far, according to Stats, LLC, the Dodgers' starting pitchers have held the Rays to a .133 average (6 for 45), which is the lowest batting average allowed by a team's starters through the first three games of the World Series since the Boston Red Sox held the Philadelphia Phillies to a .129 average in 1915. The '15 Red Sox would win the series in five games.

Kenley Jansen came on to work the bottom of the ninth and looked great…for the first two hitters. He left a fastball over the plate to the third hitter, Randy Arozarena, who ran into it for a solo home run. Jansen quickly got the next hitter, Ji-Man Choi, to line to left and end the game.

OCTOBER 24, 2020. WORLD SERIES GAME 4. DOUBLE JEOPARDY

"It ain't over 'till it's over"—YOGI BERRA

The opportunity in front of the Dodgers tonight could swing the series heavily in their favor, and they will be relying on the bats to back up twenty-four-year-old Mexican left-hander, Julio Urías. Urías has been excellent this postseason, so good that his six postseason wins are more than any other pitcher under twenty-five years old, all-time. This year, he has four playoff wins and is creeping up on some good company. Most recently, Stephen Strasburg of the Nationals in 2019 won five, Francisco Rodríguez, or K-Rod, as he was better known, won five for the Angels in his rookie season of 2002, and the Big Unit, Randy Johnson, also won five for Arizona in 2001.

Urías, exceptionally talented and not yet in his prime, had some ups and downs during the regular season, leading some to refer to him as "Curious" Urías. There has been nothing curious about him in the postseason, however, as he has been dominant on the bump. Position players have a sixth sense about pitchers when they are on the mound and can feel the confidence that spreads as those pitchers perform. Not every pitcher gives the guys playing behind him a secure feeling, but lately, Julio has been making everyone feel especially safe.

The Dodgers started the top of the first inning the same as the night before. Betts and Seager made outs before Justin Turner hit one out of the yard for a quick point. Turner's twelfth postseason home run moved him past Duke Snider for the most by a Dodger. He also became the first player in World Series history to hit first-inning home runs in back-to-back games. Another day, another two-out run scored by the Dodgers. Tonight, though, they would score every run of the seven they put on the board with two outs, bringing the postseason two-out run total to 57. A home run by Seager in the second made it 2–0. It was the eighth playoff homer for Seager this year, marking the most by a shortstop ever, and his eleventh career postseason dinger.

The home run was huge for Tampa Bay, as Randy Arozarena led off the fourth with one then Hunter Renfroe started the fifth with another. Urías certainly could have lived with giving up two solo bombs, but the one he didn't allow hurt the most. With the Dodgers up 4–2 and two men on, Pedro Báez came in to relieve Blake Treinen. The first batter Báez faced, Brandon Lowe, came up with a big swing for the third time this series to put the Rays up 5–4. The Dodgers would retake the lead in the top of the seventh on a two-out two-run single by pinch hitter Joc Pederson that barely glanced off the webbing of the glove of Lowe, who was positioned in shallow right field and diving to his right, to make it 6–5; Kevin Kiermaier lost one in the seats against Báez in the bottom of inning to tie it at six. The Dodgers seesawed back into the lead, 7–6, on an RBI single by Seager, scoring Chris Taylor, who doubled to lead off the inning. Things were only beginning to get interesting.

Lefty Adam Kolarek and "the Bazooka" Brusdar Graterol each went two-thirds of an inning and hung zeros to get to the bottom of the ninth. Kenley Jansen was coming off of two really solid outings, but Dodger fans were still nervous. If one would turn back the clock a couple of years, they would be confident that this game was over with "Kenleyfornia Love" coming into the game for the save. Japanese import Yoshi Tsutsugo pinch hit for catcher Mike Zunino and struck out swinging. One down and two to go. Kiermaier had his bat sawed in half and blooped a one-out single just past the outstretched Kiké Hernández in shallow right center. He stood at first representing the tying run while still holding what remained of the bat handle. Joey Wendle, a lefty, came off the bench to pinch hit for Yandy Díaz and flied to Pederson in left for the second out. Two down and one to get for a commanding three-games-to-one lead.

It is easy to argue that Randy Arozarena is the hottest hitter on the planet. He is not the guy you want at the plate right now with the game on the line. You can't walk him and put the potential winning run on, but you don't want to give him anything to hit right now. Jansen battled him but ended up issuing the free pass, and the Rays put the tying run in scoring position and the winning run on with two outs. Kevin Cash was short on the bench and sent up little-used Brett Phillips, who had been acquired by from Kansas City on August 27. Phillips had not come to the plate in 23 days. October baseball magnifies everything, and it is players like Phillips that sometimes become heroes. Jansen got ahead of him and got the count to one ball and two strikes. The Dodgers were one measly strike away.

Jansen, in his deliberate fashion, settled into the stretch position. He lifted his front (left) foot and pushed his body toward the plate. While pushing off the rubber with his driving right leg he released his calling card: the cutter. It approached the plate and didn't cut much. Phillips got the bat around and hit a sinking line drive into right center. Bellinger was the DH on this night due to tightness in his lower back, so he was on the bench. A.J. Pollock had started in center, but when he was lifted for a pinch hitter, Taylor moved from left to center. Keirmaier was running on contact and had a good jump. He was not going to stop until he got to the plate. Taylor had to move in and to his left to play the ball. He was trying to be aggressive with a chance to throw Kiermaier out at the plate and end the game. It wouldn't be the first time, as he had done it from left in a game against the Padres earlier in the season. The ball didn't cooperate on the two-hopper that bounced off the artificial surface, hitting the edge of the web of Taylor's glove and glancing several feet away.

Arozarena was running aggressively and had rounded third base, but he slipped and fell on his way to the plate. Phillips was trying to get in a run-down, but the Dodgers treated him as though he were invisible. Taylor recovered the ball and threw it to Max Muncy, the cut-off man. Muncy turned and relayed the ball to catcher Will Smith. The throw was a little bit to Smith's right, so he had to reach across his body to catch it. He was not aware that Arozarena had picked himself up and started back to third base. Smith apparently thought Arozarena was still coming, and would have had no way of knowing that he wasn't, so he attempted a catch and sweep tag in the same motion. The ball bounced out of the web of his glove. Arozarena realized it and reversed direction again, rumbling to the plate to score the winning run with a headfirst slide. The Dodgers were stunned. While Arozarena was still laid out and slapping home plate with his right palm, Phillips was running around the infield with his arms extended like the wings of an airplane.

Jansen pitched well. He didn't give up any hard-hit balls. The only thing he didn't do well was back up the plate on the throw home and, for some reason, was positioned several feet up the third base line. It was double jeopardy, as Jansen didn't pitch poorly to deserve the criticism he received and there were two errors charged on the play; one to Taylor for bobbling the ball and one to Smith for dropping it. It was the first time in World Series history that a game ended on a double error. The Rays tied the series up at two despite being one strike away from being down three games to one. That's baseball. Sometimes the game loves you, other times it breaks your heart.

After the game a somber Dave Roberts expressed his thoughts. "They were the best team in the American League. Those guys fight."

His counterpart in the Rays dugout returned the compliment: "They get early runs. We answer back. Then they answer again. We just couldn't stop them, and that is a credit to how talented that club is top to bottom."

The Rays won 8–7 in walk-off fashion. Due to the game ending on two errors, it is not technically a walk-off win. They didn't care, and got to enjoy the night and experience all the elation that comes with an emotional victory like that. That game was one for the ages, an instant World Series Classic. The Dodgers had a job to do now, and that was to forget what just happened and focus on Game 5.

OCTOBER 25, 2020. WORLD SERIES GAME 5. KERSHAW CLAMPDOWN

The calming presence of future Hall of Famer Clayton Kershaw is being felt around the Dodger clubhouse and in the dugout. Less than twenty hours ago, the Rays pulled off a stunning defeat. The Dodgers have scrubbed that game off with a wire brush and moved on to today. Baseball players are wired, from an early stage of their development, to think compartmentally. What happened yesterday, or five minutes ago, isn't going to change, so it is immediately relegated to the past. A player doesn't dwell on failure. Every day is a rebirth in the game of baseball where yesterday matters none.

Tyler Glasnow was making his second career World Series start after taking the loss in Game 1 against Kershaw. A couple of seasons ago, the six-foot eight-inch right-hander was probably involved in one of the most one-sided trades in recent history. Glasnow was a fifth-round pick of the Pirates in 2011 and was developing well with them. Outfielder Austin Meadows was taken by Pittsburgh in the first round two years later. Those two, along with a solid relief arm in Shane Baz, another first round pick in 2017, went to Tampa for right-handed starter Chris Archer. Archer has been hurt a lot with the Pirates, and it is painfully obvious now that he is on the back nine of his career. One Pirates executive, when I asked why they would make such a trade, told me, "Well, we had to do something."

It took only two batters for the Dodgers to do something against Glasnow tonight. Mookie led off the game with a double and scored two pitches later when Corey Seager hit a curveball for a single. If you blinked, you probably missed it. Two wild pitches and a Cody Bellinger single later, the Dodgers were up 2–0. Joc Pederson showed some "Joctober" action and led off the second with a 428-foot smash that he admired all the way out of the yard to make it 3–0.

In the bottom of the third, the Rays got on the board when Kevin Kiermaier led off with an infield single. Mike Zunino struck out looking before Yandy Díaz hit a run-scoring triple into the right field corner. Randy Arozarena got Díaz in with a single while recording his 27th hit of the postseason, a new record. Brandon Lowe struck out swinging, and Arozarena, who was on the move to second, got gunned down by Austin Barnes for a "strike 'em out, throw 'em out" inning-ending double play.

The bottom of the fourth inning was tense. Kershaw walked the first batter, Manuel Margot. Margot was a Red Sox prospect who was traded along with three others to the Padres in the deal that saw them lock down closer Craig Kimbrel to Fenway. Margot was acquired by Tampa before spring training in 2020, after playing in the Dominican Winter League for Toros del Este in La Romana. He just happened to be playing center for the eventual LIDOM champions during a game my family and I attended in La Romana this past December. The Dodgers suspected Margot would try to steal. Kershaw used his good pickoff move and Max Muncy slapped the tag on Margot as he dove safely back to first. It was close enough that Dave Roberts asked for a video review, but the call was upheld. On the next pitch to Hunter Renfroe, Margot broke for second and had the bag stolen, but the throw from Barnes sailed and second baseman Chris Taylor did not catch it. Margot went to third and Taylor was charged with an error. Renfroe then walked. Back-to-back walks by Kershaw, runners at the corners, and nobody out. Joey Wendle popped up to Seager and Willy Adames struck out. At this point, Margot took a huge gamble. Kershaw has a big stretch, placing both arms as high as they can go over his head. Being a lefty, his back is to the runner at third. With two outs and Justin Turner playing off the bag against the left-handed-hitting Kiermaier, Margot extended his lead. He had been timing Kershaw's move to the plate and was preparing a major move.

The only way Kershaw could know if a runner breaks for home is if the first baseman lets him know. Muncy was on it. He yelled at his fellow Texan, "…going home!" Without looking, Kershaw stepped off the rubber and sent the ball to Barnes, who got the tag down on a head-first-sliding Margot in the nick of time to snuff out the gutsy straight steal attempt and keep the tying run off the scoreboard. This was the turning point of this ballgame.

Muncy hit a no-doubt blast with two outs in the top of the fifth on a 99 mph Glasnow fastball. Max enjoys watching the flight of the ball maybe more than any other Dodger. He knew it was gone on contact, flicked the bat out in front of him, and got a good view of it, as it took him a while to get to first base. The Muncy bomb made it 4–2 and it was time to declare "Code Red" from the bullpen. Dustin May has had a few struggles this World Series, but Dave Roberts and first year pitching coach Mark Prior's conversation with him this week about how much confidence that they have in him may have helped. May went a scoreless inning and two-thirds, striking out Margot for the third out of the sixth. Kershaw got the first two outs of the inning on just two pitches, and the fact that he was coming out of the ball game might have been confusing to many.

The Dodgers went in with a plan for Kershaw, and that plan was that he would face 21 hitters and be done. *But he just got two outs on two pitches and is sitting on 85 pitches. Why take him out? Let him face the next man with no one on and a two-run lead, right?* Not exactly. One of the things a manager gets criticized for most is whether he took a pitcher out too soon or left him in too long. Roberts has been hammered by the fans and press for this in the past, especially regarding Kershaw. "That was the plan. We talked about it before the inning and though it was just two pitches…we stuck with the plan," Kershaw said after the game. "So, credit to Doc for that one, and D. May came in the threw the ball awesome and Victor and Blake, too. Unbelievable job by those guys tonight."

Victor González and Blake Treinen, pitching for the third consecutive day, clamped down on the Rays, combining to throw an inning and two-thirds scoreless, with Treinen closing the game. Jansen had his fill of drama the night before.

The Dodgers are up three games to two and have the upper hand in the World Series with a day off and a Texas BBQ dinner coming. My gut tells me they would trade the day off to get right back on the field, but a day off is huge for the arms to get some much-needed rest. Game 6 on Tuesday night becomes close to an all-hands-on-deck situation, with Kershaw unavailable and Urías and Buehler unlikely. Buehler and Urías could be saved for a possible Game 7, but if the right opportunity presented itself, Julio was most likely to get called into action. Who knows if we have seen the last of Kershaw in this series. Whatever happens the rest of the way, Kershaw's postseason legacy has changed for the better, as he's gone 2-0 in this series and was dominant in Game 1. The Dodgers now have a chance to wrap up their first World Series since 1988.

OCTOBER 27, 2020. WORLD SERIES GAME 6. WAIT FOR THE PLOT TWIST

It's 39 degrees out and a cool mist consumes the air. The roof will be closed for tonight's possible World Series-clinching game. Realistically, this series could already be over, if not for the bullpen breaking down in Game 2 and Game 4's two-out, two-strike, two-error, two-run play that flipped the game in favor of the Rays. There are hundreds of fans who have driven to Dodger Stadium to be together in a packed parking lot to watch this game on the big screen like they are at a drive-in movie, creating an atmosphere of community based around their love of the Dodgers.

Today's *LA Times* ran a story by Rong-Gong Lin II and Iris Lee about how local health officials are alarmed that Lakers and Dodgers fans congregating to view games and celebrate wins are ignoring protocols and possibly contributing to the spread of the virus. *"Public health officials have identified gatherings as a significant source of virus transmission in Southern California, where young adults are driving the spread of the highly contagious disease,"* it said. Cases have risen on a per-week basis in Southern California during the first week in October to twelve hundred new cases each day as of last week, according to LA County's director of public health. With cases spiking all over the country and the spikes expected to get worse as we head into winter, the hope is that we don't go so far backwards that we have to lock down again. Baseball will prevail in 2020, however, and will finish the entire schedule on time. The hope for LA is that it ends tonight.

Knowing you have a game cushion if you need it is not something that the Dodger players want in the back of their heads. As players, they are focused on winning the game in front of them. "We're not worried about a second chance, we are just worried about tonight. We're going to do whatever we can to win a ballgame tonight," Justin Turner said in a pre-game presser. Turner and his teammates would have something much more important to worry about just a few hours later.

The numbers coming into this game were rather one-sided, considering Tampa Bay was still very much in the series. The Dodgers entered the game hitting .354 with runners in scoring position in the World Series, and an even more impressive .366 with two strikes on the hitter and two outs in the inning, with four home runs in such situations. Eleven home runs have been hit by nine different players. This is something that has never been done in World Series history. There were 59 runs scored with two outs over the course of the postseason; a feat that also had never been accomplished in the history of the Fall Classic.

Randy Arozarena is playing on another level. One has to ask why the Dodgers are even pitching to him at this point. Tony Gonsolin was looking for a good start, and the Dodgers were hoping for five innings from him. Dave Roberts said before the game that Gonsolin was a legit starter and they were hoping for some length. Arozarena was there to upset that plan. Gonsolin struck out Ji-Man Choi to start the game before having to face Arozarena for the first and what would be the only time during the evening. Gonsolin wasn't ready to try his fastball on the hottest hitter on the planet, so he started him off with a slider that was called a strike as Arozarena was clearly taking all the way to get a look at Gonsolin. Tony was sticking to the plan and wanted to induce a chase to get way ahead in the count. Four pitches later, he delivered another slider, but this time he started it over the outer half of the plate and wanted it to end up maybe a foot outside. It did exactly that, but the fifth pitch of the game was swung on with Arozarena getting enough barrel on the baseball to send it over the right field wall for an opposite-field solo home run, giving the Rays a quick 1–0 lead before some of the 11,437 fans could even get in their seats. How did he hit *th*at pitch out? He finished the World Series with a record 29 postseason hits, more than anyone ever.

If the Dodgers wanted to head off into the offseason in a celebratory manner, they would have to find a way past determined Rays left-hander Blake Snell. Snell was very good in Game 2 when he struck out nine over four and two-thirds. On this night it was apparent that Snell had sharpened his sword and was ready to carve up this talented lineup, which is exactly what he did. He punched out five of the first six hitters and nine of the first thirteen. Chris Taylor and Austin Barnes were the only two hitters fortunate enough to sneak in singles against Snell, in the third and sixth innings respectively. Other than that, Snell was absolutely dominant. This was the vintage Cy Young

Snellzilla from 2018. Then, out of the realm of the unexpected, something shocking happened. Following Barnes's one-out single in the sixth, Kevin Cash came out of the first base dugout. He was coming to get Snell. Are you kidding me? The Dodgers had no idea how they were going to solve him, he had only thrown 73 pitches, and he was yanked from the ballgame while shoving a two-hit shutout at the best team in baseball. This is a decision that will haunt Cash and the Rays for the rest of time.

I realize that the Rays are different, that Snell had not pitched past the sixth inning all season, but this is an elimination game in the World Series! Ride the horse that got you there. Whatever happened to managers making decisions with their eyes and guts? The Rays have a system that got them within two wins of a World Series title, but in this game and this moment, Cash stuck with the organizational plan that Snell would not be allowed, no matter what, to face the Dodger lineup a third time, the same lineup he'd been slicing and dicing.

"I believe in me and I believe in what I was doing," the despondent pitcher said following the game. "I didn't walk anybody. For most of that game, man, I was dominating every possible outcome."

Cash put in right-hander Nick Anderson, who had been great during the regular season but had allowed runs in each of his last six appearances during the postseason. The Rays were using their formula of getting to their usually excellent bullpen. The happiest person about this move was Mookie Betts, who'd been tormented by Snell, not only in his first two at-bats, but during his time facing him in the AL East. "I was like, *I got a chance*," a smiling Betts offered after the game. "I wasn't asking any questions, though. I was just like, *Hey, your manager said you gotta go, next guy's coming in*. At that point, I tried to put an at-bat together and go from there…had he stayed in the game, he may have pitched a complete game. Once he came out of the game, it was just a breath of fresh air."

Anderson threw three pitches to Betts, with the third drilled down the left field line for a double. Barnes was held at third. A swinging strike was next on the first pitch to Corey Seager. The next pitch was in the dirt and went to the backstop, allowing Barnes to score the tying run while Betts advanced to third. With the Rays' infield in and Betts getting a good lead, the contact play was on. Seager hit a grounder to first. Betts had a great secondary lead and an even better break on contact. His headfirst slide beat Choi's throw and the Dodgers had their first lead of the game, 2–1. It took only six pitches from Anderson to lose the lead and ultimately the big prize. This was a backfire of epic proportions.

Betts twisted the dagger in Tampa Bay even deeper when leading off the bottom of the eighth with a mammoth 434-foot solo shot to left center off of hard-throwing reliever Pete Fairbanks. Fairbanks used his fastball twice to start the at-bat against Betts, but then hung a slider into another Mookie Moment. It was the second time that Betts had homered in the deciding game of a World Series, as he had also done it in Game 5 against the Dodgers in 2018 at Dodger Stadium. As euphoria was starting to creep into the Dodger dugout with the realization that a world championship was becoming more imminent, something much more sinister had infiltrated the Dodgers' bubble. Justin Turner was missing, replaced at third by Edwin Rios, without explanation, in the top of the eighth. Turner, the heart and soul of this team, was not a player who would be replaced for defense late in a game and was nowhere to be seen.

Sports Medicine Research and Testing Laboratory in South Jordan, Utah, near Salt Lake City, is the lab that has been testing and processing test samples this season. The lab reached out to MLB during the second inning to say that a Dodger player's results from yesterday came back inconclusive. The group of samples in question arrived at the lab later than normal, preventing them from getting any results to MLB before the game. Now the next and most recent set of tests would be looked at with that particular player's test expedited. It would take about two hours. Late in the seventh inning, the lab completed the test and results eventually went through the chain to the Dodgers dugout. It was the top of the eighth and Turner did not run out to his position. The game would go on without him.

Walker Buehler delivered the news to his teammates in the bullpen in the seventh. He went to the bullpen to be with his fellow pitchers and to be ready just in case he was needed, even though he was slated to start Game 7. He passed on the word of Turner's positive test. His teammates thought it was a prank. Buehler had to sell it hard to get his teammates to believe him. Once they saw Rios at third, they knew it was true.

Dave Roberts may have done his best job of handling the pitching staff with the bullpen turning in their best performance of the season, covering seven and a third scoreless innings. The best move that Roberts made, however, was the one he didn't make. Instead of going to the bullpen to close out the ninth and perhaps using a rested Kenley Jansen, as his formula has called for so many times in the past, he left Urías in to finish. He went with feel, using his eyes and his gut. It was a case of going with the hot hand, and Urías was red hot facing the last seven hitters, striking out four, including the last two, pinch hitter Mike Brosseau and shortstop Willy Adames, looking to put a big blue bow on the franchise's first World Series title in thirty-two years.

It had been two months without a positive test for Major League players and staff, and right there during the World Series, a player with the virus was participating in the game. Turner was to be isolated once notified, but once the celebration ensued, he left isolation and joined his team on the field. While his teammates and staff wanted him there because of his contributions and status on the team, he may have been spreading the virus around. Ironically, it had been Turner who led the charge to tighten up protocols back in late July, when he sent a text to some who cover to the team to let us know how over and above the players had decided to go in addition to the already established MLB protocols. He had been out front in sticking to those health and safety measures because he, as well as his teammates, knew they had a team that could win it all. He was the Dodgers' ringleader for following the rules and staying healthy and now would become the poster child for the fact that the virus can infect you no matter who you are or where you are.

Turner sent out a tweet shortly after Game 6:

> *"Thanks to everyone reaching out!! I feel great, no symptoms at all. Just experienced every emotion you can possibly imagine. Can't believe I couldn't be out there to celebrate with my guys! So proud of this team & unbelievably happy for the City of LA. #WorldSeriesChamps"*

There are many questions and thoughts about the bittersweet moment that clouds up such a fabulous time in Dodger history. First, how did he contract the virus while existing in a bubble situation for three weeks? How was he allowed back on the field if contagious? What if the Rays came back and won, then when would a Game 7 have been played? There were far more questions than answers during this time and answers that MLB and the Dodgers will certainly investigate.

MLB dodged a bullet with the Dodgers winning, and the relief expressed by Rob Manfred while presenting the World Series trophy to Chairman Mark Walter and President Stan Kasten was obvious. The team that had set the example on how to play coronavirus-free was now infected and had to stay in Texas longer than anticipated due to further testing. The fallout and the story of Turner's positive test will be felt for a while.

How is it that a pitcher who is throwing a two-hit shutout in the World Series doesn't stay in the game as long as a player who has COVID-19? This might be the most 2020 thing about base-ball in 2020.

Corey Seager was presented with the Willie Mays Award as the Most Valuable Player of the World Series and deserved not only the huge trophy but the brand-new Chevrolet Tahoe that came with it. He also won the NLCS MVP, which only seven other players have accomplished in the same postseason. "This team was incredible all throughout the year," Seager said afterward. "All throughout the postseason, all throughout the quarantine we never stopped. We were ready to go as soon as the bell was called and once it did, we kept rolling."

Much of the post-game attention, aside from Turner, was directed toward Kershaw. Teammates sought him out to hug him and talked to the press about how happy they were for him. Dave Roberts did the same when he accepted the World Series trophy on stage. The pitcher had always been the bridesmaid and never the bride, climbing to the mountaintop but never touching the summit. His two wins and solid playoff performances flipped his legacy from a guy who "can't get it done when it counts," to a guy who did. 2017's World Series probably should not count against him since the Astros batters knew what pitches he was throwing. Having the opportunity to see Kershaw's smile and raw emotion was meaningful, and to see his three kids running around on the field with him was great, too.

Mookie Betts, who doesn't tweet often and does most of his social media on Instagram, sent out a post-game message.

"THE JOB IS FINISHED!!!!! This one's for you LA – the City Champions! Enjoy the hell out of it, but you know these boys aren't done chasing rings!!!"

What's Next?

From spring training in Arizona, to the shutdown and quarantine, to Summer Camp and the 60-game season, this team had one mission. It was Betts who didn't want to step on veteran toes and contacted Kershaw to make sure it was OK with him to address the team the first day at Camelback Ranch about what it takes to win a World Series and why the team should heed his approach. He reminded the team of team weaknesses he saw in the 2018 Dodgers that his Red Sox exploited en route to winning it all. He knew what needed to be changed and what course to follow. Markus Lynn Betts, whose initials, by coincidence, are "M.L.B.," proved to be a leader and a key ingredient in putting this team over the top when it counted most. He was the biggest difference-maker in the game.

Now this 2020 season has been mercifully put to bed and there are changes on the horizon. On the active roster, there are some popular players who are now free agents, like Turner and Hernández and Pederson. First-base coach George Lombard interviewed for the Detroit Tigers managerial position and ended up accepting the Bench Coach position under new manager A.J. Hinch. Franchises will continue to streamline in the wake of a reported three billion dollars in losses, and good baseball people will lose jobs. Baseball is being forced into a reset, economically and organizationally.

In the very near future, I expect to see teams approve any means possible to add revenue streams such as more advertising on the field, and even on uniforms. There could even be naming rights deals for some of the classic ballparks like Yankee Stadium, Fenway Park, and Dodger Stadium. There will be more conversations about expansion. There will be a discussion about realignment so teams can save on travel expenses. Look for more proliferation of the sports betting industry intertwining with the game and each team's broadcasts and digital platforms. Imagine digital sports book apps that interface with each team's fanbase with the teams themselves getting a percentage of the overall handle. MLB has sent people to Las Vegas to essentially shakedown the sports books for an "integrity fee" for allowing them to use the teams' logos and "official information." The sports books collectively told MLB to take a hike, so the league is realizing, with the exception of one major property with which they are involved in a marketing deal, the MGM, they will have to do it themselves.

This pandemic will have far-reaching effects on the game, with the possibility of the temporary rule changes like two seven-inning games for doubleheaders and the "placed runner" in extra innings rule becoming permanent. The game will be impacted by the loss of valuable human resources in every department across the board, and what the game will look like in 2021 remains to be seen. The vaccines are rolling out, with Dodger Stadium being the largest site to get one in Southern California, but when will they take full effect, and when will fans be free to fill the ballparks again? The franchises need to have fans, and full capacity at stadiums is crucial. Without fans, there is no industry, and this industry is desperate to have its fans return. When they can, they will return in droves, and at some point, the base-ball industry will thrive again. When that time comes, there probably will be thirty-two teams, with sixteen in the west and sixteen in the east. The line between the American League and National League may blur and possibly disappear someday. Forget pitchers ever hitting again. The DH is more than likely to be in both leagues for sure after 2021, even when the NL reverts back to its original rules for one last defiant season.

What's Next?

This severely infectious virus has been game-changing and life-changing for many. Dodger fans should be grateful and thrilled about the World Series victory that they have waited so patiently for. The team issued a press release basically stating that there will be a celebration or even a parade of some sort, but whatever it is will have to be put off for now.

The day after the World Series concluded, and following more testing at 2:00 a.m. upon returning to the hotel from the ballpark, the players and families were tested with nose swabs. Later in the day, following a few hours of rest, the Rays were cleared to fly back to Florida. The Dodgers tested negative and were able to fly back to LA except for Turner and his wife Kourtney, who stayed behind in Texas. *USA Today* reported, citing anonymous sources within one or both the Dodgers and Rays, that the members of both teams had to self-quarantine for fourteen days upon arriving home. The Turners reportedly had to charter a private plane to get back home to Southern California. The Dodger players were tested again after returning to Dodger Stadium and were told they could only drive home or charter private planes. No commercial travel was allowed at the risk of exposing others.

This baseball season was a welcome and necessary distraction at one of the most difficult times in our nation's history, that helped to bring some semblance of normalcy and a glimpse of what can be again in the future. There were a multitude of unprecedented adjustments, and those involved seemed to get used to the piped-in crowd noise and spectatorless stadiums. The season that many didn't think would be completed was, in fact, completed against the odds and left many fans anxious for the start of the next spring training. I was along for this ride in 2020 and these are my observations and interpretations. Due to being on the bench more than I was on the air, I had time to write what you've been reading and gained more awareness of what was going on around me. As it was, the 2020 season will be remembered for the good, the bad, and the ugly. It will be remembered for how it started, the effort to make it happen, the abbreviated schedule, the divisional realignment, the rule changes, the chaos that COVID caused for certain teams, and the great World Series that concluded it all.

The 2020 Dodgers, right up to the finish line, stayed focused, their eyes squarely on the prize. They set a goal, stuck with the process, and achieved it. There will understandably be some who say that the title should have an asterisk because it was only a 60-game season. I don't agree and hope you don't either. The difficulty factor of going through this season with strict limitations and constant testing will factor in when it comes to what it took from every individual involved to complete the season. Those who were involved and who took part realize just how much more difficult this season was to pull off than a "normal" much longer season. There will be no asterisk, nor should there be one.

From The Bulldog in 1988 to The Cat Man in 2020, a lot of personalities and great talent have worn Dodger uniforms for the thirty-two years between championships and have all worked to accomplish the feat that the team pulled off. The Dodgers franchise, its players, staff, and employees are proud of what occurred this season and what it took, in every aspect, to get through it. We will never forget it. For me, it is the second time in the last three years I have been fortunate enough to be with a World Series-winning club, but with all the obstacles and all the hurdles that had to be negotiated this season, this one was the more impressive.

Now, as the Dodgers and their vast fan base bask in the glow of a World Series Championship, we who are employed in the baseball world do a reality check, collectively hold our breath, and wait for what comes next.

Epilogue

Over the course of the long and bone-chilling offseason, one could only wonder what the 2021 MLB season would look like. The many iterations that were bandied about among colleagues and friends were plentiful, and most were wrong. Whether to start on time or delay the season by a month was a major issue battled over between the league and the Players Union. The Union won and we started on time. There are a number of reasons the MLBPA wanted an on-time start that were more important to them, and they held the hammer, so it is off to work we go on a full 162-game schedule.

Vaccines are rolling out, slower than most had hoped at first, but things have sped up dramatically. On a recent Dodgers pre-spring training employee Zoom call with Dodgers President Stan Kasten and Magic Johnson, Kasten was "cautiously optimistic" that some socially distanced fans would be allowed into Dodger Stadium at an early point of the season, and was hopeful that the number of fans allowed in for 2021 would gradually grow. Magic, part of the Dodgers' ownership group, was very motivational, with a positive look ahead to 2021. He is great at making people feel good about themselves and about what they are doing.

The coronavirus is still with us, but we have better ideas how to work around it than we did when it first hit. We will not have a normal start to the Dodger broadcasts in 2021, either. We will call the games on television and the radio/TV simulcasts off of monitors from the SportsNet LA studios in El Segundo and not on-site in Arizona. This will be challenging for spring training games especially but will be handled. Also, it is expected that the broadcasters will not travel to road games, calling them remotely, at least for a while, maybe the entire season. Time will tell.

Time will also tell whether the Dodgers can repeat as World Series Champions. The addition of current NL Cy Young Award winner Trevor Bauer should add even more firepower to an already-potent pitching staff. The return of fan-favorite Justin Turner is another solid move, and some key additions to the bullpen will shore up that department. Whatever the conditions, 2021 has the potential to be as memorable, if not more so, than the COVID-infected 2020 season. The best news about baseball in 2021 is that there will be fans back in the seats to share and experience the games in person. We don't know what the numbers will be, and they will vary state to state and county to county, but fans will be back. There is finally some light at the end of the tunnel, and we are getting closer to reaching it.

Thanks so much for reliving the 2020 Dodgers World Championship season with me. I am very happy to be back in the Dodgers booth this season with Rick Monday, Charley Steiner, Duane McDonald, Joe Davis, Orel Hershiser, Nomar Garciaparra, Mike Levy, and to welcome Kirsten Watson. Our friends behind the scenes at SportsNet LA and AM 570 LA Sports along with the Dodgers' outstanding social media department do such a great job bringing you the sights and sounds of Dodger Baseball. I am honored to be part of it and honored you took the time to read to this point of the book. Let's kick COVID-19 and have another great season of Major League Baseball. Hopefully, I will see you at a World Series parade sometime soon!

Acknowledgments

Thanks so much to Craig Caples, Don Logan, the late Robert J. Blum, Ken Miller, and Marc Garda, and especially my late parents, Bill and Sheila Neverett. I will never be able to re-pay your collective belief in me.

About the Author

Tim Neverett is a play-by-play broadcaster on radio and television for the Los Angeles Dodgers, joining the club before the 2019 season, and this is his first attempt at a book. His baseball broadcasting career began in 1985, at age nineteen, announcing games for the AA Nashua Pirates of the Eastern League. He worked in AAA for ten seasons broadcasting games for the Dodgers and Padres affiliates, moving on to Colorado where he worked as a TV host and fill-in play-by-play announcer for the Colorado Rockies. Since, Neverett has called games on TV and radio for the Pittsburgh Pirates, the Boston Red Sox, and now the Dodgers. He has also broadcast numerous events at four Olympic Games, including baseball in Athens and Beijing. Over a more than thirty-year career in sports broadcasting, he has announced hundreds and hundreds of games of college football, basketball, hockey, baseball, track and field, and more on regional, national, and international television. A former award-winning talk show host, Neverett is still asked to be a regular guest on many local and national radio shows. When not at the ballpark, he serves as a professor of Sports Communications at his alma mater, Emerson College in Boston, Massachusetts. He lives both in New Hampshire and Los Angeles and is available on Twitter, Facebook, and Instagram @timneverett.